CRISS-CROSS

CRISS-CROSS

THE MAKING OF HITCHCOCK'S DAZZLING, SUBVERSIVE MASTERPIECE *STRANGERS ON A TRAIN*

STEPHEN REBELLO

RUNNING PRESS
PHILADELPHIA

Running Press
Hachette Book Group
1290 Avenue of the Americas, New York, NY 10104
www.runningpress.com
@Running_Press

First Edition: September 2025

Published by Running Press, an imprint of Hachette Book Group, Inc.
The Running Press name and logo are trademarks of Hachette Book Group, Inc.

The Hachette Speakers Bureau provides a wide range of authors for speaking events. To find out more, go to www.hachettespeakersbureau.com or email HachetteSpeakers@hbgusa.com.

Running Press books may be purchased in bulk for business, educational, or promotional use. For more information, please contact your local bookseller or the Hachette Book Group Special Markets Department at Special.Markets@hbgusa.com.

The publisher is not responsible for websites (or their content) that are not owned by the publisher.

Image credits: pages 3, 75, 99, 135 (bottom), 138 (bottom), 139, 141, 182, 208, 226: courtesy Warner Bros.; page 11, courtesy Masheter Movie Archive / Alamy Stock Photo; page 39, courtesy Everett Collection Inc / Alamy Stock Photo; pages 119, 123 (top), 128, 132, 135 (top), 138 (top), 153, 169, 172, 173, 176, 177, 179, 180, 185, 190, 201, 204, 217, 255: courtesy the Family of Ted Haworth; page 126, courtesy Ronald Grant / Warner Bros. / Alamy Stock Photo; page 136, courtesy Entertainment Pictures / Alamy Stock Photo; page 159, courtesy Smith Archive / Alamy Stock Photo; page 232, courtesy Album / Alamy Stock Photo; all other photography courtesy the author

Print book cover and interior design by Amanda Richmond

Library of Congress Cataloging-in-Publication Data
Names: Rebello, Stephen, author.
Title: Criss-cross : the making of Hitchcock's dazzling, subversive masterpiece Strangers on a train / Stephen Rebello.
Description: First edition. | Philadelphia : Running Press, 2025. | Includes bibliographical references and index.
Identifiers: LCCN 2025005174 (print) | LCCN 2025005175 (ebook) | ISBN 9780762486397 (hardcover) | ISBN 9780762486410 (ebook)
Subjects: LCSH: Strangers on a train (Motion picture) | Hitchcock, Alfred, 1899–1980—Criticism and interpretation. | Thrillers (Motion pictures)—History and criticism. | Motion pictures—Production and direction—United States.
Classification: LCC PN1997.S774545 R43 2025 (print) | LCC PN1997.S774545 (ebook) | DDC 791.43/72—dc23/eng/20250527
LC record available at https://lccn.loc.gov/2025005174
LC ebook record available at https://lccn.loc.gov/2025005175

ISBNs: 978-0-7624-8639-7 (hardcover), 978-0-7624-8641-0 (ebook)

Printed in the United States of America

LSC-C

Printing 1, 2025

"There's also a person exactly the opposite of you, like the unseen part of you, somewhere in the world, and he waits in ambush."

—PATRICIA HIGHSMITH,
Strangers on a Train

Contents

AUTHOR'S NOTE

Why This Book? Why This Movie?

By now, many of Alfred Hitchcock's fifty-three films have been analyzed, dissected, deconstructed, reevaluated, mined, parsed, and dragged for everything from high-handed symbolism to low-handed misogyny and homophobia. Happily, many of them—and Hitchcock along with them—have survived these various forms of forensic analysis. Some films have emerged transcendent. Others have been exiled to the far side of paradise, perhaps for life.

Meanwhile, a few dark gems—let alone masterworks—fly under the radar, remaining underappreciated. Funny how these Hitchcock efforts are almost invariably shot in black-and-white, aren't scored by Bernard Herrmann, and don't feature cast lists of megawatt-level stars on the order of Cary Grant, Grace Kelly, Ingrid Bergman, and James Stewart, whose personae and filmographies still matter to those who are aware that great Hollywood moviemaking didn't begin and end with the 1970s.

Strangers on a Train (1951) is one of these. Much less talked about than *North by Northwest* (1959)—justifiably celebrated for its cheeky, scintillating wit and crop-duster sequence—*Strangers on a Train* offers some of the sharpest zingers and most indelible set pieces in the entire Hitchcock canon. Though nowhere near as celebrated as *Psycho* (1960), *Strangers on a Train* delivers one of the director's most visually arresting, immaculately designed, and chilling murder sequences outside of a shower stall. In fact, I would argue that *Strangers on a Train* boasts six of the best thrill sequences Hitchcock achieved in his fifty-plus years of moviemaking. Add to these pleasures Robert Walker's towering performance as Bruno Antony, one of the dark princes of Hitchcock's gallery of disarming, boyish psychopaths—alongside the urbane "Merry Widow Murderer" Charlie Oakley, played by Joseph Cotten in *Shadow of a Doubt* (1943), and Norman Bates, Anthony Perkins's sweetly sympathetic monster-next-door in *Psycho*. *Strangers on a Train* also launched Hitchcock's association with cinematographer Robert Burks, who, throughout their twelve collaborations, defined the sumptuously elegant, velvety, and compelling "look" we now most associate with Hitchcock.

I confess *Strangers on a Train* has had a hold on me from the time I first saw it, playing on a double bill at a Cambridge, Massachusetts, revival theater while I was in my last year of high school. The cofeature was *Dial M for Murder* (1954), starring Ray Milland as an unhappily married, retired tennis pro who hires an old school acquaintance to commit the so-called perfect murder of his unfaithful wife, played by Grace Kelly. (Who hasn't thought of Milland as the older version of Farley Granger's tennis-playing character in *Strangers on a Train*, unhappily saddled with icy, motherly Anne Morton, played by Ruth Roman?) Encountering *Strangers on a Train* coincided with my own sexual awakening and confusion.

One scene in the film created a frisson I've never forgotten. Bruno Antony (Walker) has strangled the scheming, avaricious wife of tennis player Guy Haines (Farley Granger). The latter returns to his apartment late at night, exits a taxi, and as he ascends the stairs to his brownstone—the camera observing him, judging him from a low, skewed angle—a disembodied voice whispers, "Guy . . . Guy . . ." Haines descends the stairs to investigate. Slipping from behind an ornamental city gate fronting a private square, Bruno emerges from the shadows, beckoning Guy to join him, almost as if he's inviting him into a seduc-

Robert Walker as Bruno Antony lures Farley Granger as Guy Haines in what Hitchcock called "the shadows of concealment."

tive covert encounter. Guy walks up to the gate, and while Bruno stands exceedingly close behind the iron bars, his gaze flicking up and down Guy's body, he talks about the strangling of Guy's wife in unmistakably intimate, caressing tones, "There's nothing for us to worry about. I was very careful . . ." Guy calls him a madman, to which Bruno protests, "But Guy, you wanted it! We planned it together. Criss-cross!"–speaking aloud a recurring Hitchcockian theme of "transference of guilt," when one character so much as desires to, let alone *commits* a crime and another character assumes the responsibility or bears the burden of remorse for having secretly wished for the outcome of that crime (see *Shadow of a Doubt*, *I Confess* [1953], *Rear Window* [1954], *The Wrong Man* [1957], etc.). When Guy spots a police car pulling up in front of his brownstone, he instantly darts behind the gate and stands behind the bars beside Bruno as they huddle together in what Hitchcock liked to call "the shadows of concealment." Attempting to evade disclosure only makes Guy appear furtive and guilty, as though two attractive adult men might be about to indulge in—if they haven't already—a bout of risky public sex. "You're spoiling everything. You're making me come out into the open," says Bruno. When Guy calls Bruno "crazy," Bruno bristles with anger, but, not wanting to alienate Guy, he backs down, rolling his eyes and saying, "Oh, you must be tired. I've sure had a *strenuous* evening." This sexually conflicted, not especially experienced, high school kid flushed with embarrassment. It is hard to believe any queer or questioning Baby Boomer man or woman wouldn't feel the homoerotic/homophobic charge or implications of such a scene.

I remember thinking, *Is this how the world sees gay men—as twisted schemers, murderers, melodramatic drama queens, shadow people lying in wait?* Yet the heteronormative alternative the film proposes didn't look much more appealing either. A dispassionate "cover" marriage to an ice princess from a wealthy family in which everyone talks in code, too genteel and polite to ever say what they really mean? Who'd willingly sign up for that life sentence? Let's say that *Strangers on a Train* made me feel seen in ways that left me only more confused and uneasy. Only when I overheard the chattering of the post-movie audience—largely students from nearby Harvard and Massachusetts Institute of Technology—everyone was, astonishingly, talking about Bruno in a non-judgy way. He was the showstopper, an agent of chaos—he owned the movie.

A few decades later—by which time I'd long since sorted myself out nicely, thank you—I thought a lot about Bruno and Robert Walker while researching and writing about Norman Bates and Anthony Perkins for my 1990 book *Alfred Hitchcock and the Making of Psycho*. During the interview process for that book, I asked Hitchcock's close associates almost as many questions about *Strangers on a Train* as I did about *Psycho*. I'm glad I did.

Before the publication of *Alfred Hitchcock and the Making of Psycho*, dozens of people asked, "Why write about *Psycho* when Hitchcock made so much better movies?" Many of these people were longtime members of Hitchcock's professional and personal inner circle. Happily, far fewer people would ask that question today, but several did when I told them I was finally planning a second Hitchcock "making of" book, this time about *Strangers on a Train*.

So, *why?* Because I had to. Because the movie got under my skin decades ago and has stayed there ever since. Because, when I saw it again two years ago with a packed and thoroughly engaged audience, many people left the theater wondering aloud why they were just now discovering one of Hitchcock's greatest films. And because my nose told me that there might be a good backstory if I dug deep enough: the story of Patricia Highsmith writing the novel; Hitchcock's stealthy, low-cost acquisition of the film rights during a time of a career slump; how nearly every screenwriter Hitchcock approached turned him down; how the stars he most wanted weren't interested; the tensions and feuds that erupted during production; the legendary creative clashes with novelist Raymond Chandler and with studio titan Jack Warner, who wanted to replace Hitchcock when the production ran overschedule; and the against-all-odds triumph of the film that led to Hitchcock's astonishing career renaissance. It is a tale as filled with all the suspense, intrigue, suspicion, blood feuds, and unlikely alliances as one finds in a Hitchcock thriller.

And now, the dark, complex, messy, and triumphant inside story of *Strangers on a Train* and how it got that way.

—Stephen Rebello

Santa Barbara, 2025

CHAPTER ONE

HITCHCOCK ON THE WRONG TRACK

Alfred Hitchcock was in a professional slump and a personal funk. Try as the fifty-one-year-old suspense film maestro might to ignore his recent creative and commercial missteps, some journalist, movie studio executive, critic, or agent would inevitably remind him that his latest efforts paled in comparison to such past glories as his *The Man Who Knew Too Much* (1934), *The 39 Steps* (1935), and *The Lady Vanishes* (1938), each the work of an audaciously talented young man who had worked his way up the ladder in the British film industry beginning in 1919 as a title card designer. Today some have reappraised and rehabilitated the reputations of Hitchcock's efforts of the late 1940s—*The Paradine Case* (1947), *Rope* (1948), and *Under Capricorn* (1949) among them. But in 1950, Hollywood conventional wisdom declared that the director peaked with his quintessential romantic spy thriller *Notorious* (1946) and was now floundering. On February 23, 1950, the director's *Stage Fright* opened at the 5,960-seat Radio City Music Hall, Manhattan's "Showplace of the Nation." Despite that film's supporting cast of British scene-stealers and the irresistible spectacle of watching glamour-puss Marlene Dietrich effortlessly steal the show from its top-billed star, recent Best Actress Oscar–winner

Jane Wyman, the modest pleasures of the cozy, made-in-England film were lost on viewers irked by Hitchcock's use of an unreliable narrator forty-five years before viewers and critics cheered the same damn device as brilliant in *The Usual Suspects* (1995). The chronically irritable *New York Times* film critic Bosley Crowther wrote off Hitchcock's first movie of the new decade as delivering "very little sustained excitement or suspense." The *Los Angeles Times*'s Philip K. Scheuer thought the movie showed Hitchcock as "almost his old self," with such highlights as the soigné, self-mocking Dietrich becoming rattled by the bloodstained doll held by a child at a garden party and the heroine's showdown with a murderer in an empty theater as "A-one Hitchcock." *New Yorker* reviewer John McCarten termed the show "disappointing." Stanley Kauffmann's review in *The New Republic* called it "abominable." Though a critic reviewing *Stage Fright* in the British Film Institute's *Monthly Film Bulletin* wrote of Hitchcock's latest as "not without effective moments," those moments only served to "[remind] us how Hitchcock once excelled in the simple melodrama with ordinary, naturalistic backgrounds; but too much of it has the heavy, corpulent quality that made *Rope* and in particular *Under Capricorn* so lifeless and unreal."

The cognoscenti declared that one of cinema's most dazzling visual stylists—a director who complained that most movies were simply photographs of people talking—had stumbled into the trap of making overly gimmicky movies that constricted space (*Lifeboat* [1944], *Rope*), talked too much (*Under Capricorn*), or both (*Rope*). *Los Angeles Times* critic Philip K. Scheuer proved himself one of the few journalists bold enough to ask Hitchcock directly how he had lost his way. Or, in Scheuer's words, "Why this genius of sleight-of-hand, of visual magic had abandoned the camera for the microphone, or at any rate relegated it to second spot." Answered Hitchcock with unusual directness: "I wanted to find out if an actor can sustain a picture." He'd been stung by hearing a famous London stage actress answer a question about her recent work by lamenting, "Oh, my dear—I'm filming," as if she were saying, "I'm slumming." The idiosyncratic character actor Alistair Sim had told Hitchcock while filming *Stage Fright*, "When I come into a film, I abandon my instincts as an actor and put myself into the hands of the director."

Hitchcock explained,

> And so I decided I would try to make pictures in which actors would have an opportunity to give sustained performances, as they do in the theater, instead of in little bits and pieces. What takes time in picture-making? The setting up of the camera and the lighting. If you're lucky you shoot for fifteen minutes out of every two hours on a set—and perhaps four or five seconds reach the screen. So what I did was rehearse the movements of the actor with the movement of the camera, synchronizing both. The actor would get his chance.

Enter the experiments of *Lifeboat*, *Rope*, and *Under Capricorn*, the latter of which, said Hitchcock, featured a sequence "in which [Ingrid] Bergman paced the floor and soliloquized for twelve minutes straight. If any actress could do it, she could." Audiences expected many things from Hitchcock thrillers, but not soliloquizing—even if it was Bergman doing it. "It is still a visual rather than a sound medium," Hitchcock declared. "Right now I'm looking for a story. I have a big problem: to find a vehicle that will lend itself to 'the Hitchcock treatment,' to the sort of thing that people expect to see from me."

So Hitchcock—and not for the first time—found himself caught in a unique, private trap: to track down a piece of material from which he could construct the kind of entertainment audiences expected of him, only different enough to keep them coming back for more. He also vowed to follow the trend toward greater veracity. He said, "Currently, there is this chase after realism, real locations. We did that in silent films; I did it again as long ago as in *Shadow of a Doubt* shot in Santa Rosa in 1942." He began telling associates that once he landed the right literary property or original screenplay, he planned to shoot it on real locations, which was neither the norm for Hollywood at the time nor was it the inclination of an artist who, like Fellini or Bergman, preferred to work on a soundstage where he could make the world and the people he envisioned in his imagination look so much more beautiful.

But the first order of business was to find the right property, an effort he doggedly pursued in the best way he knew how: by instructing agents, friends, and business contacts to rush him the strongest, most offbeat material available. Among the unconventional ideas he considered was a "psychological melodrama," a fresh take on Shakespeare starring Cary Grant as a modern-day Hamlet. Hitchcock hired Scottish writer and editor Alan Dent, Laurence Olivier's "text advisor" on *Hamlet* (1948), to work on the screenplay. Describing the project as "one hell of a revenge thriller," Hitchcock elaborated to the press that "the plot, situations, psychology and characters will be retained, but the action and sets will be modern." Grant told columnist Earl Wilson, "We'll do it in a modern manner. For instance, 'To be or not to be' will probably read, 'What the hell do I do now?'" The publicity backfired. American playwright and writer Irving Fiske filed a preemptive $1.2 million suit accusing Grant and Hitchcock of plagiarizing his unpublished but staged *Hamlet in Modern English*. The unpleasantness only ended in 1954 when a New York federal court judge advised jurors to throw out the case as "not proven." Fiske was ordered to pay Hitchcock $5,000 to defray his legal costs. Warner Bros., Hitchcock, and Grant dropped the whole idea. When other possibilities also led Hitchcock down blind alleys, he began to despair, if not outright panic.

That panic was only exacerbated by his ongoing relationship with two major figures in his professional life at the time, Sidney Bernstein and Jack L. Warner. When *Strangers on a Train* eventually came into Hitchcock's orbit, he had an ongoing business partnership with British theater chain owner Bernstein, who had befriended the young Hitchcock in 1925 when Bernstein cofounded the London Film Society. After Hitchcock's American contract with David O. Selznick came to its bitter end with *The Paradine Case* in 1946, the director and Bernstein formed Transatlantic Pictures with the intention of shooting films in both England and the United States. For the first time in his career, Hitchcock became his own producer. Though uncredited, Bernstein also became producer on Transatlantic's first releases. But both their earlier efforts, Hitchcock's *Under Capricorn* and *Rope*, lost money for Transatlantic and for Warner Bros., which distributed them to theaters. Hitchcock's Warner Bros. deal left the option open for him to make films directly for them, or for Transatlantic with Warner distributing. When Hitchcock and Bernstein's *Stage Fright* also fell short with

Hitchcock and studio boss Jack Warner make nice for the purposes of a publicity photo.

audiences and critics, Bernstein and Hitchcock amicably dissolved Transatlantic during the filming of Hitchcock's 1953 film *I Confess*, with Bernstein concluding that the company was an unlikely contender for success. Long and protracted script difficulties seemed to plague Transatlantic productions.

Warner was a studio boss whose rapacious business practices were unrivaled even in Hollywood and whose disdain for actors ("I don't want to look at an actor while I eat," he is quoted as saying), writers ("schmucks with Underwoods"), and other creators made him one of the most despised power brokers in the business. He expected a big box-office hit from Hitchcock and never failed to remind the director that, after three movies released by Warner Bros., the director had yet to come through. Warner was many things—a hound when it came to young actresses and a studio executive who rarely bothered with day-to-day creative filmmaking issues—yet his name is synonymous with tough, sexy, impactful hit films that not only defined the Warner Bros. house style but were also highly respected and envied by other studio chiefs. On his watch the studio made the jazzy, bullet-spattered gangster classics *The Public Enemy* (1931), *Little Caesar* (1931), and *White Heat* (1949); the enduring romantic adventures *Casablanca* (1942) and *Key Largo* (1948); the snarly private-eye thrillers *The Maltese Falcon* (1941) and *The Big Sleep* (1946); the crackling, female-driven melodramas *Jezebel* (1938), *Now, Voyager* (1942), and *Mildred Pierce* (1945); and such blood-and-thunder swashbucklers as *The Adventures of Robin Hood* (1938) and *The Sea Hawk* (1940). Warner was charismatic, brash, and often clownish, and he chose stars whose swagger and vitality he simultaneously admired, despised, and coveted—tough cookies like Humphrey Bogart, James Cagney, Paul Muni, Edward G. Robinson, John Garfield, Barbara Stanwyck, Joan Blondell, Glenda Farrell, Bette Davis, and Joan Crawford. He went to the mat with his biggest stars—putting on suspension such top money-earners as

Cagney, Davis, and, most consequentially, Olivia de Havilland—who battled him in court over the abuses of the studio contract system.

Director Gottfried Reinhardt characterized Warner as someone who "derived pleasure" from grinding subordinates under his heel. Comparing him to other studio bosses, he observed: "[Columbia Pictures cofounder] Harry Cohn was a son-of-a-bitch but he did it for business. He was not a sadist. [MGM cofounder Louis B.] Mayer could be a monster but he was not mean for the sake of meanness. Jack was." Actress Jacquelyn Park, Warner's longtime mistress (she also dated Ronald Reagan in the 1950s), said, "[Warner] was so cheap he would always make sure the bills didn't stick together when he counted them. He was very, very cruel. He could turn on you, just like that."

Warner was the sort of person who thought nothing of saying to someone as powerful as Hitchcock, "I don't want it good. I want it Tuesday." To Warner, Hitchcock was "a genius who needs to be watched every minute." Out of nowhere, Warner could suddenly become as blunderingly intrusive about production minutiae as the manic, hands-on producer David O. Selznick, with whom Hitchcock clashed epically while making *Rebecca* (1940), *Spellbound* (1945), and *The Paradine Case.* Warner was infamous for bombarding directors with typed messages on pink slips, in which he weighed in on everything from the potentially censorable "perkiness" of Joan Blondell's bosom and the new shade of dye being used on Errol Flynn's moustache to why he resented paying such a high salary to Paul Muni when the thespian insisted on wearing prosthetics and wigs that hid his facial features and why Warner Bros. shouldn't bankroll the sure-to-flop Bette Davis movie about a terminally ill playgirl, *Dark Victory* (1939), which went on to pack theaters and win Oscar nominations.

The handwriting was on the wall. Hitchcock and Warner were on a collision course. The only question was: Would either of them blink?

CHAPTER TWO

HITCHCOCK VS. HIGHSMITH

In late February 1950, Harper & Brothers publicity director Ramona Hardman sent Hitchcock and his agent Lew Wasserman advance copies of *Strangers on a Train.* A new suspense novel by first-time author Patricia Highsmith, the book was set to be published on March 15, 1950. Boarding the 20th Century Limited train back to Los Angeles after the underwhelming New York opening of *Stage Fright*, Hitchcock needed a diversion. Highsmith's novel supplied it.

The premise: in the American southwest, architect Guy Haines wants to divorce his faithless wife, Miriam, so he can marry Anne Faulkner, the socially prominent daughter of a US senator. En route by train to see Miriam about his divorce plans, Haines meets Charles Anthony Bruno, a wealthy gadfly who initially appears merely to be an eccentric, aimless, and lonely alcoholic until he slowly reveals himself to also be a psychopath. Bruno suggests the idea that he and Guy, complete strangers, exchange murders. Bruno will kill Miriam and Guy will kill Bruno's despised father. Because neither man will have a motive nor any history of knowing each other or any future contact, why would the police suspect either of them? Guy writes off Bruno as a crank—until Bruno murders Miriam while Guy is in Mexico.

Bruno confesses to Guy what he has done, but Guy does not go to the police, fearing that Bruno could implicate him for having knowledge of the plan to swap murders. In the ensuing months, Bruno repeatedly materializes to remind Guy he must keep his end of their bargain. Ignored, Bruno accelerates the pressure by sending incriminating anonymous letters to people in Guy's social and professional circle. Guy succumbs to the pressure and kills Bruno's father, leaving him wracked with guilt. Bruno, unfazed, only presses for more and more of Guy's attention and company. He crashes Guy's wedding to Anne and causes great embarrassment during the events of the day. Meanwhile, a private detective, previously hired by Bruno's father to shadow his unstable son, cannot shake his deduction that Bruno not only met Guy on the train but also that Bruno might have murdered Miriam and masterminded his father's murder. Guy's evasive behavior and contradictory statements about Bruno bring him under suspicion everywhere he turns.

During a sailboat cruise, Bruno topples overboard, and Guy nearly drowns while failing to rescue him. Bruno's death shuts down the murder investigation. Over too many drinks with one of Miriam's ex-lovers, Guy guiltily confesses the truth about the murders. Miriam's ex-boyfriend blames the dead girl for her own fate and spews a vicious woman-hating tirade. The detective formerly leading the murder investigation overhears Guy's drunken admission of his crimes and confronts Guy, who surrenders himself to the police.

Highsmith's central premise excited Hitchcock—a "perfect crime" murder swap pact between perfect strangers—but he immediately envisioned the central plot device as merely a springboard for a flight of imaginative moviemaking and a roadmap to a series of splashy suspense set pieces. On publication of the novel, reviewers applauded the young Highsmith's writing style, self-assurance, and her dark exploration of themes including guilt, duality, and the deeply complicated aspects of human nature, tempered by her bilious, darkly mordant view of the world. The book came "Highly recommended" by the *New Yorker* reviewer who described Bruno as "[an] oddly ingratiating young man who has about all the complexes you ever heard of." The reviewer could just as well have been describing the memorable antagonists of past Hitchcock triumphs such as *The Lodger* (1928), *Suspicion* (1941), and *Shadow of a Doubt*, let alone such future ones in *Psycho* and *Frenzy* (1972). Other reviewers faulted Highsmith for hinging her novel on wild incongruities and coincidences that demanded suspension of belief well above and beyond the norms of the genre: "Outlandish." "Unpleasant." "Beggars belief." The critics summoned these invectives. And worse. Hitchcock scorned such critics "The Plausibles," grudgingly demanding airtight logic and reason even from pure, edge-of-the-seat entertainment. Time and again Hitchcock declared to the press, "Logic is dull" and "Films should be stronger than logic." Before the 1960s anyway, he insisted on promoting himself as an entertainer, not a highbrow artiste, a confectioner who compared his films to slices of cake, not slices of life. "Who requires logic from a slice of cake?" he facetiously asked an interviewer. No wonder Hitchcock brushed off the critics who called Highsmith's novel "tasteless," "unremittingly unpleasant," and even "depraved."

The moment Hitchcock arrived at Union Station in Los Angeles and was met by Alma Reville, his film editor, continuity supervisor, and screenwriter for the past twenty-seven years and his wife for twenty-four years, he began touting Highsmith's novel, urging Alma to read it as soon as possible before some rival moviemaker pounced on it. As always, Alma would be the final arbiter. If she shared his excitement and saw the book's filmic possibilities, then he would acquire the film rights. Alma saw what her husband saw in *Strangers on a Train* and then some. Hitchcock immediately alerted Wasserman, president of MCA Artists since 1946, to acquire Highsmith's book. As was the director's frequent modus operandi when purchasing literary material, he kept his famous name out of the negotiations until the last possible moment—the better to lowball the author on the purchase price. On April 20, 1950, Mary Patricia Highsmith, represented by her Manhattan-based literary agent, Margot Johnson, countersigned the contracts to sell Hitchcock the film rights at a bargain basement rate of $7,500 (about $97,500 today). Highsmith's agent had tried to get the price up to $10,000, but Hitchcock refused to budge. He did consent, though, to a contractual clause stipulating that should he request Highsmith's writing services, collaboration, or contribution of ideas during the film's production, then she would be given two weeks' notice, no later than October 16, 1950, and would be paid an additional $1,500 (about $20,000 today). "That wasn't a bad price for a first book and my agent upped it as much as possible," Highsmith reflected over three decades later. "I was 27 and I was working like a fool to earn a living and pay for my apartment. I didn't hang around films. I don't know if I'd ever seen *The Lady Vanishes*."

Four days later, on April 24, Hitchcock in turn sold the book rights to Warner Bros. Intra-studio Warner Bros. legal memos explicated the director's standard gambit for acquiring literary material on the cheap. According to a late-April 1950 Warner Bros. memo: "Alfred Hitchcock is to direct a film based on a novel titled *Strangers on a Train* by Patricia Highsmith under our four-picture deal with him. To cut down the purchase price of this property, Hitchcock arranged to purchase the same from the author direct [*sic*] and we in turn succeeded to Hitchcock's rights." That is, Hitchcock immediately recouped from the studio his $7,500 and relinquished to Warner Bros. all potential remake rights. Hitchcock's directing and producing deal, brokered by Wasserman, was substantially more lush, guaranteeing him 10 percent of the film's gross (i.e., the amount remaining after the studio deducted all costs incurred)—specifically, the lower of either $4 million or double the production cost. His overall Warner Bros. contract also guaranteed him a weekly salary of $3,000 ($36,900 today) for a term of 333 weeks, during which he was committed to produce and/or direct those four films.

The *Los Angeles Times* and other major US newspapers carried the announcement of Hitchcock's purchase of Highsmith's novel as the basis for a new motion picture. As if to reassure fans and critics that he was intent on making something special of *Strangers on a Train*, Hitchcock sounded genuinely excited in announcing to the press: "This is the freshest murder situation I've ever encountered. If audiences expect thrills, adventure, and action from films bearing my name, I'm not going to let them down. I'm perfectly content to provide suspense the rest of my career, if that's what's wanted from me. I like thrillers the best anyway." Filming was tentatively scheduled to begin in the fall of 1950 on East and West Coast locations, as well as on Warner Bros. soundstages in Burbank, California.

For Highsmith, even such a modest financial windfall occurred at an opportune time. Born in 1921 in Fort Worth, Texas, she was the sole child of commercial illustrator Jay Bernard Plangman and Mary Coates, who divorced ten days before her birth. Her mother, to whom she was abnormally attached and who told Patricia that she had tried to abort her by drinking turpentine, got remarried in 1924 to another illustrator, Stanley Highsmith. The newlyweds and their daughter moved to New York City that same year. Before she was even six, young Patricia felt unorthodox notions about her gender and her sexual leanings. At age twelve she experienced "the saddest year" of her life, when her mother "abandoned" her by sending her back to Fort Worth to live for a year with her maternal grandmother. She assuaged her anger and found solace in immersing herself in her grandmother's library, where she helped herself to psychiatric histories detailed by Karl Menninger in *The Human Mind*.

She hatched the idea for the book that would become *Strangers on a Train* when, in the winter of 1945, on an especially eventful subsequent trip to visit her grandmother at age seventeen, she met a "completely dissolute," very spoiled boy whom she calls "B" in her diaries. Adopted into "a wealthy family and completely worthless," B reportedly exposed her to pornographic pictures and to other unspecified diversions. Highsmith claimed this boy "was sort of the genesis of Charles Anthony Bruno," the wealthy, childlike, dangerous psychopath she would go on to make the centerpiece of her novel.

She prided herself on having the most advanced vocabulary of any student at Julia Richman High School in New York City, where she flourished despite struggling with female hormone deficiency, anorexia, and dysmenorrhea. She also developed several distracting crushes on fellow student classmates, including Judith Tuvim (the young Broadway and film star-to-be, Judy Holliday). While walking with her mother and stepfather along the Hudson River near their newly adopted upstate New York residence, she began to think about "two soulmates" who swap murders. But she let life intervene and failed to seriously develop the idea until 1947. Margot Johnson, her literary agent, sent the unfinished manuscript to Dodd, Mead & Co., who accepted it but wanted it shortened, and they offered considerably less money for the publishing rights than Johnson thought it worth. In early 1948, after a writer's residency at the Yaddo artist colony (recommended by new friend Truman Capote, whom Highsmith met at a party), she completed the novel in six weeks. In early 1949, she put the finishing touches on it and decided she liked the title *Strangers on a Train*, which was suggested by Marc Brandel, the nascent British novelist and television writer whom she nearly married, despite her many love affairs with women and his reputed bisexuality and taste for indulging his sadistic tendencies toward women.

Highsmith's participation in the film version of her first novel pretty much ended once she cashed Hitchcock's check for the film rights; the director never quite got around to requesting her counsel, denying her that extra $1,500. But it would not be the last time Patricia Highsmith would hear from Alfred Hitchcock.

CHAPTER THREE

TO CATCH A SCREENWRITER

"To make a great film, you need three things: the script, the script, and the script," Hitchcock declared. To help Hitchcock achieve his high aspirations for *Strangers on a Train*, Jack Warner advised him to join forces with a big-name writer carrying a prestigious—and a commercially exploitable—literary pedigree. Hitchcock compiled a list of first-rate writers he thought might be capable of weaving an outlandish plot—featuring two tricky, rather incongruous main characters—into a persuasive narrative and stylish entertainment. Considering the director's business acumen and his eye for the box office, especially when he so needed a major success, it goes without saying that he understood how a major writer's name on the credits could not only elevate the status of the project but also do wonders to help polish his tarnished image. "Hollywood judges one by the company one keeps," said the director, whose target list for *Strangers on a Train* included Tennessee Williams, Lillian Hellman, Arthur Miller, and William Inge. "Very few writers would touch it, none of them thought it was any good," Hitchcock told French director François Truffaut in 1962. Hitchcock stubbornly pursued prestige and reassurance in the form of two leading literary lights with whom he had previously worked. He first turned to playwright and novelist Thornton Wilder, the renowned Pulitzer Prize winner for both drama and fiction and a key contributor to the success of *Shadow of a Doubt*, Hitchcock's subversive and disquieting 1943 masterpiece in which a young small-town woman discovers that her dashing, beloved namesake uncle, Charlie, is secretly "The Merry Widow Murderer" and the target of a national manhunt. Sharing Wilder's spot atop Hitchcock's want list was novelist John Steinbeck. But he was an unlikely prospect, considering he wrote the original screen story for Hitchcock's 1944 *Lifeboat* but unsuccessfully petitioned the director and 20th Century Fox to scrub his name from the credits. He thought Hitchcock and screenwriter Jo Swerling had slanted his work in a decidedly pro-Axis direction. Tallulah Bankhead, who starred in the film, declared Steinbeck's criticism (widely shared by other political reactionaries) "moronic."

With Hitchcock's and Jack Warner's favored writers continuing to respond negatively to Patricia Highsmith's novel, the director said, "None of them could see what I saw in it," and commissioned playwright-novelist Whitfield Cook to create a treatment based only on the novel's central premise of "swapped murders." Hired in mid-May, Cook, working alongside Hitchcock, filed his treatment on June 20, 1950. Hitchcock and Cook began their story meetings in early June, and as was the director's style with all his writers, he often avoided talking about such nuts-and-bolts issues as character development, theme, and story by shifting the focus to favorite topics like gourmet food, fine wine, parties, gossip, and travel. Screenwriter Ernest Lehman, who would spend agonizingly long months writing *North by Northwest* for Hitchcock, recalled how their meetings invariably veered into discussions of which priceless wines pair best with fine foods, world travel, and choice Hollywood gossip—the more ribald the better. While preparing *Psycho* with Joseph Stefano, Hitchcock loved to pepper the screenwriter with questions about his frequent psychother-

Playwright-screenwriter and Hitchcock family intimate Whitfield Cook wrote the influential first *Strangers on a Train* treatment.

apy sessions dealing with, among other challenges, his mother issues. *Psycho* novelist Robert Bloch refused writing contracts with Hitchcock because he could not afford the luxury of spending months exploring the director's movie ideas that mostly led nowhere.

As soon as Hitchcock and Cook began collaborating, the director (with *Strangers* very much on his mind) told a *New York Times* reporter,

> As far as I'm concerned, you have suspense when you let the audience play God. Let an audience be told all the

> secrets that the [characters] do not know and they'll work like the devil for you because they know what fate is in store for the [characters]. The fact that the audience watches [characters] go blithely through atmosphere that is loaded for evil makes for real suspense. I never puzzle the audience. They're in on everything from the start, whereas the characters know nothing. One of the necessary ingredients is a series of plausible situations with people that are real. When characters are unbelievable, you never get real suspense, only surprise. I believe it is important in a story with sinister implications to use counterpoint as we will do in *Strangers on a Train*. Suspense is contrast.

Treatments for Hitchcock's projects are often virtual blueprints for expansion into full screenplays. In his work on *Strangers*, Cook clearly understood the assignment and delivered—mapping out the characters and their motivations and actions, the scene progressions, story beats and twists, long passages of key dialogue, major suspense set pieces, and imagery. Hitchcock had reason to expect good work from Cook. Since the mid-forties the dashing, witty writer had been a close family friend and traveling companion of Alfred and, sometimes separately, Alma Hitchcock. In 1944, he had written and directed the Hitchcocks' sixteen-year-old daughter Patricia "Pat" Hitchcock in the title role of a Little Miss Fix-It in a short-lived Broadway comedy *Violet*, about which one critic wrote of her performance, "Papa Hitchcock will have no scolding to do, for Pat whoops it up like a seasoned trouper." More recently Cook had cowritten the screenplay for the 1945 June Allyson comedy *The Sailor Takes a Wife* (which sold Cook on the talents and audience appeal of Allyson's costar Robert Walker) and *Stage Fright* for Hitchcock. Hitchcock hardly selected Cook as a writer out of mere friendship or sentimentality, however. As the director anticipated, the purportedly bisexual Cook responded to the novel's homoerotic undercurrents, perversity, and bleak humor. Considering the restrictions of the times, Cook touched lightly but adroitly on those aspects in his highly detailed forty-five-page treatment.

Cook's main brief from Hitchcock was to make the material less internal and far more dynamic than the novel. So instead of characterizing Guy Haines as an up-and-coming architect saddled with a libidinous, coarse, manipulative estranged wife, as Highsmith had written him, Guy became a rising tennis player with political aspirations, a more visual and active cinematic avocation and with potential elements of suspense baked right in. Rather than write Bruno as a mordant alcoholic consumed by white-hot hatred for his father and Oedipal worship of his mother and devoted to pulp-fiction detective novels and to spinning theories about perfect murders, Cook took the character in other directions.

Hitchcock arranged for Cook private screenings of *Shadow of a Doubt* and *Suspicion* (for which only studio cowardice prevented Hitchcock from filming the novel's ending, revealing in the finale that Joan Fontaine's insecure, bookish heiress character was right all along: her new husband, Johnny—a handsome, irresponsible rake played by Cary Grant—is a fortune hunter who has poisoned her). In response to revisiting those films, Cook fashioned Bruno accordingly, investing him with touches of Johnny's charm, brashness, and boyish irresponsibility laced with *Shadow*'s Uncle Charlie's cunning intelligence and chilling nihilism. As characterized by Cook, Bruno is a dapper dresser; however, unlike the impeccably buttoned-down Charlie, Bruno's sartorial flair runs to the flamboyant and garish. Both men share a penchant for smoking fine cigars and both ply older, rich women with a surface charm that barely conceals their latent savagery. For instance, when Uncle Charlie's niece interrupts his shocking diatribe about the disposability of wealthy widows by reminding him that they are human, he says, "Are they? Or are they fat, wheezing animals? And what happens to animals when they get too fat and too old?" In Cook's treatment, Bruno says about killing Miriam, "What is a life or two? Some people are better off dead." When Bruno shares with Guy one of his schemes for a perfect murder—"carbon monoxide in the garage"—it's a callback to one of the ways Uncle Charlie tries to kill his niece, young Charlie. *Shadow of a Doubt* features two fatherly gents who entertain each other nightly by discussing inventive ways to murder people; in *Strangers on a Train* two elderly society matrons make party conversation out of the violent ways they've fantasized about killing people—including their husbands.

As Cook's work on *Strangers on a Train* progressed, he further strengthened the links between Uncle Charlie and Bruno. Cook's treatment brings to the table another darkly comic element reminiscent of *Shadow of a Doubt*, among several other Hitchcock films that posit murder and menace as the stuff of everyday family conversations. In Cook's treatment, when Guy tells his fiancée's fine Washingtonian family about his disastrous meeting with the vulgar, grasping Miriam, his fiancée's young sister, Barbara, instantly chirps, "How are we going to get rid of her?"

But Hitchcock insisted on Cook's elimination of one of Highsmith's darkest and most memorable plot elements—Guy killing Bruno's father—presumably to appease censors, to give audiences a hero to root for, and to attract a movie star, often a breed who prefer being liked by audiences. To Highsmith, the change violated a primary intention of her novel and smacked of the sort of Hollywood compromise she detested. To contemporary viewers looking back on the film today, viewers who more readily embrace morally ambivalent or outright irredeemable characters in films and TV series such as *Gone Girl* (2014), the *Joker* movies (2019, 2024), *Dexter* (2006–2013), and *Barry* (2018–2023), Hitchcock's decision might seem cowardly and unnecessary. Even in

1951, smoothing out Guy's roughest edges struck some as a cop-out. After all, *Strangers on a Train* and *A Place in Sun* (1951) would open in theaters within months of each other, and the latter won massive acclaim for director George Stevens, who pulled few punches, without damaging the career of Montgomery Clift, who played an upwardly aspiring antihero who actively plans to murder his inconveniently pregnant lower-class girlfriend, or the careers of screenwriters Harry Brown and Michael Wilson, who defied Hollywood convention and won six Oscars. Not only did Charlie Chaplin call *A Place in the Sun* "the greatest movie ever made about America," but that film was also among the year's biggest moneymakers.

Cook must be credited for attempting to deepen and complicate the characters. He proposed an entirely different kind of father for Bruno—an up-by-the-bootstraps immigrant, a wifebeater, a domestic monster. Cook also brought in his own brand of subversion by creating a Bruno with affectations such as a facility for speaking French, a tendency to make flighty outbursts, and an obsession with having his delicate hands manicured by his mother because, as he puts it, "I like them to look just right." One expects no less of a strangler in a Hitchcock film, of course. These traits, along with him being the ostentatious dresser, queer-coded Bruno, make him easily read to those in the know while leaving him ambiguous enough that others read him as a (possibly) closeted, asexual, early 1950s-variety mama's boy. Cook's approach also left it up to Hitchcock's discretion—and to that of the actor he would eventually choose to play the character—how strongly to lean into the character's implied sexuality, if at all.

It is vital to view without the lens of presentism the circumstances under which *Strangers on a Train* was created. Since World War II and while the film was in the works in 1950, Wisconsin's opportunistic Republican Senator Joseph McCarthy was whipping the country into a furor over unsubstantiated, questionable, and outright false claims that the US State Department and other government agencies had become infiltrated by homosexuals. By the summer of 1950, goaded by McCarthy and his zealot allies, the senate convened a committee charged solely with investigating and routing out "the employment of homosexuals and other sex perverts in the government."

With the overwhelming support of a ginned-up public, newspaper editors, and US senators (including more than several closet cases), the entire government shifted into full overreach mode. The hysteria grew alongside a parallel crusade accusing moviemakers, actors, writers, musicians, and other artists of being communists or sympathetic "fellow travelers." Those labeled as "subversives"—and many were so labeled due solely to actual or perceived sexual orientation—got dragged before the kangaroo court and subjected to the performative and destructive theatrics of the House Un-American Activities Committee (HUAC). The government forced hundreds of civil servants to submit to lie detector tests. Meanwhile, police stepped up their surprise sweeps of gay bars and their raids on other places where so-called deviants were known to fraternize.

The options for an actor, director, or writer subpoenaed by HUAC were limited: either confess to having communist ties and provide names of other known or suspected "reds," or refuse to cooperate, risk jail time, or get placed on a blacklist that would end their Hollywood careers. Orchestrators of the blacklist succeeded in exploiting religious zealots as well as those who felt bypassed, disenfranchised, or otherwise threatened by the liberalism of President Franklin D. Roosevelt's New Deal politics. Characterized as "security risks" due to the purported high risk of blackmail, ninety-one suspected homosexuals would be fired by the State Department. Stripped of nuances and complications, McCarthyism was a thinly veiled attack on communists, Jews, liberals, nonwhites, immigrants, and homosexuals—not motivated by national security interests but rather by bigotry, ignorance, fear, and hatred. *Plus ça change.*

Hitchcock and Cook recognized the undercurrent of suspicion, secretiveness, and paranoia implicit in Highsmith's novel; Cook's film treatment reflects a similar mood and ambience without having to speak its name. Hitchcock saw the promise in Cook's work and liked it for being au courant and provocative, particularly after critics had stung his recent work for being stodgy and out of step with the times. Besides, let's also remember that Hitchcock—either in jest or in earnest—told gay actor/screenwriter Rodney Ackland (screenwriter of Hitchcock's *Number Seventeen* [1932]), "You know, if I hadn't met Alma at the right time, I could have become a poof." (If the story is true, of course, Ackland might have done Hitchcock a solid by telling him that meeting "the right woman" hardly precluded one's "becoming a poof.")

Hitchcock knew he must shake off the 1940s if he were to survive as a vital and relevant filmmaker in the 1950s. At the same time, he knew he had to toe a line, especially while witch-hunt hysteria spread like wildfire through his adopted country. After all, as recently as two years earlier, municipal censorship boards of New Bedford and Worcester, Massachusetts; Spokane and Seattle, Washington; and Atlanta, Georgia, and Memphis, Tennessee, had banned *Rope* from theaters, objecting to Hitchcock's claustrophobic thriller inspired by the real-life 1924 kidnapping and "thrill-killing" of fourteen-year-old boy Bobby Franks by brilliant, wealthy university students Nathan Leopold and Richard Loeb, who were consumed by the idea of committing "the perfect crime." The police censor board in Chicago, Illinois, barred showings of *Rope*—in which two young intellectuals host a dinner party in their swank Manhattan apartment, where they've strangled a former college mate and stuffed his corpse into a trunk, atop which they lay out a buffet—on the grounds that it was not "wholesome entertainment." Warner Bros. appealed the decision, and Chicago theaters were only permitted to show the movie on an "adults only" basis. Even among adults, a showing of the film at a Millington, Tennessee, naval base got scrubbed after a single showing in a two-day engagement.

Reacting to the banning controversy, Thomas M. Pryor's *New York Times* article of November 28, 1948, stopped just short of calling the censorship a form of harassment due to the film's hints of the homosexuality of the two main characters, played by Farley Granger (who, in his private life, self-identified as bisexual) and John Dall (who was gay). As the first inklings of the anti-gay "Lavender Scare" had begun to surface in tandem with the blacklist, Pryor's column questioned the "peculiarly aggressive attitude of censorship bodies in this instance" and let the implications hang in the air:

> At this moment local censor authorities up and down the land are having a time sniping at *Rope*, the Alfred Hitchcock melodrama currently being distributed by Warner Brothers. The picture, for the benefit of those who have not seen it, parallels a sensational murder case of some years back in that it concerns two young men who kill a friend just for the thrill of committing a murder. Not an ennobling theme, to be sure, but then it is not any worse, to put it bluntly, than any number of other crime films that have gotten by without arousing the censors.

Although Pryor admitted that it was not unusual for movies to meet with official protests, "it is not often that a picture runs into such difficulty on the scale that *Rope* has up to the moment." And then came *Strangers on a Train.*

It is fascinating, if frustrating, to note how Cook's importance to the creation of the project has been downplayed, when not ignored entirely. It would be heartbreaking and infuriating if Cook's sexuality were part of the reason for his relative anonymity, as it has been in the case of so many gay, lesbian, and bisexual artists over the years. And the irony should not be lost on anyone that Cook's work on the project was eclipsed by a brighter, heterosexual (and, incidentally, homophobic) literary eminence who was yet to become part of the story: Raymond Chandler. Yet Cook's take on *Strangers on a Train* provides an invaluable glimpse into not only the beginnings of the project but also one writer's early enduring contributions to it.

Cook's treatment established many aspects of the film as we know it, including the basic shape of the story and the progression of the scenes from beginning to end; concentrating the action in Washington, DC, and the Northeast Corridor, as opposed to Highsmith's sprawling southwestern odyssey; the antagonist's signature gold tie pin (or, in Cook's version, a gold tie chain spelling out "Bruno"); all the major elements of Bruno stalking Miriam and her "college boyfriends," including her and her friends breaking out in song on the carousel and, later, such visual elements as the shadow of Miriam's boat (astutely named *The Pluto*, the Roman god of the dead and the underworld) in the tunnel to "Magic Isle" being menacingly overtaken by the shadow of Bruno in his boat.

In his treatment, Cook paints the murder on the island in potent visual detail:

> **Bruno:** *Is your name Miriam?*
> **Miriam:** *Yeah, who are you?*

Gloved hands fly to her throat. Bruno's head passes across Miriam's face as they sway in a dance of death. Her head leans to one side, causing her glasses to fall, and as they drop on the ground, we get the faint impression of struggling feet beside them. Then, through one of the lenses, we see the elongated figures of Bruno and Miriam struggling. The figure of the girl falls forward toward us and the lens.

Also in Cook's own language directly from the treatment: "Then, a mass of hair drops into the picture beside the glasses. [Note: the spill of hair is an obviously Hitchcockian image.] Bruno's hand comes into the scene and snatches the glasses." Also front and center in Cook's treatment is the enduring element of Bruno staring straight at Guy while the heads of all the other tennis-match spectators swivel back and forth during the game.

Although, as of his June 1950 treatment, Cook had not yet devised a convincing way of establishing Guy's innocence in the finale, he had succeeded in departing radically from Highsmith's novel and creating a template for further development, in addition to nailing most of the story beats and the bravura visual touches.

With Cook's treatment, Hitchcock believed he had what he needed to prove the cinematic potential of *Strangers on a Train* to a marquee-name screenwriter who would also win Jack Warner's approval. In the meantime, the treatment aroused such interest and curiosity on the Warner Bros. lot that Bill Cagney, producing partner and brother of tough-guy film icon James Cagney (enjoying a resurgence in popularity from his 1949 gangster hit *White Heat*), approached Jack Warner's beloved older brother and studio executive Harry Warner about casting James Cagney in the role of Bruno's abusive, working-class bully father, for whom Cook and Hitchcock originally envisioned several powerful, confrontational scenes.

With Hitchcock's approval, Lew Wasserman sent Cook's work to Thornton Wilder. By 1950, Wilder had spent the past few years alternating between Broadway stage productions of his one-act play *The Happy Journey to Trenton and Camden* and writing new television plays, including *Love and How to Cure It* and *The Long Christmas Dinner*.

Hitchcock respected Wilder's feeling for humanity and his brilliance for elevating everyday language to the level of philosophy and poetry, especially after the writer shared many personal reminiscences during meetings when preparing *Shadow of a Doubt*, the 1943 crown jewel project for which Wilder initially felt little enthusiasm beyond financial. But Hitchcock offered $10,000 (about $193,000 today) for five weeks' work, a sum that would keep Wilder's widowed mother and two sisters financially secure. Wilder eventually warmed up to Hitchcock and the project, so much so that in a May 26, 1942, letter to his sister Isabel (a novelist, biographer, and his agent) he wrote, "Work, work, work. But it's really good. For hours Hitchcock and I with glowing eyes and excited laughter plot out how the information—the dreadful information [about Uncle Charlie's homicidal nature]—is gradually revealed to the audience and the characters. And I will say that I've written some good scenes. And with that old Wilder poignance about family life going on behind it."' On June 11, 1942, Wilder assured his friend, forty-six-year-old stage actress Ruth Gordon, that he recommended Hitchcock cast her as "Emma Newton," mother of the heroine in *Shadow of a Doubt*: "Honest, Ruthie, the [script] is good. At the end we descend to a little fee-fo-fi-fum [*sic*], but for the most part its [*sic*] honest suspense and poignancy and terror."

On June 16, 1942, Wilder wrote his friend and associate Robert Maynard Hutchins about the "murder-script" that brought him to Hitchcock and Hollywood: "I wanted to make some more money for my dependents in the event of a long war. I came cynically, and what happened? I'm fascinated. Our work is very good. It's not literature. But the wrestling with the sheer craft, the calculation in a mosaic of exposition, is bracing."

Wilder agreed to complete his work on the *Shadow of a Doubt* script during a train trip from California to Miami, Florida, where he was set to report for Army basic training on June 27, 1942. The picture opened to excellent reviews on January 12, 1943, with Wilder (who received a "Special Thanks" credit) coming in for a fair share of the critics' praise.

It's small wonder that Hitchcock—who often cited *Shadow of a Doubt* as his favorite film—was so enthused about the prospect of reuniting with Wilder for *Strangers on a Train*. But it is intriguing to speculate on the deeper reasons why, beyond the writer's extraordinary talent and their happy prior collaborative experience. It is well known that Hitchcock was a deep repository of show business gossip; he chose screenwriters as strategically as he did actors, particularly when he knew some secret personal idiosyncrasy or appetite of theirs. Hitchcock was aware of Wilder's repressed attraction to men. It is also tempting to speculate whether Hitchcock also knew that Wilder, like Bruno Antony, seethed with animosity toward his wealthy, domineering father, Amos Parker Wilder, the editor, journalist, church deacon, and part owner of a Wisconsin newspaper. Each summer the young Wilder got sent off to local farms to perform intense physical labor, with the aim, according to Amos Wilder, of "ridding him of his peculiar gait and certain effeminate ways." At age twenty-eight Wilder wrote to his older sibling Amos Niven Wilder about their father: "There are times when I feel his perpetual and repetitive monologue is trying to swamp my personality and I get an awful rage."

If Hitchcock's gossip network or his conversations with Wilder had not clued him into the specifics of Wilder's prickly father-son dynamics, then the director could easily have discerned it from his work. After all, Hitchcock had attended a performance of the original 1942 Elia Kazan–directed Broadway production of Wilder's *The Skin of Our Teeth*, in which a father (played by Fredric March) and his obnoxious, Cain-like son (played by Montgomery Clift) come to near-fatal blows. But Wilder harbored other shadows, like the twin brother who died at birth, a signal event that influenced his work in its preoccupation with themes of duality, alter egos, and twinning. Think of the intense, almost telepathic bond Wilder helped build into the relationship between young Charlie Newton (played by Teresa Wright) and her suave, homicidal uncle (Joseph Cotten) in *Shadow of a Doubt*. And then there was Wilder's homosexuality, which remained unacknowledged until late in his life. In his 1967 novel *The Eighth Day*, published forty-one years after his father's death, Wilder created a plot that turned on a son murdering his violent father. He wrote in a letter, "Art is confession; art is the secret told. . . . But art is not only the desire to tell one's secret; it is the desire to tell it and hide it at the same time. And the secret is nothing more than the whole drama of the inner life."

Wilder had been writing for Hollywood since 1934, toiling on never-made versions of the story of Joan of Arc for Katharine Hepburn and a *Twelfth Night* for Marion Davies, as well as turning down the chance to write a Greta Garbo movie he felt was unworthy of her talents and his. He might have been a temperamentally and experientially apt partner to assist Hitchcock in taking Whitfield Cook's treatment to its next level. But the creator of *Our Town*, *The Matchmaker*, and *The Bridge of San Luis Rey* found *Strangers on a Train* too gimmicky, bleak, and tawdry to tempt him into reuniting with Hitchcock. Never one to take rejection lightly, Hitchcock was hurt and disappointed by Wilder's response. But he turned immediately to another giant: Dashiell Hammett, whose impact on crime and thriller literature places him securely in the company of Poe and Sir Arthur Conan Doyle.

Courting Hammett was probably a fool's errand on Hitchcock's part. At age fifty-six and suffering from debilitating bouts of poor health, worsened by heavy drinking, Hammett had published nothing new in seventeen long years. Decades past the literary glories and financial bounty afforded him by the publication of ninety short stories, five novels, and subsequent film versions of his seminal *The Thin Man* (1934), *The Maltese Falcon*, and *The Glass Key* (1950), in 1950 Hammett accepted an incentive of $10,000 ($130,000 today) from director William Wyler and Paramount Pictures to lure him back to Hollywood to work on the screenplay of *Detective Story* (1951), Sidney Kingsley's

1949 Broadway hit. Hammett mustered enough confidence to think he could begin writing again—telling his longtime on-and-off lover, playwright Lillian Hellman, that he could put himself right if only he could stay locked in a room with the typewriter. But he could not. He apparently dabbled a bit on *Detective Story* and, at the same time, on Wyler's script for *Sister Carrie*, but not enough to earn a writing credit. So Hammett's work for Wyler gained no more traction than such other recent offers as the chance to pen a new William Powell picture, a General John Pershing biographical film for Darryl F. Zanuck at 20th Century Fox, or a movie José Ferrer wanted to do based on Hammett's intoxicatingly atmospheric short story "Night Shade."

It was during this time that Hammett's agent informed him of Hitchcock's interest in hiring him. But at this sad stage of the once-towering author's life, he knew it was beyond him. Skipping town owing Paramount $10,000, he became a hermit and rented what Hellman called an "ugly little country cottage," where he spent the last four years of his life with her before dying of lung cancer in 1961.

Hitchcock also reached out to the brilliant Ben Hecht, upon whom he'd relied—sometimes credited, sometimes not—for *Foreign Correspondent* (1940), *Spellbound*, *Lifeboat*, *Notorious*, *The Paradine Case*, and *Rope*. Hecht, dubbed "the Shakespeare of Hollywood," told Hitchcock he was unable to offer him anything more than a quick rewrite and patch-up work once someone else had written a full screenplay. Similarly, Hitchcock failed to arouse interest from Lillian Hellman, Clifford Odets, or Arthur Laurents (who had adapted Patrick Hamilton's 1929 play for Hitchcock's *Rope*). Lamented Hitchcock, "Eight writers and not a single one was interested—nor did any like the story, for that matter." He elaborated, "I just couldn't find anyone to work on it. They all felt my first draft was so flat and factual that they couldn't see one iota of quality in it, yet the whole film was there if you visualized it."

There was bad blood between marquee-name screenwriter-novelist Raymond Chandler and Alfred Hitchcock.

Hitchcock remained committed to Whitfield Cook's treatment, but to further refine the narrative and create crackling dialogue—and to satisfy Jack Warner's insistence on a star name—he redoubled his efforts to pursue a top-tier, household-name novelist. In late June Warner began urging Hitchcock to consider collaborating on the script with the hardboiled fiction maestro Raymond Chandler, creator of the fictional character Philip Marlowe and author of *The Big Sleep*; *Farewell, My*

Lovely; *The High Window*; and *The Lady in the Lake*. Hitchcock agreed. Although Warner would not officially greenlight the production without a viable shooting script, the studio chief was sufficiently excited by the idea of a Hitchcock–Chandler collaboration to authorize Hitchcock to dispatch a second-unit crew to shoot necessary background, crowd, and atmospheric footage of the 1950 Davis Cup matches between Australia and the United States, held in New York at the West Side Tennis Club in Forest Hills, New York, August 25–27.

Before then, however, negotiations began for Chandler's writing service and continued into early July. On August 9, 1950, national newspapers carried the official press release: "Raymond Chandler, famous writer of mystery stories, has been assigned by Warner Bros. to write the screenplay *Strangers on a Train* for Alfred Hitchcock." Straight out of the gate, the perpetually aggrieved Chandler objected to the word "assigned" and so told his agent, Ray Stark, and Warner Bros. It marked the start of a rocky relationship with Hitchcock, although the director had nothing to do with the publicity release. But, then again, Chandler, who made Los Angeles and its environs synonymous with noir, maintained a fraught relationship with Hollywood—and, for that matter, much of the world beyond.

In a way, the animosity began with Billy Wilder deciding to direct a screen version of James M. Cain's 1936 thriller *Double Indemnity*. Hollywood's guardians of morality at the Hays Office instantly flagged the sexy, snarly, and violent book as unfilmable. Screenwriter Charles Brackett temporarily broke off his eleven-film partnership with Wilder over the project, telling him, "No, it's too grim for me." So Wilder tried getting Cain himself to collaborate on the script, but at the time the fifty-two-year-old writer was busy writing *Western Union* (1941) for Fox. Wilder turned to Chandler, who, according to Wilder, had never set foot on a movie studio lot and was mostly eking out a living by writing pulp fiction for *Black Mask* magazine and stringing tennis rackets as a side hustle. Wilder brought in Chandler for a meeting and gave him a copy of Cain's *Double Indemnity* to read. "I read that story. It's absolute shit," Chandler told the director the following day. Writing about Cain to his publisher, Alfred Knopf, Chandler described him as "every kind of writer I detest, a *faux naïf*, a dirty little boy with a piece of chalk and a board fence and nobody looking. Such people are the offal of literature, not because they write about dirty things but because they do it in a dirty way." Wilder attributed Chandler's disdain of Cain to envy of his financial success.

Nevertheless, Chandler accepted the job on a Friday, asked Wilder for a sample screenplay so that he could learn the form, and startled the director by asking whether he wanted the completed script a week from Monday. Ten days later, when Chandler delivered eighty pages of what Wilder described as "absolute bullshit," the director laid down the law for what would follow: a close collaboration with four months of daily meetings from 9:00 a.m. to roughly 4:30 p.m. Things got contentious quickly, with each man eventually going public with his list of grievances about the other, including how Wilder considered Chandler "a dilettante" and wound up observing, "There was a lot of Hitler in Chandler." The thin-skinned, hard-drinking writer wrote a resignation letter after Wilder, wielding a riding crop, dared to tell him to close the office's Venetian blinds without adding a "please." Another time Chandler fumed when Wilder downed three pre-lunch martinis and held phone conversations with "obviously young girls," spending fifteen minutes on just one call. ("Sex was rampant at the time," Wilder said, but, as for Chandler, "He just could not take it, because he was impotent, I guess.") Chandler later characterized Wilder as rude, uncooperative and—why not?—a Nazi. They so grew to despise each other that they decided to divide their workdays into shifts. One would arrive early at Paramount to work on his slice of the screenplay, and when finished for the day, he would clock out so the other writer could clock in and work alone. Concluded Wilder, "He was a mess, but he could write a beautiful sentence. 'There is nothing as empty as an empty swimming pool.' That is a great line." It sure is. Now go try to film it.

Chandler nursed his grudges. When Wilder completed *Double Indemnity*, Paramount held a preview screening in Westwood. Chandler was AWOL, but James M. Cain was there, and Wilder claimed that, after the screening, the author wept in gratitude over the many changes the director and Chandler had made to improve the source material. Though brilliant, *Double Indemnity* was only a middling success with critics. Neither was the movie the big box-office success its makers and Paramount had expected it would be. Despite earning seven Oscar nominations, it won none. Among the film's biggest admirers was Hitchcock, who rarely praised other directors yet wrote Wilder: "Dear Sir. I had the very great pleasure of seeing a lovely picture the other night and would like to say that the two most important words after '*Double Indemnity*' are 'Billy Wilder.'"

It is not known whether Hitchcock's unusually gracious letter sparked a conversation between him and Wilder about Chandler or anything else. But Wilder could have saved Hitchcock much agony over Chandler had he warned him of the gifted, fifty-eight-year-old Chandler's eccentricities and limitations. In any case, on July 7, 1950, Hitchcock's legal team closed the deal with agent Ray Stark for his new client Chandler to write the *Strangers on a Train* screenplay. Said H. N. Swanson, a friend of Hitchcock's and the legendary literary agent who sold the motion picture rights to Hollywood for such writers as F. Scott Fitzgerald, James M. Cain, William Faulkner, John O'Hara, Paul Gallico, Charles Bennett, and Raymond Chandler himself (for whom he sold *The Big Sleep* to Warner Bros.):

> Hitch never casually shopped for a "next picture." He always expected me to find "something different." He was

> relentless about it. He'd found that "something different" in *Strangers on a Train* and was more excited about it than he'd been in years. He told me the troubles he'd been having with the adaptation and the good writers who had already turned him down. We had talked for years about Ray [Chandler] and how much Hitch liked his work. So, I put the two of them together—at Hitch's personal request.

Financially, at least, the timing was right for Chandler, who had recently written the first chapter of a new novel but quickly abandoned the idea without having anything more promising on the immediate horizon. In early July the Hitchcock office had rushed Chandler a copy of Highsmith's novel, and after reading it, he dismissed it as "a silly enough story" and decried it for "advocating nihilism, moral anarchy, and homosexuality, a license for murderous compulsion." One might think that such moral outrage would have been enough to put him off the project entirely, as it had apparently done for other writers before him. But the prospect of writing it intrigued Chandler, and besides, even the legendarily penny-pinching Jack Warner and mighty Hitchcock acceded to Chandler's list of non-negotiables. Ray Stark's July 7, 1950, deal memo for Chandler stipulated as follows:

> *Chandler will start as of July 10, 1950.*
>
> *His compensation will be $2,550 per week [about $33,000 now], on a week-to-week basis, with a five-week guarantee.*
>
> *He will work from La Jolla, California [note: 130 miles from Warner Bros. Studios].*
>
> *Warner Brothers agrees to pay Chandler's secretary $50.00 [or $651 today] a week.*

Also included in the memo was a request to Warner Bros. story editor Finlay McDermid; Chandler wanted the studio to supply him with the exact type of manuscript paper he was expected to use. The studio complied.

Chandler's contract required him to devise a new story treatment, a rewrite of that treatment after consultation with Hitchcock, a complete screenplay, and one revised screenplay. It is remarkable that Hitchcock agreed to Chandler's demand that their work sessions take place at his home at 6005 Camino de la Costa in La Jolla, a 130-mile trek from Warner Bros., requiring Hitchcock to board an early-afternoon plane from Los Angeles to San Diego, then take a limousine to La Jolla, and back again. Consider it a measure of how much Hitchcock expected the screenplay could gain from Chandler's gift for characterization and smart, crackling dialogue. Consider it also an indicator that Chandler had been expecting to work solo and without the intercession of anyone, especially an opinionated and exacting film director. Quipped an H. N. Swanson Office memo about the imperious demand Chandler made of the equally imperious Hitchcock, "Since the mountain won't come to Mohammad, Mohammad is going down." "Down" referred to the wealthy, sleepy San Diego beach town enclave in which Chandler lived and described as "a nice place for old people and their parents" and so quiet "it's almost like being dead."

Despite Hitchcock's admiration of Chandler's work and Chandler's curiosity about Hitchcock, the writer got things off to a contentious start when he announced during their first meeting how unworthy of his and Hitchcock's efforts he thought Highsmith's book was. Still, Chandler appeared willing to make a go of the assignment, writing to close friend Hamish "Jamie" Hamilton, his London-based book publisher since 1939, "Why am I doing it? Partly because I thought I might like Hitch, which I do, and partly because one gets tired of saying no, and because one day I might want to say yes and not get asked."

From the outset, though, Hitchcock and Chandler were bad casting. For one thing, Chandler disapproved of Hitchcock bringing along to their San Diego story meetings screenwriter and production assistant Barbara ("Bobby") Keon, who had worked with the director since the 1940s. (At one point, Chandler would refer to Keon as one of Hitchcock's "henchmen.") Where Chandler preferred to dive headfirst into meetings, Hitchcock insisted upon a more leisurely and oblique approach. The director was perfectly content to lavish time on questions about where and on what the other had most recently dined, who else had also been there, and above all, what industry gossip had been gleaned along the way.

Nevertheless, the Warner Bros.' top brass were thrilled by the prospect of what Chandler and Hitchcock would concoct together. In a July 7, 1950, letter and parcel to Chandler, the studio's story department head Finlay McDermid, who was also a screenwriter, enthused,

> I am delighted that you will be working with Alfred Hitchcock on *Strangers on a Train.* Ray Stark relayed to me your request for some of our cockle paper, which I am sending separately. Also, I am enclosing, herewith, a copy of the screenplay of *The Big Sleep*, in case your secretary would like to know something about our screenplay form. (And anyhow you might find it entertaining.)

In the letter McDermid went on to remind Chandler of their first and only previous meeting in 1946, when he escorted the writer to and from a Warner Bros. screening room presenting a private showing of the Howard Hawks–directed movie version of Chandler's 1939 novel *The Big Sleep.*

Chandler learned quickly that, when it came to *Strangers on a Train*, the character of homicidal Bruno Antony commanded the lion's share of Hitchcock's interest. "The stronger the villain, the stronger the movie," Hitchcock insisted, and even the contrarian Chandler found no reason to debate the point. Every detail of Bruno fascinated Hitchcock, and he (and Whitfield Cook) had already discussed such matters on a granular level, right down to the food Bruno would order on the train. As Hitchcock explained,

> Preferences in food characterize people. I have always given it careful consideration so that my characters never eat "out of character." Bruno orders with gusto and with an interest in what he is going to eat—lamb chops, French fries, and chocolate ice cream. And the chocolate ice cream is probably what he thought about first. Bruno is rather a child. He is also something of a hedonist. Guy, on the other hand, shows little interest in eating the lunch, apparently having given it no advance thought, in contrast to Bruno, and he merely orders what seems his routine choice, a hamburger and coffee.

Bruno's menu sounds suspiciously like what Hitchcock might have ordered for himself. In any case, Chandler did not bother to hide that he found such conversation excruciatingly dull and pointless.

Deep fundamental issues soon dramatically divided Chandler and Hitchcock. Long before the novelist had signed his deal, Hitchcock and Whitfield Cook had already spent considerable time calibrating the intended homoerotic subtext and discussing signature visual motifs and bravura sequences that critics and audiences alike would later recognize as prime examples of "the Hitchcock Touch." Not surprisingly, Chandler tried to find ways to put his distinctive spin on the project. Isn't that why Hitchcock hired him, after all? Chandler wrote to Ray Stark,

> Hitchcock seems to be a very considerate and polite man, but he is full of little suggestions and ideas, which have a

> cramping effect on a writer's initiative. You are in a position of a fighter who can't get set because he is continuously being kept off balance. . . . He is always ready to sacrifice dramatic logic (insofar as it exists) for the sake of a camera effect or mood effect.

To help guide his way toward a more Chandlerian *Strangers*, featuring sharp dialogue and rich characterizations (no one expected great film plotting from Chandler), he would hammer Hitchcock with questions that he insisted audiences would expect to have answered, questions of logic that he believed Highsmith had dodged in the novel and worried that Hitchcock appeared all too willing to ignore. For example, when the intrusive, combustible, and clearly insane Bruno corners Guy Haines on the train, why doesn't the tennis player simply get up and move to another car? When Guy learns that Bruno has killed his ex-wife, why doesn't he go straight to the police? Why is the basically decent—if dull—Guy so indecisive and passive? Decades of collaborating with logic-minded writers and intrusive producers like David O. Selznick had taught Hitchcock how to feint, dodge, and deflect such pertinent questions. "Logic is dull," he would chide writers, adding, "If the character did what you are suggesting, we wouldn't have a movie." To silence inquisitive actors, Hitchcock would say, "Because the script and I tell you to." Chandler explained his frustration with Hitchcock's work methods, "The thing that amuses me about Hitchcock is the way he directs a film in his head before he knows what the story is. You find yourself trying to rationalize the shots he wants to make rather than the story. Every time you get set, he jabs you by wanting to do a love scene on top of the Jefferson Memorial or something like that."

There was one plot turn on which Chandler refused to relent: Guy's inexplicable transition to cold-blooded killer when he kills Bruno's father—though Hitchcock had long given up that plot twist of

Highsmith's. The writer instead sold Hitchcock on the notion that Guy only pretended that he had plans to kill the senior Mr. Antony, when he instead wants to confront Bruno's father by urging him to take action to stop his dangerously unhinged son. Chandler's argument hinged on Highsmith being able to "get away with murder" as a novelist in ways that a screenwriter never could. He embedded the following note in the first script pages he wrote for Guy and Bruno's initial shared scenes on the train:

> I nearly went crazy myself trying to block out this scene. I hate to say how many times I did it. It's darn near impossible to write, because consider what you have to put over:
>
> 1) A perfectly decent young man (Guy) agrees to murder a man he doesn't know, has never seen, in order to keep a maniac from giving himself away and from tormenting the nice young man.
>
> 2) From a character point of view, the audience will not believe the nice young man is going to kill anybody or has any idea of killing anybody.
>
> 3) Nevertheless, the nice young man has to convince Bruno and a reasonable percentage of the audience that what he is about to do is logical and inevitable. This conviction may not outlast the scene, but it has to be there, or else what the hell are the boys talking about?
>
> 4) All through this scene (supposing it can be written this way) we are flirting with the ludicrous. If it is not written and played exactly right, it will be absurd. The reason for

> this is that the situation actually is ludicrous in its essence, and this can only be overcome by developing a sort of superficial menace, which really has nothing to do with the business at hand.
>
> 5) Or am I still crazy?

—

As Chandler struggled with the differences between writing for readers versus writing for viewers, he continued to voice his issues to an increasingly impatient Hitchcock, who was under relentless pressure from Jack Warner and the "front office" for a satisfactory screenplay. Chandler's messages to Hitchcock only increased the director's suspicion that his screenwriter was stalling and had developed a case of "cold feet." Wrote Chandler,

> The question I should really like to have answered, although I don't expect an answer to it in this lifetime, is why in the course of nailing the frame of a film together so much energy and thought are invariably expended, and have to be expended, in exactly this sort of contest between a superficial reasonableness and a fundamental idiocy? Why do film stories always have to have this element of the grotesque? Whose fault is it? Is it anybody's fault? Or is it something inseparable from the making of motion pictures? Is it the price you pay for trying to make a dream look as if it really happened? I think possibly it is.
>
> When you read a story, you accept its implausibility and extravagances because they are no more fantastic than the conventions of the medium itself. But when you look at real

people, moving against a real background, and hear them speaking real words, your imagination is anesthetized. You accept what you see and hear, but you do not complement it from the resources of your imagination. The motion picture is like a picture of a lady in a half-piece bathing suit. If she wore a few more clothes, you might be intrigued. If she wore no clothes at all, you might be shocked. But the way it is, you are occupied with noticing that her knees are too bony and her toenails too large. The modern film tries too hard to be real. Its techniques of illusion are so perfect that it requires no contribution from the audience but a mouthful of popcorn.

The more real you make Guy and Bruno, the more unreal you make their relationship, the more it stands in need of rationalization and justification. You would like to ignore this and pass on, but you can't. You have to face it, because you have deliberately brought the audience to the point of realizing that what this story is about [is] the horror of an absurdity become real—an absurdity (please notice because this is very important) which falls just short of being impossible. If you wrote a story about a man who woke up in the morning with three arms, your story would be about what happened to him as a result of this extra arm. You would not have to justify his having it. That would be the premise. But the premise of this story is not that a nice young man might in certain circumstances murder a total stranger just to appease a lunatic. That is the end result. The premise is that if you shake hands with a maniac, you may have sold your soul to the devil.

Chandler's meetings with Hitchcock plodded along as the writer's contractual deadline for delivery of the first draft treatment loomed. Perhaps due to Hitchcock's indirect, confrontation-averse communication style, Chandler presumed—not unlike Bruno presumes of Guy—that he and Hitchcock were on the same page despite some temperamental and creative differences. In fact, however, they were imagining almost entirely different films—so much so that Hitchcock was already on the hunt for another screenwriter. He just didn't bother to inform Chandler or Jack Warner. With Warner pressing Hitchcock to confirm a hard production start date, Chandler obliged by promising to speed up completion of the first-draft treatment, which he delivered on July 28. But even the highlights of that treatment underscore the vast gulf between what Hitchcock expected and what Chandler was prepared to (or able to?) deliver. Chandler commits an unforgivable screenwriting sin: he tells instead of shows. As bad or worse? Chandler's gifts for creating mood, intriguing characters, and crackling dialogue were scarcely to be found.

Chandler's first effort so dispirited Hitchcock that he did not show it to Jack Warner, who—in that absence of knowledge—was now entertaining the possibility that both the first and second production units might begin shooting at the end of August—*if* Hitchcock and Chandler came up with a screenplay he liked. Behind the scenes, Hitchcock instructed Chandler to make cuts and revisions to the treatment and, above all, return to what the director thought was the best material in Whitfield Cook's earlier treatment.

On August 1, Chandler responded with a four-page revised synopsis that culled some of the best of Cook's work; Hitchcock gave him a half-hearted go-ahead to expand this synopsis into a full screenplay. Chandler accelerated his pace, delivering 38 screenplay pages on August 5 and another 68 pages on August 12; on August 25, he tendered a complete 144-page first draft screenplay. From September 2 to 30,

Chandler filed, in sections, revisions to that draft. The script begins with the arresting image of two pairs of feet in contrasting styles of shoes heading to the train. There is considerable reason to suspect that this imagery came from Hitchcock, especially considering the visual signatures Chandler deleted from his draft—Miriam's strangulation reflected in the eyeglasses, the swiveling heads of the tennis spectators except for Bruno staring at Guy, and Bruno appearing like an unsightly stain on the white stairs of the Jefferson Memorial. (Or was he intended as a visual manifestation of Washington's 1950s paranoia about imaginary homosexual infiltrators lying in wait to lure government employees into selling government secrets?) In any event, reading Chandler's screenplay pages, it is difficult to escape the impression that Hitchcock's brand of visual storytelling—"pure cinema," as he liked to call it—utterly eluded Chandler.

What works best in Chandler's screenplay drafts? Some of the dialogue has verve, and even the stolid Anne gets off a few good zingers. It does feature a familiar scene that Chandler described as his and Hitchcock's "stop-gap" until they came up with something better: Guy stealthily enters Mr. Antony's bedroom and finds Bruno in the bed. Hitchcock not only liked it; he also embroidered a detail. Bruno startles Guy by emerging from under the covers still wearing his formal attire from the party at the Morton residence. Chandler awaited Hitchcock's reaction to the script but didn't get one. Chandler wrote to Ray Stark, "I don't know whether he likes it or whether he thinks it stinks. The only method I have of deducing an answer to this question is that I was allowed to finish it." Instead, Warner Bros. story department head Finlay McDermid, not Hitchcock, delivered to Chandler a report of the Breen Office's censorship objections.

The self-censorship board of the Motion Picture Code, launched in 1934, was charged with monitoring Hollywood films for unacceptable motion picture content—anything from, in the language of the Code, "pointed profanity" and "licentious or suggestive nudity" to "ridicule of the clergy" and "any inferences of sex perversion." First formulated in the 1920s by Will H. Hays and enforced in the 1950s by his successor, Joseph Breen, the Code's true power lay in its ability to deem any film noncompliant toward the Code and effectively bar it from distribution to theaters. No wonder screenplays needed to be vetted before a film headed into production.

Through the decades, Alfred Hitchcock was among the directors who did all he could to subvert and skirt the Code, expose it for its absurdity, and contribute to its eventual weakening. So, the Code forbids any depiction of so-called sex perversion? Hitchcock answers with the character of housekeeper Mrs. Danvers in the 1940 film *Rebecca* and does so through lighting, movement, and the superb performance of Judith Anderson as she reverentially talks about her late mistress while running her fingers over her lingerie and other personal items. So, the Code restricts people from kissing for any more than three seconds, does it? In *Notorious* in 1946, Hitchcock responds with an intimate two-minute-forty-five-second scene with the camera tracking so close to Ingrid Bergman and Cary Grant that we are virtually voyeurs as the gorgeous duo intimately nuzzle, make small talk, and constantly kiss—but break every three seconds as they simply cross a room.

Wrote the Breen Office after reviewing Chandler's screenplay,

> As set up at present, Guy and all our sympathetic characters are the ones who are pressing for a divorce [from Miriam]. If instead, Miriam had wanted the divorce and Guy had made some attempts to hold the marriage together but then had accepted the situation, the Breen office would find this phase of the plot more acceptable. Guy, returning to see Miriam would find that she had changed her mind again and he would still have the same reactions.

McDermid informed Chandler that the Breen Office also expressed "concerns" about

> the rather bald way in which the treatment shows Bruno's home life in a literal manner and the equally bald manner in which Ann [*sic*], Barbara and other sympathetic characters disclose the point that there is a latent murderer in everyone. I have assured the Breen Office representative that these elements will not be so blatantly expressed in the [final] screenplay and that Ann's thrill over the mistaken thought that Guy has killed for her will also be carefully expressed.
>
> I pass these things on to you with the assurance that you can cope with such problems. *Strangers on a Train* will, I know, be a much more impelling, convincing drama after it receives its transfusion of Chandler dialogue and characterization.

If only it had.

In his essential book *Hitchcock at Work* (1999), Bill Krohn rightfully questions how closely the censors read Chandler's work. If so, how could they have missed some of Chandler's pointedly homoerotic dialogue for and homophobic dialogue *about* Bruno? Or his image of Bruno pausing at the window of a dress shop, the better to "see his reflection take his place among the actual models of women in their various stylized postures"? What to make of the censors' shrugging off a scene in which a young messenger delivering Bruno a package (at the tennis club where Guy is playing) reacts in disgust—spitting on the ground and raising his middle finger—believeing that the older man is trying to make a pass at him? And how could the Breen office possibly miss the point of Guy telling Bruno that "his type" is always "theatrical"? Unless, of course, all of this and more flew completely over their heads?

Given the disdain Chandler had displayed toward gay characters in his books (despicable although hardly atypical for its time), let alone his apparent discomfort with all things sexual, one wonders how much his homophobia infected his attitude toward the project, especially considering the elements that Whitfield Cook had subtly woven into his treatment in which Bruno is a full-blown mama's boy, a French-speaking snob and dilettante, a gourmand, and showy fashion plate—in other words, in simplistic 1950s terms, a coded homosexual. It is likely that Chandler would try to talk Hitchcock out of indulging in these touches. But it is equally unlikely that this would have made any difference to Hitchcock, whose films often contain, for better or worse, coded queer or sexually conflicted villains, sometimes as murderers, murder suspects, or figures of fun (*Blackmail* [1929], *The Lady Vanishes, Rebecca, Suspicion, Shadow of a Doubt, Psycho*). Not only did the Hitchcocks enjoy the company of many gay friends, but Hitchcock's casts are also filled with gay and bisexual actors.

Nevertheless, with no recent communication from Hitchcock, Chandler decided on his own not only to respond to the Breen Office's complaints but to also make alterations based upon communications from McDermid. The latter had indicated that Hitchcock remained unsatisfied with Chandler's handling of Guy and Bruno's first meeting and advised Chandler to take an approach more along the lines of "You do me a favor. I do you a favor." That is: a crisscross rather than Chandler's proposal of having the two characters stop the movie dead in its tracks with a dry, psychiatric discussion of murder. For its divergence from and similarities to the *Strangers on a Train* Hitchcock eventually made, the revised second draft is most noteworthy for:

- When Guy first spots Bruno's flashy tie pin on the train and comments on it, Bruno blushes and is "almost puppyish in his friendliness."

- When Miriam and Guy meet to discuss their divorce and future in a hometown malt and milkshake hangout for teens, Miriam so angers the waitress, a former schoolmate, that the latter says, "Once a tramp, always a tramp." In petty retaliation, Miriam steals the tip Guy leaves for the waitress.

- Bruno's mother, Mrs. Antony, becomes a "handsome, soigné woman in her late 40s, early 50s." An attached, unsigned, handwritten note suggests such potential casting ideas as the sly sophisticates Irene Dunne or Claudette Colbert, two stars with whom Hitchcock had wanted to work since the 1940s. Also floated as possibilities were Myrna Loy and Joan Fontaine (the latter Hitchcock's 1940s-era protégée known for her career-making roles in the director's *Rebecca* and *Suspicion*).

- Chandler builds up the scene of Bruno waiting outside Miriam's place of employment–a family business, Joyce's Hat Shop–where "a husky, leering young man" picks her up and hustles her into his flashy convertible car. "I want to ride the merry-go-round lots," says Miriam. Her date says, leering at her, "You ain't going to spend the night on the merry-go-round."

- This draft introduces the moment at the amusement park when Bruno spitefully bursts the balloon of the bratty little boy.

- Guy slugs Bruno when the latter turns up at his apartment and callously tells him he has killed Miriam.

- After Miriam's murder, Chandler proposes a two-minute montage (over two script pages) of various Metcalf citizens verbally damning Miriam with the sort of sexist judgments that some today would call "slut-shaming."

- When Bruno appears on the steps of the Jefferson Memorial, Anne and Guy both notice him as they walk past.

- Chandler—with the assistance/goading of Hitchcock?—makes a banquet of the scene in which Bruno materializes in the Fossil Hall of the Smithsonian Museum of Natural History, where he comes closer and closer to Guy and Anne by zigzagging in and out of the rows of giant dinosaur displays. It's one of the few moments that, at least visually, feels distinctively Hitchcockian.

- During Guy's tennis match sequence, this draft introduces the recurring motif of Bruno hearing the carousel calliope in his memory and seeing the spinning merry-go-round in the lenses of Barbara's glasses.

- Mrs. Antony chides her husband's warning that Bruno is again becoming dangerous by saying, "Why, Bruno couldn't frighten a sparrow." *Or harm a fly?*

- He describes Bruno as "a casual, cheerful, slightly impudent young man of 24 or 25, well-dressed in a sloppy sort of way"; Guy, however, is "a serious, almost solemn young fellow of about the same age. He has a sensitive face and is a little shy."

With his submission of this second full screenplay draft (which Hitchcock also pointedly ignored), Chandler had fulfilled the terms of his contract and made it clear to his agent that, going forward, he would prefer working only with a director "who realizes that what is said and how it is said is more important than shooting it upside down through a glass of champagne."

It was clear—to Hitchcock, at least—that the Hitchcock-Chandler experiment was long over. Chandler had come to experience those summertime story meetings with Hitchcock as "god-awful jabber sessions which seem to be an inevitable although painful part of the picture business." He had even come to resent Hitchcock's presence in his own La Jolla home—which had been one of Chandler's imperious requirements in the first place—and abhorred even the sight of the director sipping tea while parked on Chandler's davenport. Even the pretense of civility had so vanished from early July to mid-August that, on their penultimate mid-August attempt at collaborating in person, Chandler stood at the front door watching Hitchcock's car arrive and, as the director alighted, Chandler said aloud, "Look at that fat bastard trying to get out of his limousine!" When his secretary warned that he'd be overheard, Chandler snapped, "What do I care?" Chandler likened Hitchcock's silences to "Chinese water torture." Observed longtime Hitchcock assistant producer and assistant director Herbert Coleman, "Hitch disliked confrontation. It made him terribly uncomfortable. If he was unhappy with someone, he would rarely speak directly about the reasons. He let others do that for him."

In their final meeting at Chandler's home on August 21, Chandler drunkenly harangued Hitchcock with an old complaint—the gross deficiencies of the source material and of the project itself. Hitchcock rose and, without uttering a word, simply walked out on Chandler mid-tirade. Returning to his production office, he stonily announced to Barbara Keon, his associate producer, "He's through." There was no equivocation on Hitchcock's part. The personal meetings stopped. Likewise the phone calls. Although it galled Hitchcock to do it, he authorized the studio to pay off Chandler with a $40,000 check (about $520,000 today) for his work. A decade after Hitchcock terminated the relationship, the director, talking with director François Truffaut, summarized his problems with Chandler thus: "We didn't get along. It has never worked well when I have collaborated with another mystery writer. We'd sit together searching for an idea and I'd say, 'Why not do it this way?' He'd say, 'Well, if you can think it out, what do you want me for?' The work he did was not good."

The experience confused and apparently bruised Chandler, who concluded, "The fallacy of this operation was my being involved at all, because it is obvious to me now, and must have been obvious to many people long since, that a Hitchcock picture has to be all Hitchcock. . . . [The screenplay] has too much Ray in it and not enough Hitchcock." If only that were true. In reality, he failed to deliver even the Chandlerian hallmarks that drew Jack Warner and Hitchcock to his work in the first place. The Raymond Chandler who made critics and readers fall in love with his moody, snarly, brainy trench coat–clad heroes and nefarious, alluring heroines seemed to have deserted him entirely.

As far as Hitchcock was concerned, the writer had long since proven himself unfit for the assignment. Chandler's letters in the days just before his sacking express his resentments, bewilderment, and frailties. In a letter to literary agent Bernice Baumgarten dated September 13, 1950, Chandler wrote,

> I'm still slaving away on this Hitchcock thing, which you may or may not have heard about. Some days I think it is fun and other days I think it is damn foolishness. The money looks good, but as a matter of fact it isn't. I'm too conscientious and, although I do not work nearly as fast as I would have worked twenty years ago, I still work faster than the job requires or has any reason to expect. For the most part the work is boring, unreal, and I have no feeling that this is the kind of thing I can do better than anybody else. Suspense as an absolute quality has never seemed to

> me very important. At best it is a secondary growth, and at worst an attempt to make something out of nothing.

Putting a fine point upon his assessment of Hitchcock, Chandler wrote in a letter to Jamie Hamilton dated September 28, 1950,

> There seems to be the general opinion about Hitchcock that he has shot his wad but that is always a dangerous assumption with a man of any talent. He is definitely a man of talent, but he belongs to a type which is rather dull outside its particular skill. Some moviemakers, like some writers, seem to do their work without committing more than a small part of their real abilities. They belong to the class [that] I class the amateurs; when they are big enough they are geniuses. Others can do some particular thing extremely well, but you would never think they had it in them merely by meeting them. These are the technicians. I'd say Hitch belongs to this group, but of course I don't really know the man.

Hitchcock instructed Warner Bros. to inform Chandler that he was officially terminated as of Saturday, September 24, 1950, and the studio took him off the payroll the following day. On September 26, agent Ray Stark told the studio, rather foolishly, that Chandler himself was terminating. *You can't fire me! I quit!*

This left Hitchcock virtually back at square one. As if to throw yet another monkey wrench into the movie's fateful journey, *Strangers on a Train* looked as if it might even lose its title when MGM considered the name a potential threat to the success of their own similarly titled movie and registered their concern with the Warner Bros. legal department. The movie in question was *Man on a Train*, an Anthony

Mann-directed Abraham Lincoln assassination thriller starring Dick Powell, for which MGM had proposed a November 1951 release, a year later. Warner Bros.' legal department countered that they saw no problem, as the only similarity was the title—a title known from Patricia Highsmith's novel. In the end, MGM retitled their film *The Tall Target* and rescheduled it to open in August 1951, two months after the release of *Strangers on a Train.* With that crisis averted, Jack Warner chose that precise moment to pounce, telling Hitchcock that he intended to kill *Strangers on a Train* for creative and budgetary concerns. Hitchcock knew this was no idle threat. Said Vincent Sherman, who directed many of Warner's biggest stars in such films as *All Through the Night* (1942), *Old Acquaintance* (1943), *Mr. Skeffington* (1944), and *The Adventures of Don Juan* (1949),

> Jack Warner hired and fired people and canceled pictures like that! If he got tired of a project, an actor, producer, director complaining about money or about some creative difference they might have about a movie, if they protested, he'd just look out the window and say, "Whose name is on that water tower out there?" And when the business tightened up because we were losing audiences to TV and the studios lost ownership of their theaters because of the Consent Decree, he got even tighter with budgets. People in town used to say, "If you could make it at Warner Bros., you could make it anywhere."

Hitchcock was also aware that, as early as December 18, 1947, Warner had been firing off dire internal studio memos to Steve Trilling, his second in command: "I can't impress enough upon you emphatically enough the importance of cutting the budgets. Everything must come down and anyone who doesn't want to cooperate I'm afraid will just have to. We are fighting a hell of a battle and you must tell every director and writer in no uncertain terms."

Threatened with the very real possibility of Jack Warner icing *Strangers on a Train*, Hitchcock resolved to deliver to the studio boss a "temporary shooting script" based largely on his and Whitfield Cook's treatment–in three weeks or less. Although he had already decided to use nothing of Chandler's work, he opted to twist the knife just a little. In the scene during which Guy returns to the Morton house after being grilled by the police, Hitchcock told associates that he planned to add an in-joke that would remain in the final film. Blink and you'll miss it, but the heroine's precocious young sister Barbara, played by Hitchcock's daughter, Pat, is seen reading a paperback novel: Raymond Chandler's *The Big Sleep*.

Hitchcock convinced Warner to let him make this last-ditch effort. It was around this time that Hitchcock provided an update to Patricia Highsmith, who recalled, "I was in New York. He was in California. He rang me once to report on his progress and said, 'I'm having trouble. I've just sacked my second screenwriter.'" The director doubled back to Ben Hecht, who informed him that he was still too busy. Or was he simply uninterested? Instead, Hecht recommended Czenzi Ormonde. Described as "a fair-haired beauty with long, shimmering hair," the forty-four-year-old novelist from Tacoma, Washington, had worked as a secretary to producer Samuel Goldwyn. By 1950 she was employed as a literary assistant to Hecht himself. Even on Hecht's recommendation, Jack Warner informed Hitchcock that Ormonde was approved but only as "the end of the line": without an acceptable screenplay in hand by November 30, Warner would officially cancel the production. There were several reasons for Warner's willingness to cut the project loose, not the least of which was that his studio was suddenly in the throes of their biggest production boom in two years, with eight movies before the cameras, including *A Streetcar Named Desire*, *Lullaby of*

Studio chief Jack Warner only approved Ben Hecht protégée Czenzi Ormonde as Hitchcock's final hope of getting a workable screenplay.

Broadway, *The Enforcer*, *Goodbye My Fancy*, *Inside the Walls of Folsom Prison*, and *Along the Great Divide*. Warner was so bullish about the studio's new product that he didn't think the studio needed *Strangers on a Train* among its 1951 releases—if it ever did.

Hitchcock was under the gun, and now he'd brought on a writer who was by no means a sure bet. Yes, Ormonde earned good notices for her first novel in 1948, an anecdotal Bohemian family childhood memoir titled *Laughter from Downstairs*, but she was unproven as a screenwriter. Ben Hecht said she had the stuff, so Hitchcock agreed to meet her in his office. Ormonde recalled, "When he told [me] Raymond Chandler had worked on it, I wondered what I was doing there, being a great fan of Mr. Chandler's." The writer expected that all a Chandler script needed was a few revisions. But when Ormonde wanted to see Chandler's screenplay, Hitchcock pinched his nose with one hand, picked up the script with the thumb and forefinger of his other hand, dangled the screenplay over the wastebasket, and dropped it. He announced, "Now, we start with page one." He told her Chandler had not even written a single line of dialogue worth using. He also told her Highsmith's story in detail, advised her to forget it, and said he wanted them to go back to Whitfield Cook's treatment.

With Chandler out of the way, Hitchcock and Warner Bros. officially hired Ormonde on September 30 on a week-to-week basis at a weekly salary of $500 (about $6,500 in today's terms), a long way down from Chandler's $2,550 per week. Hitchcock supervised and advised Ormonde, who wrote ingeniously and quickly, cherry-picking some of the best elements of Cook's work and, yes, even a soupçon of Chandler's, but she went off in her own direction as well. Ormonde delivered the first fifty-two pages of the new screenplay on October 21, 1950, and rapidly made thirty-three revisions at the director's request and five additional suggested revisions on October 28. The fifty-two subsequent revisions she made from November 4 to 25 gave Hitchcock a full script that won a green light from Jack Warner and an official start date; Hitchcock was authorized to begin choosing his cast and crew. Ormonde recalled, "Mr. Hitchcock had an urgent time schedule imposed on him by the front office, one of his abominations along with policemen and confrontations. After I began the script and he saw that it was going well, he left for the east [coast] to shoot exteriors. He liked what was happening with the story and felt confident that he would approve of what was written while he was away. He particularly enjoyed the buildup I gave to Bruno's mother and sent to London for Marion Lorne to play the part."

Hitchcock required Ormonde to make thirty more small revisions to the script from November 25 to December 2. He also thought the dialogue needed a polish. To speed things up and to outrun Warner's continued ambivalence toward the project, Hitchcock assigned scenarist and production associate Barbara Keon to work alongside Ormonde on completing these alterations. Keon had previously worked for Hitchcock on *Rebecca*, *Spellbound*, *Notorious*, and *The Paradine Case*. Modified pages 101 to 137 of the 153-page script arrived on November 11, and further revisions were made that same day. The Hitchcocks, Ormonde, and Keon worked together on November 12 and again on November 18 and 25, the latter being the day the final pages were tendered. Keon provided seventeen further dialogue revisions between November 25 and December 16.

These revisions included clarifying the central plot by using the term "crisscross" by having Bruno say, "I do your murder, you do mine"; specifying the exact details of the decoration and engraving of Guy's cigarette lighter as it appears in the film; and reimagining Bruno's mother from a fading former Ziegfeld showgirl and actress to an emotionally addled older woman with a tenuous grasp on reality.

Clearly, Ormonde did not start from ground zero, as Hitchcock told interviewers for years. She tightened, streamlined, and shed the expositional bloat. Barbara Keon's (and Ormonde's) dialogue improved significantly on Cook's work and far surpassed Chandler's. While the screenplay never rose to the peak level Hitchcock had hoped for—for example, *Shadow of a Doubt* or *Notorious*—he nonetheless believed that with his direction, the right casting, and some good luck, the film could work. The script stamped FINAL was a compilation, primarily created from October 21 to November 25, 1950. The cover and title page read "by Czenzi Ormonde (revisions by Alfred Hitchcock and Barbara Keon)."

By all accounts, Hitchcock and Ormonde's collaboration was congenial and drama-free. Definitive Hitchcock biographer Patrick McGilligan quotes Ormonde as confirming her personal experience of witnessing Alfred Hitchcock's much-publicized fear of police. Ormonde recalled being behind the wheel one day when she drove Hitchcock off the Warner Bros. lot and they encountered the usual slow-and-go traffic. When Ormonde suddenly spotted in her rearview mirror a motorcycle cop materializing and following them, she glanced over and saw Hitchcock becoming visibly agitated. She assured him that she had been driving under the legal speed limit. At a traffic stop, however, the policeman swerved his motorcycle in front of their car and pulled up alongside them. The officer said, "I saw you and Mr. Hitchcock leave the studio. I want to tell him I never miss a Hitchcock film. They are the greatest." Ormonde remained silent but Hitchcock looked frozen, as if "he didn't hear what was said, perhaps had not heard it. Fists were clenched, face was pale, his eyes stared ahead. Visibly, this was a very frightened man."

Both Hitchcock and Ormonde wanted Chandler's name kept off the film's credits. Hitchcock met with Jack Warner and told him so, but the studio boss exerted pressure on Hitchcock to retain Chandler's first-position credit. Chandler's name seemed a worthy one to exploit, especially for a film Warner thought needed all the prestige and box-office help it could get.

With the script coming together, Hitchcock also focused on hiring his crew. *Strangers* marked the first of what would go on to be twelve collaborations with cinematographer Robert Burks. Burks, then forty-one, had begun in the business at age nineteen in the Warner Bros. special effects unit before working himself up to becoming the film industry's youngest director of photography at age thirty-five. Jack

Warner agreed to assign Burks to Hitchcock after the cameraman had proven his worth on a mixed bag of the studio's output, including *Task Force* (1949), *The Fountainhead* (1949), and *The Glass Menagerie* (1950). Temperamentally and artistically, he and Hitchcock would prove to be a match made in cinematic heaven, one of the most rewarding and aesthetically influential collaborations of the director's career.

Multi-Oscar-winning production designer-director William Cameron Menzies (*Gone with the Wind* [1939], *Rebecca, Foreign Correspondent*) recommended thirty-four-year-old art director Edward S. Haworth (better known as Ted) to Hitchcock. Haworth had learned under Menzies the crucial importance of storyboarding an entire film shot by shot in preproduction. *Strangers on a Train* would mark Haworth's first credit as art director; his previous film credits billed him as production designer. Haworth told author Vincent LoBrutto in 1992,

> [Hitchcock's] way of communicating was to sit down and literally draw three lines and say, "Do you have the idea?" . . . Those lines had composition; they had light and dark. Hitch didn't spend an ounce of time more than he had to convey the idea. I would make sketches, and Hitch would approve or not approve them. Hitch was one of the few directors who knew exactly what it was going to be by the time he went on the set. He would say, "I need space here because when two people are angry, they almost always distance themselves from each other and start yelling." He would sit down and think about what he wanted to do with the set in detail. He would say, "Everybody get lost for a few minutes," and chase everybody out of the room but never the art director. He was just an absolute gem to work for.

Other key assignees included editor William Ziegler (*I'll Be Seeing You* [1944], *Rope*), camera operator Leonard South (*The Fountainhead*; *Strangers on a Train* marked his first of fifteen Hitchcock films), second cameraman William Schurr (*The Public Enemy*; *Strangers* was the first of his five with Hitchcock), costume designer Leah Rhodes (*Now, Voyager*; she apprenticed under the legendary Orry-Kelly, the studio's chief costume designer from 1932 to 1944), men's wardrobe Robert O'Dell (*A Streetcar Named Desire*), topflight set decorator George James Hopkins (*Casablanca*, *Mildred Pierce*, four-time Oscar-winner-to-be), and script supervisor Rita Michaels (*The Glass Menagerie*; marking her first of three successive Hitchcock assignments). Finally, after Warner Bros. erroneously announced Max Steiner as Hitchcock's musical composer, Dimitri Tiomkin (*It's a Wonderful Life* [1946], *Red River* [1948], *High Noon* [1952]) joined the team of collaborators.

As Ormonde worked on the script—which she would continue to do even while the film was in production—Raymond Chandler began communicating directly with the studio again through letters to Finlay McDermid. In a letter to Chandler dated November 5, 1950, the studio executive referred to complaints lodged by Chandler in a November 2 letter as stemming "from a failure of the communication system between Burbank and La Jolla" and explained why they preferred writers to be in closer proximity to producers, directors, "and other individuals who make up the corporation." McDermid expressed (whether it was true or not) that he had been under the impression that Hitchcock and Chandler had been maintaining regular contact during their entire period of collaboration.

And then McDermid delivered Warner Bros.' coup de grâce to Chandler: "In the near future I will have to send out tentative writing credits. Would you have any objection to sharing a screenplay credit if it develops that the writer now working on the script seems entitled to that distinction?" That's when Chandler first learned that Ormonde, another Ray Stark client, was "the writer now working on the script." Chandler fired off a letter to Stark to express his fury over what he saw as another in a long trail of Hollywood betrayals: "It's one thing to be stabbed in the back without having your agent supply the knife." In late November Stark slipped Chandler a copy of the "Raymond Chandler and Czenzi Ormonde" script. Chandler fired Stark immediately and went back to H. N. Swanson. Predictably, Chandler loathed the Ormonde-Keon-Hitchcock screenplay. Just as predictably, he wanted Hitchcock to know just how much he loathed it:

December 6th, 1950

Dear Hitch,

In spite of your wide and generous disregard of my communications on the subject of the script of Strangers on a Train and your failure to make any comment on it, and in spite of not having heard a word from you since I began the writing of the actual screenplay–for all of which I might say I bear no malice, since this sort of procedure seems to be part of the standard Hollywood depravity–in spite of this and in spite of this extremely cumbersome sentence, I feel that I should, just for the record, pass you a few comments on what is termed the final script. I could understand your finding fault with my script in this or that way, thinking that such and such a scene was too long or such and such a mechanism was too awkward. I could understand you changing your mind about the things you specifically wanted, because some of such changes might have been imposed on you from without. What I cannot understand is your permitting a script which after all had some life and vitality to be reduced

> *to such a flabby mass of clichés, a group of faceless characters, and the kind of dialogue every screenwriter is taught not to write–the kind that says everything twice and leaves nothing to be implied by the actor or the camera. Of course you must have had your reasons but, to use a phrase once coined by Max Beerbohm, it would take a "far less brilliant mind than mine" to guess what they were.*
>
> *Regardless of whether or not my name appears on the screen among the credits, I'm not afraid that anybody will think I wrote this stuff. They'll know damn well I didn't. I shouldn't have minded in the least if you had produced a better script–believe me. I shouldn't. But if you wanted something written in skim milk, why on earth did you bother to come to me in the first place? What a waste of money! What a waste of time! It's no answer to say that I was well paid. Nobody can be adequately paid for wasting his time.*

Chandler was not done venting his spleen. In a December 15 letter to agent H. N. Swanson, one of whose agency colleagues had sent the writer a clipping about *Strangers on a Train*, Chandler called himself "fantastically uninterested in [that] project and with everyone who had anything to do with getting it up." Lobbing a volley at Ray Stark and Hitchcock, Chander complained that "if I'd had an agent who was any good, he would have told me what to expect from our fat little friend," i.e., a certain suspense film director who "has hardly any feeling for dialogue and none at all for plausibility. I don't know whether he is scared or just terribly conceited–perhaps a little of both–but it's clear that he won't let anything get into the picture which he can't at least say he thought of."

A million-dollar question surrounding the *Strangers on a Train* screenplay: How, if at all, do Cook's, Chandler's, and Team Ormonde's contributions intersect? It's impossible to answer definitively. But Bill Krohn's book *Hitchcock at Work* provides at least one glimpse. Consider the phone booth scene that follows Guy and Miriam's angry confrontation in the music shop. In Chandler's script, Guy's conversation with Anne climaxes with him shouting, "I'd like to . . . !" To which Ormonde, Alma Reville, Alfred Hitchcock, or Barbara Keon added: ". . . strangle her!" Then Hitchcock, Ormonde, and editor William H. Ziegler devised the idea of an editing "dissolve" from Guy's expression of rage to a close view of Bruno's flexing hands, as if to strangle someone when, in fact, he is only flexing after a manicure. The final contribution came from Hitchcock's written instruction to editor William Ziegler to minimize the time spent lingering on Bruno's hands. That's how collaborative the moviemaking process can be.

With a working screenplay in hand, Hitchcock now had to wrangle one more time with the censors over the screenplay while beginning the casting process.

CHAPTER FOUR

HITCHCOCK OUTWITS THE BREEN OFFICE

In both 1950 and 1951, Hollywood's eight most prolific studios submitted roughly two thousand screenplays, rough cuts, and release prints seeking the Production Code's seal of approval. A production failing to clear the moral and political bar set by the panel of movie censors—commonly known as "the Hays Office"—could be denied a numbered Production Code certification, and that spelled big publicity (often a good thing) but also the threat that the movie may be barred from theaters (an unthinkably expensive calamity). Hitchcock and Jack Warner carefully reviewed the several exceptions the censor took to the final script. Although most of them may sound ridiculous today—as they surely must have to Hitchcock—they had to be addressed. For instance, the tipsy Professor Collins, whom Guy Haines encounters on the train, "will not be offensively drunk in this sequence." Breen also raised issues about a speech in which the deluded Mrs. Antony announces her suspicion that her son is going away for "a weekend with a girl" rather than going away to murder a woman. Breen wanted Hitchcock to entirely delete Anne's supportive speech to Guy after Miriam's murder:

"Even if you had done it, I'd have stuck by you. Even if you'd had anything to do with it, I would have gone into hiding with you anywhere." (It was cut.) Breen voiced serious objections to Bruno's demonstration of strangling Mrs. Cunningham at the Morton's party, warning that, in filming the scene, Hitchcock's close-ups "should not be such as to show any objectionable details of the strangling but should be handled largely by suggestion." Even with the slight modifications Hitchcock made in the shooting and editing process, that scene would go on to arouse such wrath from local censorship boards across the country that it got cut (or substantially edited) from prints shown in several of the more conservative American theatrical markets.

The censors also leveled complaints about Mrs. Cunningham's fellow dowager Mrs. Anderson suggesting to Bruno, "How about a little arsenic?" (as a way of murdering a loved one) and suggested substituting the word "poison." During the carousel showdown between Guy and Bruno, Hollywood's guardians of morality demanded that Hitchcock "Handle with care to avoid unacceptable brutality." Hence, no kicking, kneeing, or bloodied knuckles—all of which, of course, the director ignored. Breen also demanded elimination of the words "jeez," "damn," and "hell"—traditionally the kinds of things Hitchcock would add to a screenplay simply as diversionary bargaining chips. Additionally, when a mother in the amusement park crowd finds her young son a survivor of the merry-go-round crash and utters, "Thank God," Breen insisted that it "must be delivered reverently." In the script's final moments, when a minister interrupts Guy and Anne on their train trip, intended as a lightly comical callback to Bruno's first encounter with Guy, the censor preferred the character to be someone "not connected with the church." The final clause of Breen's letters was usually the boilerplate: "You understand, of course, that our final judgment will be based upon the finished picture."

Hitchcock participated in a conference with Breen on October 27, and ever the master entertainer and prevaricator, he solemnly assured

"You don't mind if I borrow your neck for a moment?" asks Bruno (Robert Walker) of a smitten Washington biddy (Norma Varden). After all, especially at a senator's dinner party, it's all fun and games until someone nearly gets strangled, right?

the censor and his staff of fellow bluestockings that their concerns would be fully addressed and that he would uphold the moral sanctimony of Mom, apple pie, and the moral purity of the U.S. of A. Nevertheless, Hitchcock had slipped in several lines of dialogue and situations as sleight-of-hand tactics that he was perfectly willing to cut to prove how amenable he was. Think of it as his own version of "crisscross": "I'll cut *this* if you let *that* stay in the picture." These included Bruno's reference to murder as "part of natural law" although "not against the laws of nature"; Breen reminded Hitchcock that he had previously agreed to cut such references. Although the director plowed ahead and filmed that bit of dialogue, in the end he reluctantly cut it as a sop to the censor because he didn't think it was all that vital.

The references to Guy and Miriam's divorce were another sticking point. Hitchcock had promised to remedy these, but, very pointedly, he and Ormonde had deliberately ignored their commitment. The Breen Office assured him they were merely trying to be helpful "to avoid any flavor . . . that your sympathetic lead, Guy, is trying to break up his marriage with Miriam so as to marry Anne." Breen suggested Hitchcock should underscore that Miriam had run out on Guy in the first place and demanded a divorce despite Guy's protests and, "Later, when Miriam refused to return to him, Guy had reluctantly agreed to the divorce and had only then become involved with Anne"—Guy's rage now stems from Miriam wanting to renege on her agreement. Breen asserted, "The important thing in this scene is to stress the fact that your unsympathetic character, Miriam, is the person who is trying to break up the marriage." Although Hitchcock put up with Breen's parsing, he had a more provocative plot twist up his sleeve: as in the novel, Miriam announces that she is pregnant with another man's child. Breen, like a rube fooled by the sleight-of-hand of a magician on a carnival midway, signed off on it. Hitchcock breezed through Breen's objections. He portrayed Miriam as the marital partner seeking divorce and poked no obvious fun at the clergyman on the train (although the bit still gets laughs). Breen persisted, however, demanding Hitchcock remove two bits of dialogue: an exclamation of "My God!" from Senator Morton and, more offensively (at least to Breen), Bruno uttering "Nuts!"—which, Breen warned, was a specifically "forbidden term" according to the "Thou shall not" list of the Motion Picture Association of America. And as for Hitchcock's solemn vow to cooperate, in the filming and editing, Hitchcock let Bruno kick Guy's knuckles while the latter hangs for dear life onto the whirling carousel. But to cover his tracks, Hitchcock made certain that the makeup artist, Gordon Bau, create marks on Guy's hands that audiences could interpret as dirt from Bruno's shoes rather than blood.

The biggest win of all for Highsmith, Whitfield Cook, and Hitchcock? Breen and company said nothing about the undercurrent of Bruno's homoerotic yen for Guy. According to screenwriter Czenzi Ormonde, however, the homoerotic elements of *Strangers on a Train* are products of other people's imaginations or projections. "It doesn't exist in the script or in the film," she said. Apparently either Hitchcock did not clue her in or she was rather obtuse, although talented.

Can one blame Hitchcock for refusing to take these people seriously and for his treating the censorship negotiations like a game of chicken? In any case, Hitchcock had lost a few and won more than a few in Round One with the censors. The Breen Office was pleased. Jack Warner was relieved. But once the filming was completed, Round Two awaited.

CHAPTER FIVE

CASTING A SPELL

"What is directing, after all, but 90% casting? If you put Cary Grant or James Stewart in the movie, the audience is already on your side," said Alfred Hitchcock, who believed that getting the cast he wanted exponentially increased his odds of more fully realizing his creative vision. However, he only rarely got the actors he wanted. *Strangers on a Train* required kid-glove casting, and the director had two stars in mind almost from the outset. In casting discussions with Alma Reville and Barbara Keon, Hitchcock announced his intention to pursue two of the hottest young leading men in the business to play the ambitious tennis player and the maniacal mama's boy. Character descriptions in Hitchcock's screenplays tend to be especially rich and specific. Not only did they serve as inducements to the actors considering the jobs, but they were also written to provide cues to costume, hair, and makeup experts; production designers; and cinematographers. These persuasive, beautifully written character thumbnails appear in Raymond Chandler's final screenplay draft before Hitchcock sacked him:

> *Bruno Antony, about 25 years old, wears his expensive clothes with the tweedy nonchalance of a young man who has always had the best. He has the friendly eye of a stray*

puppy who wants to be liked, and the same wistful appeal for forgiveness when his impudence lands him in the doghouse. In the moments when his candor becomes shrewd calculation, it is all the more frightening because of his disarming charm and cultured exterior. It is as if a beautifully finished door, carved of the finest wood, were warping noticeably, and through tiny cracks one could only glimpse the crumbling chaos hidden inside—and even then, not believe it.

For the Bruno role, Montgomery Clift topped Hitchcock's casting shortlist. The handsome Clift's brooding, naturalistic performances for

Montgomery Clift, "the most promising star on the Hollywood horizon," was Hitchcock's top choice to portray what Raymond Chandler described as the "crumbling chaos hidden inside" the insane Bruno Antony.

such directors as Howard Hawks in *Red River* (1948), Fred Zinnemann in *The Search* (1948), and William Wyler in *The Heiress* (1949) had impressed filmmakers, fellow actors, and the public alike. Like most filmmakers, Hitchcock was eager for the chance to work with the fiercely independent thirty-year-old, whose halting speech, emotional authenticity, and sensitive, other-worldly presence inspired journalists to praise him as "the most promising star on the Hollywood horizon." Hitchcock had, without success, previously pursued Clift to star as Brandon Shaw, one of the two coded gay "thrill-killers" in his 1948 film *Rope*. Instead, theater actor and fledgling Warner Bros. contract player John Dall (*The Corn Is Green* [1948]) got the role. Playwright Arthur Laurents, who adapted Patrick Hamilton's 1929 play *Rope's End* for Hitchcock's film version and was a frequent Hitchcock dinner and party guest along with others in the director's circle, observed how the director delighted in being in the know about the sexual preferences of Hollywood's leading men and women. But the turbulent and complex Clift, whose longest romantic relationships were with such famous men as Jerome Robbins and Roddy McDowall, shunned *Strangers on a Train*, most likely to shield his private life and protect his rising career.

To plead the case with Clift, Hitchcock asked for intervention from his longtime friend and professional ally Katherine "Kay" Brown, the formidable MCA agent who represented Clift. But to no avail. Clift rejected the offer, forcing Hitchcock to expand the casting list with input from Reville and Keon. Today, even Hitchcock's typed and handwritten notes about potential Clift alternatives suggests the upheavals that Hitchcock and the movie business were undergoing at the time. During World War II, 90 million people flocked to movie theaters weekly as a primary entertainment source when discretionary money was readily available, but travel options were crimped due to tire shortages and gasoline rationing. Just after the war ended in 1945, though, housing boomed, sending millions to relocate to the suburbs, often far away from the once-thriving urban movie palaces. Then, competition from television mushroomed so rapidly that, by 1950, moviegoing plummeted by 20 to 30 percent among households with TV sets. As if those losses weren't enough, the government pursued an antitrust case that accused the major studios of keeping a stranglehold on film distribution and exhibition because they owned 65 percent of the nation's first-run film theaters, spelling the end of theater ownership for the studios. When profits at Warner Bros. alone tumbled from $22 million in 1947 to $10 million in 1949, Jack Warner cut loose the long-term contracts of the studio's major stars Humphrey Bogart, Bette Davis, James Cagney, Olivia de Havilland, and Barbara Stanwyck. Other studios followed suit with their stables of players. Such old-guard audience favorites as Cary Grant, Gregory Peck, James Stewart, and Henry Fonda felt the pushback as studios promoted the new, young, unproven—but much less expensive—breed of 1950s hopefuls.

Hence, Jack Warner's drive to persuade Hitchcock to cut production costs to the marrow for *Strangers on a Train*. Warner lobbied Hitchcock to consider casting—as a cost saver—several major roles from among the studio's roster of remaining contract stars. Hitchcock, presumably half-heartedly, agreed to at least consider the list Warner sent him. On it were Dennis Morgan, Robert Hutton, Dane Clark, William Prince, and Ronald Reagan (the mind reels). For Anne, the names included Lauren Bacall, Patricia Neal, Faye Emerson, and Ruth Roman. No wonder Hitchcock stalled Warner over casting—briefly, anyway. Intent on landing the right Bruno, the director briefly entertained the possibly calamitous, possibly brilliant notion of testing twenty-six-year-old Marlon Brando, fresh from his *A Streetcar Named Desire* stage triumph; Jack Warner was all for it because he desperately wanted to land Brando for a multi-picture deal. But every studio boss, producer, and director at the time was chasing Brando, whom one journalist dubbed, "the Valentino of the bop generation." With Elia Kazan preparing to direct Brando in Warner

Bros.' movie version of *Streetcar*, however, Hitchcock would have had to push back the *Strangers* start date. Unacceptable.

Meanwhile, phone calls, telegrams, and personal entreaties barraged the Hitchcock office on behalf of a herd of young (and young-ish) bucks representing Old and New Hollywood and wanting to star in a Hitchcock picture—at least until they heard the details and implications of the script. These included Paul Newman, Jack Lemmon, Richard Widmark, Rock Hudson, Dana Andrews, John Cassavetes, Sterling Hayden, Ralph Meeker, Guy Madison, Roddy McDowall, Tony Curtis, and more. Few sparked much interest in Hitchcock, who preferred to capitalize on the element of surprise by casting against type. "One always wants to avoid the cliché," said the director. "As they are in life, murderers and villains should be attractive, charming, suave. After all, that's part of how they attract their victims."

Hitchcock could be an artful dodger and a tale spinner when it came to talking to the press about his theories of filmmaking, but when it came to casting, he walked it like he talked it. In 1926 he had surprised and intrigued the press and public by hiring the enormously popular actor-playwright-composer and bona fide matinee idol Ivor Novello to star as the shadowy "Is he or isn't he Jack the Ripper?" figure in *The Lodger*. In the 1940s, Hitchcock chose the debonair light-comedy star Cary Grant to play an irresponsible, charming cad who might be a murderer in *Suspicion*, callow hunk Gregory Peck to portray a troubled amnesiac and possible killer in *Spellbound*, and honey-voiced romantic leading man Joseph Cotten to embody a suave, psychotic murderer of lonely, wealthy widows in *Shadow of a Doubt*. For *Strangers on a Train* the director finally met with Jack Warner to announce whom he had chosen as his three target actors, and two of them would need to be borrowed from the studios that had them under contract. True to form, for Bruno Antony, his mind was now set on the popular and charming Robert Walker, known best for playing boys next door and young enlisted men in such MGM movies as *See Here, Private Hargrove* (1944), *Thirty Seconds Over Tokyo* (1944) with Spencer Tracy, and *The Clock* (1945) with Judy Garland.

As for Guy Haines, Chandler's last script described him as

> *well-dressed because he can now afford to be. His life of hard work and dedication to a purpose has sobered the laugh lines on his face, but his sense of humor is still alive. His fine reputation as a tennis player has not altered his unassuming personality, nor dimmed his ambition to play an important role some day in government. He is executive assistant to Senator Burton [eventually renamed Morton]. Like most honest and forthright people, he makes the mistake of measuring other people's motives by his own high principles and is consequently shocked and hurt by chicanery in others. But he is learning to accept people for what they are, not what they ought to be. Although he is firm in his likes and dislikes he sometimes sacrifices his own comfort to avoid being labeled a snob. He is quick to take advantage of an opportunity but would turn his back on one if it made him a self-seeker.*

William Holden consistently topped Hitchcock's wish list for the role. But Hitchcock had been trying to sign the *Golden Boy* (1939) actor for starring roles since his 1940s spy thrillers *Foreign Correspondent* and *Saboteur* (1942). In 1950 the thirty-two-year-old Holden, who had been knocking around Hollywood since the late 1930s, was finally about to score his biggest breakthrough playing the cynical, opportunistic screenwriter who winds up floating dead in a Silent Era–movie queen's swimming pool in *Sunset Boulevard* (1950). Said Billy Wilder, who directed both Holden's Oscar-nominated performance in that brilliantly

William Holden was Hitchcock's ideal Guy Haines, but the complicated, macho leading man eluded two decades of the director's attempts to cast him in films.

corrosive masterwork (originally meant to star Montgomery Clift, who withdrew) and Holden's later Oscar-winning turn in *Stalag 17* (1953), "Every woman was in love with him." Hitchcock wasn't alone in sensing that Holden was about to become one of–if not *the*–quintessential Hollywood leading man of the 1950s. Making an end run around Jack Warner, the director messengered the Ormonde script to Holden's agent, Charles K. Feldman.

As Hitchcock awaited Holden's reply, he announced to Warner his choice to play Anne, described by Chandler as "a beautiful, high-spirited,

Had studio boss Jack Warner not overruled Hitchcock, *Strangers on a Train* would have marked the young Grace Kelly's first of four films for the director.

and well-bred young woman. She is the daughter of Senator [Morton] and acts as her father's hostess in Washington, D.C. In this capacity she observes the conventional protocol of diplomatic circles, yet manages it with warmth, simplicity, and capacity to love." Hitchcock wanted to direct the feature film debut of a twenty-one-year-old model and rising theater and television actress named Grace Kelly.

That's when Jack Warner began the horse trading for which he was infamous. He agreed to pay what it would take to borrow Holden from Paramount and Walker from MGM, but to offset those significant expenses, Hitchcock would need to agree to cast Warner Bros.' contract player Ruth Roman instead of Kelly. Although the husky-voiced, sultry Roman had recently tested to star in Cecil B. DeMille's *Samson and Delilah* (1949), and Jack Warner was pressuring Elia Kazan to cast her as Stella Kowalski in his film of *A Streetcar Named Desire* (Kazan strenuously resisted the pressure), Hitchcock thought the twenty-eight-year-old actress was completely unsuitable for the role of a witty, head-strong, and subtly sexy Washington hostess and politician's daughter. (As for Kelly, Hitchcock would need to wait three years before casting her in her first of three films for him, *Dial M for Murder*—and by then, Warner Bros. would have to pay her nearly ten times what she would have cost for *Strangers on a Train*.) But for now, Hitchcock was saddled with the earthy, raven-haired Roman in a role that Hitchcock envisioned for a patrician, elegant blonde like Kelly, who would go on to become one of his all-time ideal leading ladies and a lifelong friend.

The contrast between Roman and Kelly could scarcely be more apparent to Hitchcock. Where Kelly was strictly Philadelphia Main Line, Roman pulled herself up from a hardscrabble working-class Revere Beach, Massachusetts, background, where her father worked as a side-show barker in the carnival he owned and her dancer mother was the snake handler. Kelly attended the American Academy of Dramatic Arts, while Roman had to make do with third-tier theatrical schools in Boston. Kelly debuted on Broadway at age eighteen opposite Raymond Massey; Roman moved to New York and, struggling to find theater work, toiled as a cigarette girl in a restaurant, checked hats at a night-club, and modeled for crime magazines—sometimes all in the same day. Kelly acted in about sixty live broadcast television shows and four Broadway productions; Roman spent 1943 through 1949 toiling in bit parts, small roles, and a thirteen-episode serial before catching such better breaks as playing the wife of Kirk Douglas in the well-received 1949 boxing drama *Champion* and, the same year, appearing in the suspense thriller *The Window* (a film that Hitchcock forever resented being compared to or confused with his *Rear Window*). Jack Warner signed Roman to a long-term Warner Bros. contract that same year.

Suddenly, she landed on the cover of *Life* magazine with a headline saluting her so-called rapid rise, although it was playing mostly forgettable molls and sexpots, including a second-fiddle stint opposite Bette Davis in the risible *Beyond the Forest* (1949). That was the movie that persuaded Jack Warner to cancel Davis's contract and from which campy dialogue—"What a dump!"—achieved immortality in Edward Albee's *Who's Afraid of Virginia Woolf?*

In October of 1950, Warner made sure that Roman won headlines for being the first actor officially cast in *Strangers on a Train.* Wrote Edwin Schallert dutifully in his *Los Angeles Times* column of October 16: "Necessarily this means much for the comparatively new Warner luminary, because Hitchcock pictures always attract attention to their personnel." Meanwhile, the chic Kelly kept working in TV and on stage until a good-girl role opposite Gary Cooper in the landmark Fred Zinnemann–directed, multi-Oscar-nominated western *High Noon*, her breakthrough, was just around the corner. On seeing Kelly in the film, Hitchcock thought her "rather mousy" despite noting her obvious star quality.

After signing for *Strangers on a Train*, Ruth Roman told the press how she had earlier hoped to be cast by Hitchcock in his psychological thriller *Spellbound*, saying,

> Mr. Hitchcock was kindness itself, but he told me I simply wasn't right for the role [of the sexually provocative young psychiatric patient played by Rhonda Fleming], and Hitchcock politely told me so. I was heartbroken. But it has given me a triumphant feeling to know that five years later I am the right type for a Hitchcock production. I've always wanted to work for him and so, better late than never, I am immensely proud to be cast as the heroine in *Strangers on a Train.*

Although John Derek wanted to accept Hitchcock's offer of the Guy Haines role, Columbia Pictures studio boss Harry Cohn refused to loan out the rising young contract player.

She also told the press how excited she was that Hitchcock insisted on her wearing "a smart, new short hairdo and style-setting clothes designed by Leah Rhodes." Neither Roman's manner nor her press interviews would do anything to endear her to Hitchcock.

In the end, though, Hitchcock's casting master plan collapsed under the weight of its own ambitions. When macho, melancholic William Holden turned down Hitchcock for the role of Guy, the director made a rebound offer to newcomer John Derek. The strikingly handsome twenty-four-year-old was a client of gay talent agent Henry Willson, whose beefcake stable also included Rock Hudson, Guy Madison, Tab Hunter, Robert Wagner, Kerwin Matthews, and Rory Calhoun. Derek captured Hitchcock's notice when he played Broderick Crawford's son in Robert Rossen's prestigious Oscar-winner *All the King's Men* (1949) and, the same year, the ruthless pretty-boy killer in director Nicholas Ray's *Knock on Any Door* (1949), in which he stole some thunder from no-less-a-star Humphrey Bogart, who also produced the film.

Bogart had bought the film rights to the 1947 Dorothy B. Hughes thriller novel *In a Lonely Place* and originally planned to produce it with Derek playing the leading role of a multiple murderer. However, Bogart decided to shift the tone and focus of that 1950 film, aging up the central character and playing the role himself. Meanwhile, Derek—dismissed by the *New York Times* critic Bosley Crowther as "plainly an idol for the girls"—wanted to accept Hitchcock's offer. But Columbia Pictures tyrant Harry Cohn, who kept Derek under his thumb in a seven-year contract, capriciously refused to let Hitchcock borrow him; instead, he shoved Derek into *Rogues of Sherwood Forest* (1950) and *Mask of the Avenger* (1951), films as dire and forgettable as they sound. Even fan magazines of the era featured stories asking whether Cohn was intentionally quashing the young actor's career. "Is Hollywood Destroying John Derek?" asked one title. Said Derek years later, "I never liked acting. I used to go to the directors of my films and say, 'I'm not an actor but I'll turn up on time and know my words.' I really wasn't good at it but if I could have had the acting career predicted for me, Columbia killed it by not letting me do things like work for Hitchcock." Hitchcock liked actors who, he observed, "do nothing well. It's the best kind of acting. Some actors and actresses make faces. I call it scribbling all over their faces. The actor who makes his face blank but you can't look away from them? They invite the audience to identify with them."

Hitchcock forever regretted not landing a Montgomery Clift or William Holden–level talent for *Strangers on a Train*—as much for financial reasons as creative. He said,

> One is always compromising about almost everything. You compromise on casting when you put a star in a role. If

> you were making a film purely for artistic purposes—I really hate the word "artistic"—a film that is fully integrated as far as characters are concerned, you certainly cast it with unknown people, just as the novelist casts his novel with unknown people. But with stars we bend a little bit and don't quite get the character we had in mind. So, there is where compromise starts. On the other hand, from the audience's point of view, the star helps because he or she increases the potency of the story. To take a crude example: if the heroine is tied to a railroad track and the train is bearing down on her, and the audience doesn't know who she is, it will say, "How awful, the poor woman is going to be killed." But if it's a star like Claudette Colbert or Greer Garson, then they are going to scream because it's like a relative being run over. The effectiveness is increased one hundred-fold.

Frustrated and running out of time, Hitchcock pivoted from Derek to the twenty-five-year-old, California-born Farley Granger, whom he had previously cast as Phillip, the jittery counterpoint to John Dall's steely, brainy provocateur in *Rope*. Like Derek, Granger was a pinup boy and bobby-soxers' delight. His standing in Hollywood might best be encapsulated in the story of when he tried to impress Marlon Brando at a party in the early 1950s by vowing he was committed to studying with legendary acting teachers Sanford Meisner and Brando's own muse, Stella Adler, to help spur his intention to exit Hollywood and transition to serious stage work. According to Brando's sister, the actress Jocelyn Brando, her brother stood silently behind Granger, making cruel faces and gestures to mock Granger's aspirations as pretensions. As writer (and Granger's former lover) Arthur Laurents spilled to interviewer Patrick McGilligan years later, referring obliquely to the amiable, if comparatively lightweight Granger, "*Rope* could have been marvelous if [Hitchcock] had been able to cast it the way he wanted to, with Cary Grant [as Rupert Cadell, the older Nietzschean aesthete] and Monty Clift. But since Cary Grant was at best bisexual and Monty was gay, they were scared to death and they wouldn't do it. So Hitchcock got Jimmy Stewart as one of the leads [instead of Grant], and he was dead wrong for the part." Granger fired back at Laurents–who wrote the screenplay–when he observed of *Rope* in an interview for the American Film Institute, "We would have had a better movie if we'd had a better script."

As an inexperienced seventeen-year-old, Farley Granger had sent a photo of himself and a bio that led to a successful screen test and seven-year contract with producer Samuel Goldwyn, and since then he had been chafing under that powerful independent producer's control of his career. Other Goldwyn contract players included Dana Andrews, Guy Madison, Virginia Mayo, Cathy O'Donnell, and Danny Kaye, each of whom had their own views of Goldwyn. Granger complained that the producer was underpaying him ("Oh, boy! A hundred bucks a week [about $2,000 today] in 1942," he told an interviewer) while wasting him in dull, decorative supporting roles. *The North Star* (1943) or *Enchantment* (1948), anyone? Granger looked like a much stronger candidate for stardom when Goldwyn loaned him out to RKO Pictures and director Nicholas Ray to play a fugitive star-crossed young lover in the fascinating 1948 crime melodrama *They Live by Night*. Reteamed the next year with the same appealingly vulnerable costar Cathy O'Donnell in *Side Street* (1949), Granger also did well as a young father-to-be who, trying to provide for his pregnant wife, takes a fatal step into crime that brings the world down around him. Granger wrote of those days in his autobiography, "Goldwyn wanted so much money to loan me out to other studios that very few of them wanted to negotiate with him. They had their own young stars under contract, who were being paid as little as I was. They would think, 'Why should I build Granger up for Goldwyn?'"

Fed up with Hollywood and after a string of flops, Granger got put on suspension for infuriating Goldwyn by refusing to do yet another of what the actor called his "moody youth" roles. Instead, he lit off to Europe for nearly five months, prowling through France, England, Austria, Germany, and Italy for the very first time. Granger took considerable flak from fan magazine writers such as the one in *Photoplay*, who wrote, "We ain't sayin' whether Farley's right or wrong, but we know a lot of ambitious actors who would give their shirts to get just one of the parts Farley's turned down." Granger returned to the United States and patched up things with Goldwyn, but he kept actively on the lookout for better opportunities. Perhaps his luckiest shot of all came when the Goldwyn office informed him on a Friday that he had a Monday morning meeting at Hitchcock's Bel-Air home at 10957 Bellagio Road. Over tea on the terrace of his home that directly overlooked the Bel-Air Country Club golf course, Hitchcock entertained Granger with the plot of *Strangers on a Train*, complete with asides about how he planned to film what he called the movie's "six big showstoppers"—the "strangling" of the dowager at the Washington society party, the murder at the amusement park, the tennis match in which Bruno only has eyes for Guy, Bruno's struggle to retrieve Guy's cigarette lighter from the storm drain, Guy's nighttime visit to Bruno's father, and the spectacular, out-of-control merry-go-round battle royale between Guy and Bruno.

Having initiated early preparatory work with production designer and storyboard illustrator Ted Haworth, Hitchcock was prepared to show Granger a large binder of compelling images that laid out the story and camera angles from start to finish. Hitchcock described these images, readily available to all crewmembers, as not only a "time-saver" but also an "immense help, especially to players to more immediately convey the mood feeling of their roles. Rushes never come as a complete surprise and these drawings are an aid to those not as visual-minded as I am." Having thoroughly discussed with designer Leah

Rhodes (Oscar winner for 1948's *Adventures of Don Juan*) his costuming concepts for each major character, Hitchcock detailed to Granger exactly how Guy Haines would be dressed in the opening scene: loosely structured wool-tweed sportscoat, white button-down shirt, conservative checkered tie under a dark sweater vest, and brogues.

"I was enthralled," Granger recalled. "Hearing a story told by Hitch was almost as good as seeing the film." When Hitchcock finished his pitch and asked whether Granger liked what he heard, the actor enthused, "I think it's great." "Good," Hitchcock replied, "because you're playing Guy"—news that so excited Granger that he recalled he nearly "jumped out of my skin." When Hitchcock asked Granger who he thought should play Bruno, Granger had no response. "Well, what would you think of Robert Walker?" What indeed? "I thought Bob Walker was a terrific idea," Granger said. "Walker had been the boy next door in movies for so long." Then Hitchcock leaned in and said, grinning and referring to the recent headline-making reports of Walker's emotional volatility, erratic behavior, and struggles with alcohol and depression, "Farley, wouldn't it be interesting if something happened on our film?" Granger thought the comment was "macabre" at the time but wondered whether the famously puckish and provocative director was only trying to shock him. The best response he could dredge up was, "Oh, Hitch . . ."

It might have miffed Granger that Goldwyn was only too happy to loan him out (at a great profit) to Hitchcock, but he was eager for the role, saying, "I had a great time when I worked for Hitchcock before in *Rope*. I knew what a lot I could learn working for that great director again. And there was more to it than that. I play a healthy, happy, tennis-playing character in *Strangers on a Train*—and that's the kind of role I want to play from now on." Hitchcock could not have avoided seeing an item about Granger that appeared in the "Inside Stuff" section of the widely read *Photoplay* magazine days after their meeting:

"Hollywood is talking about Farley Granger and his change of heart. After the public reaction to *Rope*, he wasn't eager to appear in another Alfred Hitchcock production. Farley's first picture since his return from Europe will be *Strangers on a Train*, directed by you-know-who." In any case, Hitchcock cast Granger at the eleventh hour, only four days before the actor would need to report to New York to begin filming.

What remains unknown today is just how deeply Hitchcock and Granger discussed the worrisome headlines and rumors that had recently damaged Robert Walker's reputation. One of the tortured and often combative actor's few truly close and trusted friends, journalist Jim Henaghan (son of Gwen Verdon, the legendary Broadway musical star and muse of Bob Fosse), once described Walker as a "scalawag." The Salt Lake City–born Walker grew up the fourth of four sons, skinny, sensitive, volatile, and embarrassed by chronic acne and impaired vision. He got shipped off to military school when his tendency to pick fights with his peers became unmanageable to his parents, whom he thought never loved nor wanted him. Taken under wing by a wealthy Manhattan aunt, Walker expressed interest in acting but doubted he had the looks or even the drive to make a dent. Still, in 1938 his aunt provided the twenty-year-old full tuition to attend the American Academy of Dramatic Arts, where he fell in love with a shy, introverted nineteen-year-old Oklahoma-born fellow student named Phyllis Isley.

The socially awkward duo found support and comfort in each other, married in 1939, shared a one-room Greenwich Village walkup apartment, and performed together in shows at the Cherry Lane Theater. They quickly had two sons, Robert Walker Jr. (born in 1940) and Michael Walker (1941). When they moved to California, where Isley tried to break into movies, she landed a five-year contract at Republic Pictures, known best for westerns and B-movie melodramas. Meanwhile, the literary-minded Walker eked out a living by reading manuscripts for an agent. But it was Walker who first got important work in show business, as his mellifluous voice made him a highly sought-after radio actor. Although Isley was ready to give up on Hollywood, she caught the eye of producer David O. Selznick when he auditioned her to star in the movie version of the popular 1939 novel and 1949 Broadway hit *Claudia*. She didn't stick the landing (Dorothy Maguire, who starred in the play, got the job), but the smitten Selznick signed Isley to a seven-year contract. He propelled her to the front of the line of more experienced contenders, including Anne Baxter, Teresa Wright, Gene Tierney, and Linda Darnell, and installed her in the plum leading role in *The Song of Bernadette* (1943). With her every move now carefully controlled by the infatuated, long-married Selznick, Isley was renamed Jennifer Jones, scored an Oscar for her first important film role, and got promoted as an overnight movie star. The day after she won the Academy Award, Jones—several times cited by the Women's Press Association as "the year's most uncooperative actress"—filed for divorce from Walker. It broke him. He checked into a hotel and drank himself into oblivion.

Meanwhile, Walker's agent arranged a screen test for a key role in the Robert Taylor–starring war picture *Bataan* (1943). Walker aced the test and made such a splash in the movie that MGM signed him to a long-term contract. Tay Garnett, the director of the wartime hit, summarized the appeal of the new young star as a "talented, sensitive, fey guy who combines the comic abilities of Jack Lemmon and Bob Montgomery with a heart-grabbing, little-boy-lost appeal." Walker scored an even bigger triumph as an Army draftee in the hit military comedy *See Here, Private Hargrove*, delivering a performance that moved one critic to write of the actor's final scene in the movie, "it wasn't the script or the story that lent this touch of immortality, it was Robert Walker himself. For a moment, up there on the screen, he was all the men of that time. Gallantry and hope, courage and enthusiasm were there, and I felt like getting to my feet and cheering. Only I had a lump in my throat." Walker's star rose even faster than Jones's, who began distancing herself even further from her distraught and broken-hearted ex-husband, who nonetheless continued to be a devoted father to their two sons.

By the time Walker accepted Selznick's cruel and sadistic 1944 offer to play Jennifer Jones's doomed boyfriend in the World War II home-front drama *Since You Went Away*, Walker's costar and friend Keenan Wynn, who had loved clowning around with him while making the *Hargrove* movie just months before, was stunned to encounter a different Walker:

> The happy-go-lucky guy I'd worked with was transformed overnight into a morose and melancholy shadow of his former self. [Working with Jennifer Jones] became a nightmare for Bob. Did Selznick do what he was doing maliciously? I don't know. But it was heartless to bring Bob together with his estranged wife for intimate love scenes. The film became emotionally disastrous for Bob.

Van Johnson, who made *Thirty Seconds Over Tokyo* with Walker, recalled, "He was often very remote. It broke your heart to see the guy. I don't, however, recall his being difficult during the filming–just lost in a world of his own." When not working on films, Walker was given to violent, self-destructive mood swings, during which he'd punch walls or smash his fists into plate-glass windows. Coworkers praised his unique talent and found him so vulnerable and unguarded that they expressed anguish at being unable to help ease his emotional pain. His movies continued to be moneymakers, and MGM paired him with top stars, including Hedy Lamarr, Ava Gardner, and June Allyson. He charmed audiences but was hostile to the press and antagonistic to Metro's executives. He loathed Hollywood and talked often of getting out. Privately, he was in torment, and it only worsened when the press announced that David and Irene Selznick were divorcing, leaving the lovestruck mogul and Jennifer Jones free to marry.

The career-damaging headlines began in 1948. While driving slightly inebriated, Walker struck a truck. There was no damage to the driver nor the truck, but Walker had fled the scene and the police charged him with hit-and-run while under the influence. To the press, the once sweet, gangly, boyish Walker was now an unruly drunk. Another arrest, in 1949, after he and a young woman shared drinks at a bar near his modest Wilshire Boulevard apartment, sealed his fate. Failing a sobriety test, he was taken to jail by the police. Objecting to the way he was treated, he punched one of the cops and then got into a melee when several other officers joined in. MGM executive Dore Schary issued him an ultimatum: commit himself for psychiatric treatment at the Menninger Clinic or leave show business to get on with the business of dying. Walker told friends that he knew something was deeply wrong and wanted help desperately. He remained for six months at the Menninger—except for a breakout that led to the Topeka, Kansas, police picking him up for disorderly behavior. While in custody, he smashed most of the windows in the station. Upon his release from the clinic, he returned to Hollywood and impulsively married but quickly divorced Barbara Ford (daughter of director John Ford). In Ford's divorce petition, she charged that she had found herself married to a man who wanted to be a husband "in name only."

Deeply humiliated by his stint at Menninger and his impulsive second marriage, Walker struggled to convince Hollywood that he was employable and reliable. Hitchcock had a special affinity for spotting capable actors trapped by their public image (examples include Ivor Novello, Cary Grant, Joan Fontaine, James Stewart, Doris Day, Janet Leigh, and Anthony Perkins). So he invited Walker to his Warner Bros. office, where he described in detail the role of Bruno Antony, the turns of the plot, and his costuming, as he had with Granger. Hitchcock envi-

Frustrated when Warner Bros.' costume designers failed to find a ready-made version of the gaudy necktie Hitchcock envisioned for Robert Walker's Bruno, the director personally designed one and had copies expensively custom-made.

sioned Bruno sporting a brilliant-blue, multi-striped suit with a white silk pocket square, white shirt with pinned shirt collar, French cuffs and dark cufflinks, spectator shoes, and a tie pin reading *Bruno*. Why such specificity? Said Edith Head, who worked on more than eleven Hitchcock pictures, "[He] dresses a character to express psychology. He is the only person who works on a script with such detail that a designer could go ahead and make the clothes without discussing them with him. It's so completely lucid. Hitchcock will send me a script, and if I say, 'Hitch, what do you like?' he will reply, 'My dear Edith, just read the script.' That's all. Until you have sketches ready to show him, there's no point in asking him what he likes." But why so much emphasis on color for a black-and-white film? Because Hitchcock, the complete filmmaker, knew exactly how those colors would either absorb or bounce light, how they would "read" on camera. Bruno's final sartorial detail specified by Hitchcock was a navy-blue silk tie decorated with three hand-painted red-orange lobsters, measuring, the director specified, exactly two-and-a-half inches long and two inches wide. Hitchcock was so adamant about the tie that when the studio costumers Leah Rhodes and Robert O'Dell came up empty after scouring men's clothing stores for such a tie in Hollywood, Beverly Hills, and downtown Los Angeles, Hitchcock himself designed the necktie and ordered three custom-made copies at a total cost of what today would be nearly $1,000. Hitchcock told Granger that he already knew that he planned to pay off the lobster-claw reference: he would direct the actor playing Bruno to hold his hands in as clawlike a way as possible in the strangulation scenes in the amusement park and the party at the Morton's home, as well as in the scene in which Bruno struggles to retrieve from the storm drain Guy's incriminating cigarette lighter.

The director also told Walker that his character would smoke thin, expensive Cuban cigars (Walker had quit smoking only a few days before filming began) and that, for the manicure scene with the actress playing his mother, he would be dressed in black satin pajamas with white piping and, over it, an especially flashy shawl-collar dressing gown. Although costume designer Leah Rhodes provided preliminary sketches for the robe of black-tinged green with neon-bright abstract figures, she would instead pull from the Warner wardrobe department an Orry-Kelly-designed black dressing gown with light green, purple, and magenta planet-like shapes originally worn by Monty Woolley in 1942 in *The Man Who Came to Dinner*. Hitchcock heartily approved. Said Walker,

> I'm a conservative Brooks Brothers dresser who goes for sober, somber shades. So the colors Hitchcock and the costumer described to me were, let's say, "remote." But

> Hitchcock said, "Bob, all this strangeness will contribute to characterizing Bruno's neurotic quirks." So I began to see that Bruno would be the sort of a fellow who'd be in favor of these attention-getting styles and colors. He's an introvert who deliberately acts like an extrovert. And I intend to wear my lobster tie on dates to see if it murders them, too. Time will tell if it'll become a fashion fad for the rest of my life.

Walker and Hitchcock clicked instantly, and the actor told reporters, "I accepted the role on the spot." Walker was thrilled to be sought after by Hitchcock, telling friends that the director boosted his ego by assuring him that he was his first and only choice for the role of Bruno—only a few in Hollywood knew otherwise. Before Walker arrived home from his meeting with Hitchcock, the director had already arranged delivery of a copy of Highsmith's novel with a note: "To help you get under the skin of the weirdo you'll be playing."

For a time, though, MGM threatened to punish Walker for his well-publicized antisocial behaviors by refusing to let Hitchcock borrow him. Walker found himself championed by the often-venomous doyenne of Hollywood gossip Hedda Hopper. Hopper's nationally syndicated column of October 13, 1950, headlined, "Walker Eager to Do Film with Hitchcock," presented Walker as "worried he may not get to play the best part of his career," a role Walker describes as one "any actor would cut off his right arm to play." Walker said that doing Hitchcock's film "would mean the start of my career." Hopper dropped hints that Walker had other offers from producers David O. Selznick, Howard Hughes, and Hal Wallis, adding, "I don't think Bob needs to worry. I'm sure if Metro hasn't anything for him, they'll lend him to Hitchcock."

Three days later Hopper gave Walker another headline story. Metro had loaned Walker to Warner Bros., and Hopper crowed, "the part will be a real switch for Bob. He plays a fellow who's loaded with outward charm but has murder in his heart. Bob is getting away from all those all-American boy roles which started with *Private Hargrove*."

Years later, Farley Granger recalled that Walker, after reading the book and script, gleefully confided to him that he planned to play Bruno as homosexual. This exchange reminds one of Martin Landau telling the press it was *his* idea to play as gay Leonard, the assistant and henchman of the spy portrayed by James Mason, in *North by Northwest*. In fact, the clues are so evident in Ernest Lehman's screenplay that they may as well have been color-coded in lavender. But Granger, who hailed from an era when studio publicists trained stars to be charming but evasive, insisted that such conversations he had with Walker never involved Hitchcock. Granger, who could be frustratingly vague in interviews, told author John Billheimer, "We never discussed any homoerotic attraction Walker's character had for me, but I think Hitch did that with Walker, and he just asked me to act normal and not be aware of too much undercurrent. Of course, Hitch understood all of this, and he knew what he could do and what we could do."

What he—that is, Walker—could and did do playing Bruno was remarkable. By turns charming, dashing, awkward, vulnerable, chilling, barely suppressing rage, and stalker-like, he bats his lashes and looks Granger up and down in about as queer-coded a way as a Hollywood leading man could get away with on screen in the 1950s. His Bruno is marvelously charismatic and funny, nasally growling out a line of dialogue about his father, "I get so sore at him sometimes, I want to kill him!"—sounding a bit like a homegrown Peter Lorre. Catch the sinewy, lithe way he moves across the room wearing that florid dressing gown when a butler announces his phone call to Guy has been put through. "Sorry, father, long distance," he says like an exultant, petulant teenager rushing toward a phone call with a secret crush. Is it entirely plausible that Walker and Granger somehow never talked about how each would handle the cat-and-mouse seduction that is endemic to the entire movie? Granger told another interviewer, "It was 1950. We didn't talk about things that didn't exist! But Hitchcock knew what he wanted to be able to get away with. He might have been indirect in dealing with sexual things in his films, but he had a strong instinct for them. He thought everyone was doing something physical and nasty behind every closed door—except himself: He withdrew; he wouldn't be part of it."

Turning next to choosing his supporting players—often Hitchcock's favorite characters and his favorite roles to cast—the director focused on who might be right for the juicy role of the conniving, unapologetically sexual Miriam Haines, whose face, according to the Chandler screenplay, "is pretty because it is still young. There is a vain immaturity and shallowness about her which she will never outgrow. She is self-centered and vindictive but is confident that she is irresistible to any man. She wears harlequin glasses, and the myopic lenses tend to make her eyes look as small as her calculating little brain." Hitchcock considered Miriam a small but crucial role, so he asked the casting department to cast a wide net. He lamented, "I much prefer to cast these roles in England where the theater gives one access to much more unusual sorts of actors."

The studio's list of possibilities even included thirty-year-old Shelley Winters, who at the time was, ironically, relentlessly lobbying director George Stevens to cast her in the somewhat analogous role in *A Place in the Sun* of the sympathetic, pregnant, blue-collar young woman who becomes inconvenient when upwardly mobile Montgomery Clift wants to marry socially prominent beauty Elizabeth Taylor. Offscreen, since 1949, Winters had been enjoying a well-publicized, on-and-off romantic romp with Farley Granger, who broke off his years-long relationship with Arthur Laurents when Winters entered the picture; still, Granger enjoyed a fling with composer and conductor Leonard Bernstein at the same time as he and Winters were carrying on. In any case, Winters didn't interest Hitchcock. But the actress would later visit Granger (her costar in a joyless RKO comedy *Behave Yourself!* [1951] that hit theaters four months after *Strangers on a Train*) on the set, invariably demanding to pose for publicity still photographer Durward "Bud" Graybill with Granger for lovey-dovey shots or playing chess with the more cerebral, publicity-averse Robert Walker.

For months, casting director Jack Bowers had been vetting a range of lesser-known potential candidates to play Miriam before narrowing down the candidates to seven—ranging from refreshingly small-town pretty women to drop-dead glamorous mantraps—each of whom screen tested for Hitchcock's consideration at Warner Bros. on November 19, 1950. Bowers and Robert Burks shot a series of sound and photographic tests of actresses vying to play Miriam, including Claudia Barrett (*White Heat*), Helena Carter (best known for *Invaders from Mars* [1953]), Ruth Conte (TV's *Chevron Theater* [1952]), Cynthia Corley (*Mr. Peabody and the Mermaid* [1948]), Virginia Gibson (*Goodbye, My Fancy* [1951]), Dorothy Hart (*I Was a Communist for the F.B.I.* [1951]), and Meg Randall (*Ma and Pa Kettle* [1949]). Hitchcock's pick was twenty-five-year-old Laura Elliott, whose talents were being wasted under contract at Paramount. Elliott, who enjoyed perfect vision, would go on to be ambivalent about Hitchcock requiring her to wear thick eyeglass lenses for the role. Elliott recalled,

> I think the glasses were very instrumental, though. Mr. Hitchcock—you see, I still say "Mr. Hitchcock"—said, "Go to this eyeglass place and pick out some glasses." "Well, what kind?" "Whatever you want to pick up." I found those particular glasses you see in the film, and they made six pairs. We had two pairs that were medium lenses and I never once saw those. And there were two pairs that were just clear glass, for long shots, and there were two with those very, very thick lenses—so thick that I could not see the blur of my hand passing in front of my face. If you can

> imagine, all I could see through them was just a little bit out of the sides. And that was the pair Hitchcock wanted me to wear because they made the eyes look very small—very "pig-eyed," as he called it.

The actress further recalled,

> I had heard about the Miriam Haines role from Jean Ruth, a young contract player at Paramount. She came from musical comedy and after she'd auditioned for *Strangers on a Train*, she said, "Oh, it's perfect for me." And I thought, "Well, she and I look nothing alike, our personalities are nothing alike. There's no way it would be right for me." So I didn't think anything more about it. I guess they kept searching and my agent called one day—this is like three or

Hitchcock chose thick-lensed eyeglasses for Laura Elliott to wear as Guy Haines's mercenary estranged wife. The director liked the "pig-eyed" look the glasses gave her, but that choice forced Elliott to perform her scenes functionally blind.

> four months later—and said, "Laura, you have an interview over at Warner Bros. on this Hitchcock picture." I said, "Well . . . I don't think I'm right for that," but he said, "Go. Just go to the interview." So I went over there and read the only big dialogue scene there was, set in the music store. It wasn't with Farley Granger, but I've totally forgotten who did the scene with me. [All the candidates for Miriam tested opposite actor-screenwriter Warren Douglas, *The Man I Love* (1947).] I just loved that scene. I auditioned and the casting directors loved it. I had not even met Hitchcock, had no direction from him. What each of us brought to the role that day was what we brought to the role on our own. I tested and, just as simple as that, my agent called and said, "You got the role." I was thrilled.

The Chandler screenplay's description of another key supporting role, Barbara Morton, Anne's younger sister, reads, "a lively seventeen-year-old who loves excitement, says exactly what she thinks and rarely thinks before she says it. Superficially, in height and figure, she resembles Miriam. She also wears glasses." Hitchcock considered several actresses; however, his daughter, Pat, had not initially been among them. About to graduate from London's prestigious Royal Academy of Dramatic Art, she had been told by the principal that she had "a comedy face." She had won promising reviews as the star of two short-lived Broadway shows and made a charming 1950 movie debut in a small speaking role in her father's *Stage Fright*. But it was Pat's new agent, Edith Van Cleve, who urged Hitchcock to consider his daughter for the role of Barbara, just as Pat's former agent, Katherine "Kay" Brown, had done earlier without success, before she stopped representing actors and began to focus entirely on literary talents. As a talent and literary scout, the well-respected Brown had a storied history as the person

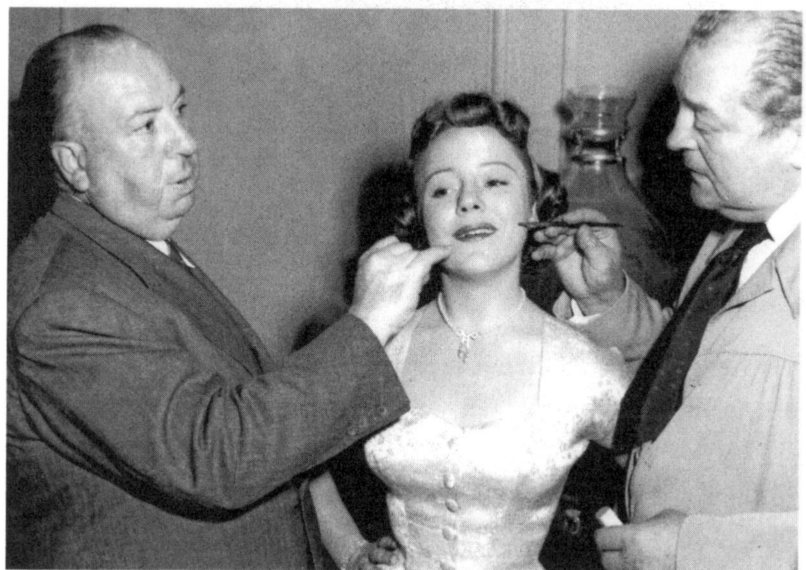

For the role of the heroine's outspoken sister, Hitchcock only considered his twenty-two-year-old actress daughter Pat when her agent insisted he give her a screen test.

who persuaded Alfred Hitchcock to sign his first American contract as well as convinced Ingrid Bergman and Laurence Olivier to leave their native countries and pursue Hollywood careers. She also brought to the attention of producer David O. Selznick both the novels *Rebecca* (for which she lobbied Olivier to director Hitchcock and Selznick as their best choice for the male lead) and *Gone with the Wind*. Later, after becoming an agent at MCA, Brown represented Montgomery Clift, Alec Guinness, Rex Harrison, Lillian Hellman, Isak Dinesen, and Arthur Miller, among others.

Despite his respect for Brown's taste, prowess, and track record, Hitchcock could not imagine his daughter in the Barbara Morton role; however, at Brown's insistence, he screen tested Pat. Said Pat Hitchcock,

> I would have loved it if he had believed more in nepotism so that I could have done more pictures with him. He only cast people he thought were absolutely right for the part. I

> was graduating from RADA and about to go into rep in Nottingham. He did so much preparation before he ever walked onto the set that he was able to devote a lot of time for the actors. If he didn't like something he'd very quietly come up to someone and say, "I think it might be better if you tried it in such and such a way." You did that and it was right.

When Hitchcock mentioned to Jack Warner that he was considering casting his daughter, the studio head dragged out one of his perennial witticisms: "I told Albert Einstein when I met him, 'I have a theory of relativity, too. I never hire them.'" (Warner conveniently forgot that his stepdaughter Joy Page made her screen debut in *Casablanca* as the young Bulgarian newlywed.)

Hitchcock had a field day casting Mrs. Antony, psychopathic Bruno's mother, who was described in the final shooting script as "a gentle, once-pretty woman whose pastel exterior harbors a tigress-like determination to protect her son. She has found reality too harsh for her sensibilities, refuses to face it–if it is determinantal to Bruno–and seeks peace of mind at the easel where she squeezes paint directly on the canvas from the tube, and prefers a palette knife to a brush." Earlier Hitchcock held discussions about significantly amping up the Oedipal charge between the twisted Bruno and his stylish, younger ex-actress and former Ziegfeld showgirl mother by casting as Mrs. Antony a star of the caliber and allure of Claudette Colbert, Irene Dunne, Mary Astor, Tallulah Bankhead (*Lifeboat*), or Madeleine Carroll (his stunning blonde star of *The 39 Steps* and *The Secret Agent* [1936]), but all that ended when the role was reconceived. Still, Hollywood columnists floated Judith Anderson's name, and Hitchcock's erstwhile Mrs. Danvers from *Rebecca* might have been intriguing had she played Bruno's mother in the brittle, hard-edged style of her Ann Treadwell character in *Laura* (1944). Instead, though, for a movie Hitchcock feared could become far too serious, he preferred someone adept at delivering a light comedic touch and dotty eccentricity, qualities he found to be as irresistible as they were rare. Warner's casting chief, Jack Bowers, suggested Ethel Barrymore, Helen Hayes, and Fay Bainter, each of whom may have been fine so far as they went, but Hitchcock gravitated toward such less expected candidates as Miriam Hopkins and Billie Burke.

Hitchcock's inspired, left-field choice was Marion Lorne, an American Academy of Dramatic Arts alum who had debuted on Broadway in 1905, and from the 1920s through the late 1930s, she had achieved great success working and living in London with her actor-playwright-producer husband, Walter C. Hackett (*The White Sister*, a hit 1909 play made into a film four times, the first in 1915 and the last in 1960). After Hackett's 1944 death, Lorne returned to Broadway, where, in 1948, she achieved renown when she replaced Josephine Hull as the tipsy, fluttery-fingered sister of Elwood P. Dowd in the original Broadway production of *Harvey*. Hitchcock had known Lorne for her London stage work and was newly impressed by her *Harvey* performance, which capitalized on her delightful gift for scatterbrained befuddlement and indignant mumbling. Although the sixty-eight-year-old was virtually unknown in the United States at the time, Hitchcock offered Lorne her very first role in a feature motion picture. As for the redoubtable English-American character actress Norma Varden, familiar from appearances in *Casablanca*, *The Major and the Minor* (1942), and *White Cliffs of Dover* (1944), Hitchcock liked her enough to cast her in the small but memorable role of haughty Washingtonian society-type Mrs. Cunningham, whom Bruno nearly strangles at a cocktail party.

Leo G. Carroll, who could qualify as a Hitchcock stock-company member, having appeared in six of the director's movies, including *Rebecca*, *Suspicion*, *Spellbound*, and *North by Northwest*, fit the bill as Senator Morton: "a distinguished fifty, a man with great pride in tradition, family, and his career." The Weedon Bec, Northamptonshire-born

Carroll had debuted on stage in 1912 and appeared in numerous Broadway plays, including the long-running original 1941 production of Patrick Hamilton's *Angel Street* (better known in the United States for the movie version, *Gaslight* [1944]) before returning to the screen in such films as *Wuthering Heights* (1939) and *Father of the Bride* (1950). In the film Carroll embodies good ole hidebound American conservatism (even with a British accent that Hitchcock heard as "sufficiently Bostonian"), expressed in his comments about Bruno being, variously, "a bit weird" and having "an unusual personality" (queer coding, 1950s style). For Miriam's Boyfriend #1 and Boyfriend #2 in the amusement park murder sequence, Hitchcock chose, respectively, Tommy Farrell (the son of actress Glenda Farrell and who would also go on to appear as the elevator operator in Cary Grant's office building in *North by Northwest*) and Roland Morris (a young actor who regularly performed on radio series and in the film *The Accused* [1949]). But doing the movie was a special event for the twenty-six-year-old Farrell, who said,

> Besides the excitement of being in a Hitchcock movie, doing this was like coming back home after many years. When mother was a star with Warners, I used to come over after school and visit her every day. Why, the Warner lot was my playground. Most of the crew members on *Strangers* were no strangers to me. I was used to working nights, too, because Tony Curtis, Janet Leigh, and I were among the people who'd make these amateur 16mm movies at night—fifteen, twenty-minute movies—the first movies ever directed by Jerry Lewis. Don Maguire [writer of *Tootsie* and several Martin and Lewis comedies] wrote them, they had titles like *The Sol Schwartz Story* and *How to Smuggle a Hernia Across the Border*. They were very funny, to us, and every one of them had the same musical soundtrack, the *Captain from Castile*.

Warner Bros. also announced that Hitchcock had cast tennis great Don Budge in an undisclosed role (but likely as Guy's tennis opponent) in the film's most important tennis match sequence. But once the filming dates were lined up, Budge—the only man to win the Triple Crown at the same tournament and achieve consecutive wins of the Australian, French, Wimbledon, and US Opens—was precluded from fulfilling the role because of his prior commitment to the Australian Tennis Tour. Meanwhile, in advance of the location filming, complex negotiations were underway between the Warner Bros. legal department, various professional tennis associations, and the West Side Tennis Club in Forest Hills, Queens, New York City. The legal eagles were obliged to allay concerns about potential lawsuits over invasion of the privacy of the spectators, referees, linemen, ball boys, and players. There was also the need to avoid prejudicing the amateur standing of the players themselves. In the end, the studio got permissions from ball boys Bill Shay, Greg Connolly, John Jeffers, Donald Matteo, Don De Jardin, Barry Murtha, Barry Fleischman, Pete Gardiner, Jerry Grogan, and Harry Segerita to make their movie debuts in the film. And for payment of $1—along with a promise that long shots would be employed whenever possible—the US Lawn Tennis Association president Lawrence A. Baker granted Hitchcock and company the right to shoot the Davis Cup and National Championships for limited use in the film.

With his cast locked in, Hitchcock was primed to begin principal photography. Even though he had Barbara Keon and Alma Reville Hitchcock continuing to rework significant portions of the screenplay, the director felt sufficiently confident and prepared enough to have the luxury of worrying about other less pressing matters. For one, what was he going to do about the title of the film he was about to make?

CHAPTER SIX

HITCHCOCK BACK ON TRACK

Alfred Hitchcock flew from the West Coast to New York and reported to work on October 18, 1950. The following day he was joined by assistant director Mel Dellar, director of photography Robert Burks, camera operator Bill Schurr, camera assistant Leonard South, script supervisor Rita Michaels, men's wardrobe coordinator Bob O'Dell, assistant location manager Charles Bonniwell, prop man Armor Marlow, and others. Farley Granger and Robert Walker arrived on October 19, along with actors Robert Gist and John Doucette, the film's Detectives Leslie Hennessey and Hammond, respectively. Ruth Roman would join the company on October 31. First on the schedule would be ten days of location shooting in New York; Washington, DC; and Danbury, Connecticut; the latter known since the 1850s as the manufacturing Hat Capital of the World.

The last-ditch script revision efforts of Keon and the Hitchcocks required many coast-to-coast phone calls, cables, and late-night work sessions, but their talent, dedication, and sheer panic produced enough script pages to convince Jack Warner to officially authorize the studio's location manager Bill Guthrie to lock down the last few location filming permits required for New York and

Washington, DC. Meanwhile, even though Jack Warner had given Hitchcock and company his hard-won green light, the studio boss cabled Hitchcock, warning that he expected to read new screenplay pages daily and would approve or not approve them at his discretion. The threat hung in the air.

Before he began hinting to reporters that he planned to change the film's title, Hitchcock complained to Alma Reville and his associate Barbara Keon that *Strangers on a Train* sounded like a B-movie or a 1930s romance that might have starred Kay Francis, Warner Bros.' highest-paid female star from 1930 to 1936 (perhaps because the swank fashion-plate Francis starred in *Strangers in Love* in 1932?). Hitchcock separately asked his trusted associates and the Warner Bros. publicity and promotional departments to submit ideas for alternate titles. As he wrote in a memo, "Let's come up with something memorable and preferably of the one-word variety like *Suspicion*, *Notorious*, *Spellbound*." Apparently, the juxtaposition of the words "strangers" and "train" bothered Hitchcock, who recalled turning down the chance to direct a 1936 Gainsborough Pictures comedy-thriller titled *Strangers on a Honeymoon*. Being an astute businessman, he was also acutely aware of recent box-office disappointments featuring "train" or "strangers" in their titles, such as the 1943 Robert Mitchum marital thriller *When Strangers Marry*, directed by William Castle, the Deanna Durbin mystery *Lady on a Train* (1945), director John Huston's Jennifer Jones–John Garfield adventure romance *We Were Strangers* (1949), and Warner Bros.' own 1950 Ginger Rogers–Dennis Morgan romantic comedy *Perfect Strangers*. By November and for months after, *Criss-Cross* began to be listed as the "alternate title" for *Strangers on a Train*, appearing on internal memos and other studio documents. However, that title had already been claimed by the 1949 Burt Lancaster–Yvonne De Carlo crime drama based on a novel of the same name, so Hitchcock tabled his concerns over the title to deal with more pressing matters.

For one thing, he was wracked by uncertainty about whether the early location scouting trips he and Bill Guthrie had taken from July 14 to 16 had produced sites in small-town Connecticut; Forest Hills, Queens; and Washington, DC, equal to those he had chosen in Santa Rosa, California, for *Shadow of a Doubt*. Nevertheless, he had to start filming his movie. After the company's arrival in New York on October 19, Hitchcock spent the day with his crew doing last-minute location scouting ahead of the first day of filming at Pennsylvania Station in New York City. From there, they were scheduled to shift to such Washington, DC, locations as the Jefferson Memorial and the National Gallery of Art (the revised locale of a scene of Bruno stalking Guy and Anne, which had been formerly slated as a more visually complex, low-speed pursuit scene set among the prehistoric dinosaur fossils at the Smithsonian).

In anticipation of their beginning work together on October 20, Walker and Granger spent the day together exploring the nation's capital, investigating the tourist spots, hitting it off, and realizing how much they were looking forward to working together and for Hitchcock, about whom Walker posed lots of questions to Granger. During that initial day of filming, Hitchcock did something remarkable: in uncharacteristically high spirits, he announced to his cast and crew that with *Strangers on a Train*, he felt he was finally and officially about to make what he regarded as his first truly American film—although he'd been working in America since 1939. Recalled Leonard South, who was there when Hitchcock made his remarks and began his twenty-five-year, fourteen-film association with the director when he was hired as camera operator on *Strangers on a Train*, "He was a different man on this picture. He told us his previous work didn't matter." Hitchcock's excitement proved infectious, especially to Robert Walker, who according to several of his coworkers, was visibly enthused about the film. Nationally syndicated columnist Sidney Skolsky reported from the set that Walker looked "reinvigorated," had a "tremendous rapport" with Hitchcock, and was "terribly excited about tackling such a different role from the nice-kid roles that put him on the map."

If Robert Walker's first day of shooting led Hitchcock to expect (or hope for?) chaos from his film's star, or if Granger worried about whether his emotionally embattled coworker's personal demons might resurface, they need not have. Hitchcock and company encountered numerous delays while filming at Pennsylvania Station due to the crowds who gathered to watch the filming, ogle the two leading men, and all too often, stare straight into cinematographer Robert Burks's camera. However, neither the fans nor the delays flustered Walker, whose female fans had turned up in droves. With Hitchcock's blessing, Robert Burks and makeup artist Gordan Bau had calmed the acutely physically self-conscious Walker by shooting preproduction tests that proved he would be optimally lit and sympathetically made-up to minimize signs of his facial scarring. That helped free Walker to focus solely on his performance. Said Burks of Walker, "Bob was so skilled and knew exactly what to do with that character. Hitchcock quickly saw that he'd be one of the ones who'd walk off with the movie. I'd glance over at Hitchcock in his director's chair and he'd be smiling when Bob would say a line in a surprising way or toss in a gesture. He was magnetic." He was also by turns silkily seductive, explosively deranged, terrifying, and as he promised Granger, about as queer as an actor could afford to be in a 1950s movie. "He was marvelous in the part, he really was," said Granger.

After shooting ended for the day on October 20, Hitchcock and Farley Granger amused themselves by riding the Senate Subway, the miniature railway shuttle through underground tunnels that connect the Senate and the Capitol Buildings. Local newspapers reported Hitchcock and Granger's rides, and the actor responded to a journalist's obvious question by saying,

> Mr. Hitchcock assured Bob Walker, Ruth Roman, and me that he won't put us through anything scary aboard the underground Senate Subway in *Strangers on a Train.* You can bet there'll be plenty of other jolts in it, though. It's my second picture with Hitch so I've warned Ruth and Bob to beware if he gets a dreamy kind of gleam in his eye and says, "Wouldn't it be amusing if . . . ?" That usually means he's seen or remembered some famous, perfectly innocent locale and suddenly thought of a diabolical way of using it in a picture. He's a wizard.

On October 20 a relaxed Hitchcock and his leading men enjoyed an evening of fine dining and excellent wine at the venerable Martin's Tavern in the Georgetown neighborhood. Hitchcock was pleased to observe the easy chemistry, rapport, and friendly rivalry between Walker and Granger. He informed them that they had been invited for post-dinner brandy and coffee at the home of *Washington Post* theater critic Richard Coe. After one drink and chitchat with the amiable and intelligent Coe, Hitchcock bowed out—"It's way past my bedtime, gentlemen," he explained. However, encouraging his stars to remain, he departed and took their limousine back to his hotel. After an hour more with their gracious host, Granger could not help noticing that Walker was growing tipsier and slurring his words. So he thanked their host and begged off, with Coe calling them a cab. Once back in his hotel room, Walker flopped onto the bed, and Granger helped make him more comfortable by removing his shoes and jacket. Walker appeared ready to doze off, but as Granger was about to leave, Walker gripped his arm and frantically begged, "Please, please, don't leave me alone! Don't leave me!" Granger admitted, "He scared the hell out of me." Walker began tearfully pouring out his anguish over losing Jennifer Jones to "that son-of-a-bitch Selznick"—the immensely powerful and profligate Hollywood producer, womanizer, compulsive gambler, and speed addict twice her age who possessed the resources to fulfill his promises of giving Jones a big movie career.

Granger, recalling how Walker had the earliest call for the next morning's shooting, sat down on the other bed and tried lending his costar a sympathetic ear until, as Granger told it, both men eventually fell asleep. The next thing Granger knew, the phone was jangling and it was broad daylight. Recalled Granger, "The driver of Bob's car was calling from the lobby. Bob had an earlier start time than I did. I stalled the driver for a half hour." Meanwhile, Granger called assistant director Mel Dellar, explained that Walker had a rough night, and offered to make himself ready in a half hour so Walker could catch up on his sleep. Dellar assured him it would be no problem, as Hitchcock would only be filming the tracking dolly shots of their feet traveling through Penn Station. Hitchcock made no comment when Granger reported for work instead of Walker. When Walker arrived at noon, he said nothing about the previous evening. Neither actor ever mentioned it again. Nor was Walker ever late again.

Although the scenes set aboard the train were scheduled to be filmed on Ted Haworth's accurate and meticulously detailed sets built on Warner Bros.' Burbank soundstages, the actual train shown in exterior shots was the Pennsylvania Express's Congressional Limited. The sixteen-car commuter streamliner train featured four parlor cars for first-class passengers, two dining cars with an adjacent kitchen, an observation car, and a club car lounge. The Congressional left Penn Station in the early morning and ran daily three-and-a-half-hour trips between New York City and Washington, DC. The train was famous for providing kid-glove service and amenities to its clientele, composed of not only holiday travelers but also businessmen, politicians, and government workers. It traveled at speeds up to eighty miles per hour and made seven scheduled stops. The Congressional made no

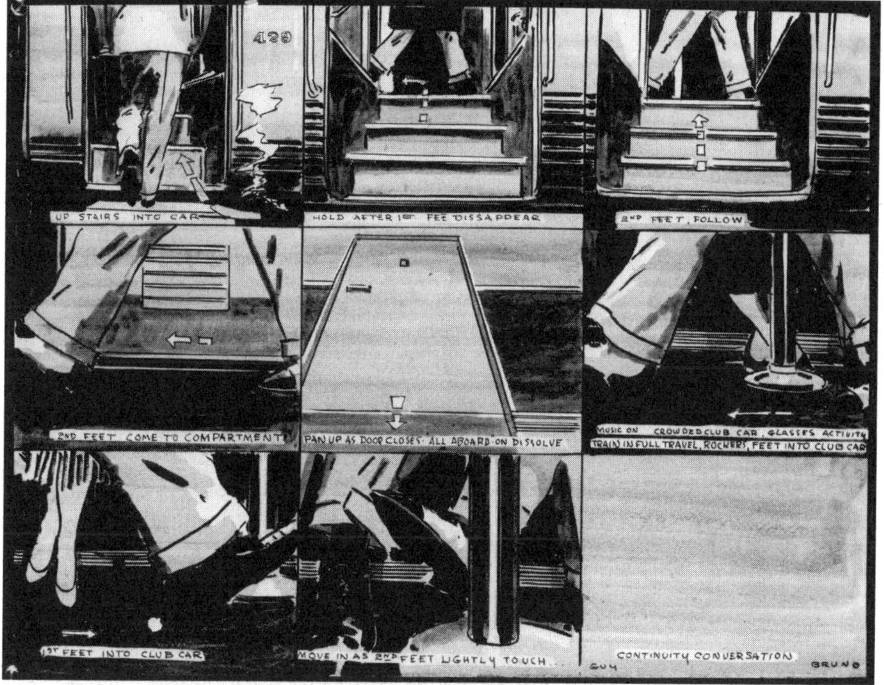

Art director Ted Haworth's storyboard production sketches for Bruno stepping onto the train, seating himself, and his two-toned shoe being brushed by Guy's.

provisions for checked baggage—not even for famous movie directors lugging double-bass fiddles.

—

With the primary Pennsylvania Station footage completed late in the evening on October 21 (a second-unit crew shot there for five additional days), the company moved on to the Danbury, Connecticut, railroad station on Saturday, October 22, for filming moments involving Walker, Granger, Robert Gist, and John Doucette. That same day Hitchcock walked the head of his second-unit crew, special effects expert and cameraman Hans F. Koenekamp, through a series of establishing shots that he wanted him to capture in Danbury. During Hitchcock's preproduction location trip, he informed several mystified locals that he specifically chose the city as the movie's town of Metcalf because he liked the pattern of the curved railway tracks and the symmetry of the canopy at the Danbury Railroad Station at 120 White Street. Local newspapers reported hundreds of residents turning out to watch Hitchcock and company filming outside Hein's Record Store on Main Street. For a scene of Bruno arriving in town, Robert Walker can be glimpsed backgrounded by the sign outside the popular local spot that read "Ray's Danbury Diner." The director spotted the goof, convened the appropriate crewmembers, and drawled, "Wouldn't you agree we've missed a rather significant geographical detail? Please see to it, gentlemen." Within the hour the sign was replaced by another reading "Ray's Metcalf Diner," and filming resumed. (Look closely enough in the film, though, and both signs are visible.) Hitchcock liked the slow-paced, lived-in feel of Danbury and even hired several residents for extra work, including Walter Brosz, whom he spotted working his job as Danbury Railroad Station portee and put him before the cameras doing the same work once he finished his shift. "He lends local veracity," Hitchcock told a reporter for a regional paper. The press also reported scores of local teenage girls showing up to ogle Farley Granger as Hitchcock filmed him disembarking the train as Metcalf local hero Guy Haines. Each time the action required Granger to light a cigarette and toss away the match, starstruck young women rushed to pick up that match as a souvenir.

Before leaving Danbury, Hitchcock decided to shoot his walk-on cameo appearance—an event he usually sprang on his crews only at the last minute. As it had been loosely planned, the moment—a playful take on the movie's overarching "doubles" motif—would involve Farley Granger hurrying to exit a train car at the Danbury Station while Hitchcock struggles to climb on as he carried a double-bass, an analogue for his rotund figure. Their director was Pat Hitchcock, whose father gave her a single suggestion: "Get it over quickly." She did and quipped to a local reporter visiting the set, "You know, I think my father has a future as an actor." When she suggested a retake, during which she told Granger to shoot Hitchcock a look of recognition (seriously, why?), Hitchcock complied, pretending to be greatly annoyed. Hitchcock joked to a reporter,

> When she wanted to become an actress, I told her, "If you're going to be an actress, be an intelligent one." If she now wants to become a director, all I can say is that she's been paying attention and she did rather well today. You'd have to ask Mr. Granger what he thought of her. As for me, don't tell her so, but I found her rather demanding. After all, you saw her demand a retake.

Said Hitchcock to a *Boston Globe* reporter about his cameo appearances,

> It's something of a cycle. In *Spellbound*, I carried a violin. My principal prop in *The Paradine Case* was a viola. In *Strangers on a Train*, I have graduated to a bull-fiddle. In my next picture after this one, don't be surprised if I start with a piccolo and end with a tuba. Then in the picture after that, perhaps I will start with the percussion instruments beginning with the triangle and wind up with a bass drum. Why do I do it, you ask? I guess it's the ham in me.

Hitchcock being Hitchcock, to further thread the needle when it came to the "doubles" theme, had already prepared for what amounted to a sly second cameo appearance by having Farley Granger carry on the train a copy of *Alfred Hitchcock's Fireside Book of Suspense*, a 1947 thriller anthology book featuring the director's photo on the back cover. (The book contained a tale by William Irish, who, as Cornell Woolrich, wrote the basis for *Rear Window*, "It Had to Be Murder," as well as another by Robert Bloch, who would go on to win fame as the author of the 1959 novel *Psycho*.)

—

Hitchcock only meant to shoot in Connecticut for three days before he and the company were scheduled to fly to Washington, DC, to film there for another three days. However, bad weather kept wreaking havoc with the schedule and canceling their flights, so they wound up in Connecticut for several more days until they gave up entirely on plane travel and switched, appropriately enough, to trains. Once in Washington, they quickly captured exteriors and interiors (West Wing) of the National Gallery of Art and the Jefferson Memorial. Hitchcock and Burks were struck by how, even in longshots, Walker was fully present and intensely effective, especially when the director spent part of October 25 filming the chilling traveling shot of Bruno—the man who has a plan to blow up the White House—staring hawklike at Guy while standing menacingly atop the hallowed steps of the Lincoln Memorial at 2 Lincoln Memorial Circle NW, Washington, DC. (It would take seventy-one years for reality to eclipse fiction, when, on January 6, 2021, armed insurrectionists supportive of President Donald Trump stormed the Capitol Building intending to inflict harm, create chaos, and overturn the certification of a presidential election in an attempted coup.)

Bad weather shadowed the company to Washington until finally, on Friday, October 27, weather conditions improved sufficiently to clear Hitchcock and crew to fly from Washington back to Los Angeles. Warner Bros. had reserved for Hitchcock Soundstages 1, 5, 14, 15, and 22 on the Burbank studio lot. Studio 1 holds a special place in Hollywood history. Such Golden Age directors and stars as William Wyler, John Huston, Bette Davis, James Cagney, and Joan Crawford came to regard Stage 1, built in 1936 and measuring roughly 11,000 square feet, as a good-luck soundstage. On that stage were filmed classic scenes in *Jezebel*;

Top: Ted Haworth's storyboards for the fateful conversation on the train between Guy and Bruno match the finished film amazingly well. Bottom: Haworth's stylish glass-and-chrome set was based on the Pennsylvania Railroad's Congressional Limited.

Dark Victory; *The Letter* (1940); *Now, Voyager*; *Yankee Doodle Dandy* (1942); *The Treasure of the Sierra Madre* (1948); and *Mildred Pierce*. For *Strangers on a Train*, Hitchcock filmed the Mortons' Washington society soirée in honor of Monsieur and Madame Darville (played by Georges Renavent and Odette Myrtil), Miriam and Guy's confrontation in the Metcalf music store, close-ups and medium shots of Bruno strangling Miriam on the amusement park's Isle of Love, medium shots and close-ups of Bruno and Guy trading punches on the carousel, and the reactions of other riders as the carousel whirls out of control. On Stage 15 were built the interiors of the Antony mansion, including the entrance foyer, hall, living room, and bedroom of the senior Mr. Antony. Prior to *Strangers on a Train*, Stage 15—built in 1927 and one of the studio's larger soundstages, at 22,660 feet—hosted the production of big-scope scenes for *Golddiggers of 1935* (1935), *Anthony Adverse* (1936), and *Mildred Pierce*.

Filming resumed on Monday, October 31, on Stage 22, where Hitchcock shot Granger and Walker's opening scenes set in the train's stunning Ted Haworth–designed glass-and-chrome parlor and dining cars. Hitchcock and Haworth knew that the train compartment interiors would provide the backdrop for inevitably dialogue-heavy but dramatically crucial scenes. Hitchcock's directive to Haworth had been: "Let's give the audience interesting things to look at and discover as I cut between the actors and move the camera when I must." Haworth came through beautifully, though technical problems cropped up when the vibration and shaking of the train's floor constantly and dangerously disrupted the stability of the lights and camera. To correct the glitch, Robert Burks and his crew rethought the lighting scheme and switched to a boom-mounted camera. That same day Hitchcock filmed an additional round of hair tests with his daughter and Ruth Roman, the latter of whose hairstyles by Myrl Stoltz continually dissatisfied the director.

Meanwhile, the press ran with an odd story about how Farley Granger and Pat Hitchcock were spotted crawling around searching the grass and shrubs outside the popular, celebrity-friendly Smoke House Restaurant directly across from the Warner Bros. lot. Apparently, on her way out of the eatery after lunch, Pat Hitchcock had bitten into a piece of hard candy and lost a tooth. When she and Granger couldn't find it, they reportedly stopped traffic to search the sidewalk along busy Barham Boulevard. Pat desperately wanted to find the tooth to avoid causing any production delays. Her father sent her to the studio dentist, who made the temporary repair that allowed Pat to finish shooting her scenes for the day.

November 1 saw the company moving to Stage 5, where both the club car lounge and Bruno's private train compartment had been built to Hitchcock's and Haworth's exacting specifications. There, Hitchcock directed Walker and Granger in some of their most crackling and memorable moments of the film. The advance planning of the camera angles and set-ups by the director and cinematographer kept the filming running smoothly and helped ensure a vibrancy and pace in the editing process. The daily production notes indicate several retakes required for Granger and none for Walker. The dark chemistry and subtext generated by the two actors—let alone their rehearsals together—helped keep things humming along. On the same day, Hitchcock was delighted that Farley Granger graciously assisted with the filming of both Ruth Roman's and Pat Hitchcock's costume tests.

Hitchcock knew he would soon need to begin filming Farley Granger in action on the tennis court. The day Hitchcock signed Granger to appear in the film, he had also wisely hired as his star's coach Jack Cushingham, tennis instructor to such stars as Cary Grant (who recommended him to Hitchcock), Errol Flynn, Rita Hayworth, and Spencer Tracy. Hitchcock, still discomfited by the prospect of handling the tennis sequences in a visually dynamic but authentic way, also asked

Hollywood's favorite tennis coach Jack Cushingham (standing, with Ruth Roman and Farley Granger seated) coached Granger, choreographed the tennis scenes, and appeared in the film as Guy Haines's opponent, Fred Reynolds.

Cushingham to act as the film's (paid but uncredited) technical advisor; it was Cushingham who helped predesign, stage, and choreograph the film's important tennis scenes. The photogenic, thirty-one-year-old Cushingham (often mistaken for the young Charlton Heston) would also appear in the film as Guy Haines's tennis opponent, Fred Reynolds. In the meantime, Cushingham put Granger through his paces daily, coaching him through long bouts of jumping rope to improve his footwork and build up his endurance. He also helped the actor correct faults in his serves, backhands, forehands, and volleys. To his credit, Granger was so committed that he skipped numerous lunch breaks to practice with Cushingham on the Warner Bros. tennis courts, where smitten studio secretaries began gathering daily in ever-increasing numbers. Explained Granger, "I practiced with Jack all the time. I couldn't let myself or Hitch down. The tennis stuff had to look convincing."

Hitchcock's anxiety about filming the tennis sequences didn't abate, however. Despite assistant director Dellar's bullish report about the excellent quality of the background footage he had captured that past July in Forest Hills for the Davis Cup Matches and the National Lawn Tennis Championships, Hitchcock insisted, sight unseen, on augmenting that footage by filming additional crowd scenes, atmosphere, and close-ups at the tennis courts at South Gate Park in South Gate, California, approximately twenty-two miles south of the Warner Bros. lot. From November 2 through 4, with temperatures soaring over 90 degrees, the director filmed gameplay close shots of Granger and Cushingham. Said Cushingham, who had minutely choreographed the match, "Farley Granger and I rehearsed that sequence over and over precisely as if it were a big fight scene or a musical number. It had to be done that way so that [we] knew exactly where the camera needed to be. And of course, [Granger and I] needed to know how close or far to the camera [we] needed to be in every shot."

On that day of shooting, as many as several hundred spectators broke through police barricades and rushed Granger. According to one newspaper reporter's account, they "lustily demand[ed] the autograph of their favorite actor as well as a closer look." The incident forced the company to temporarily halt shooting while Granger pressed flesh and signed autograph books. Meanwhile, the day wore on, and thermometers peaked at 92 degrees. Although Granger reportedly remained good humored, the pressure, heat, and fan adulation took their toll. The actor growled at Hitchcock as he was about to shoot another take: "If one more person comes up to me and wisecracks, 'Tennis, anyone?' I will hit him over the head with this racquet."

Hitchcock wanted to heighten the tennis sequence with the brand of visual punch and inventiveness audiences and critics expected of him. To that end, he and cinematographer Burks experimented by filming some of the footage from the subjective POV of the racquets, with the

Filming in 90-plus-degree weather at South Gate Park, Farley Granger displayed the form and ease it took him months to develop by studying with Jack Cushingham, coach to other such film stars as Cary Grant, Rita Hayworth, Errol Flynn, and Spencer Tracy.

ball approaching them. They also shot subjective POV images of the racquets swinging and smashing the ball straight toward the camera. (This is three years before Jack Warner would force him to shoot *Dial M for Murder* in 3D, and Hitchcock, partly in retaliation, deliberately refused to film silly, clichéd 3D effects and instead kept the 3D effects subtle and immersive.) Granger and Cushingham utilized specially constructed rubber racquets while filming these POV shots. As Hitchcock commented, "I had two doubles for Farley Granger in the tennis scenes. I even had a machine made for that scene that could project balls right toward the camera. Granger was always hitting right into the camera lens. We had to have a very strong spring arrangement so that the ball could go way over the camera just before we cut away." In the final editing sessions with William H. Ziegler, though, Hitchcock used next to nothing of this experimental footage because he and the editor agreed it looked "too gimmicky."

While at South Gate, Hitchcock also filmed Walker, as Bruno, sitting among the crowded spectator stands, where, as described in the screenplay, "The heads of the people in the bleachers move from side to side, to follow the play on the court. One head is not moving. It is staring at Guy. It is Bruno." The brilliant set-up sounds like simplicity itself, yet achieving the effect did not come easily. Walker admitted,

> I had trouble getting it. I kept having to fight my natural tendency for my head to bob and to stop myself from letting my eyes move back and forth during the match. Hitchcock just waited very patiently and, finally, he told me that I'd done it the way he wanted. That's when I commented that the whole episode reminded me of a Charles Addams drawing come to life with me as the principal character. Hitchcock had a wide grin on his face.

And that grin probably erupted because Hitchcock's unvoiced inspiration for the scene was indeed a *New Yorker* cartoon by the mordantly funny Charles Addams, two of whose originals resided in Hitchcock's personal art collection. In "Sad Movie," the 1946 *New Yorker* cartoon Hitchcock had in mind, gnomelike Uncle Fester chuckles in a movie theater while the rest of the audience is in tears. In 1956 another Addams *New Yorker* cartoon, "The Man of One Note," would inspire Hitchcock's droll creation of an impassive-looking musician whose sole job during the playing of "The Storm Cloud Cantata" in the Royal Albert Hall concert scene in *The Man Who Knew Too Much* is to crash the cymbals at a climactic moment in the musical piece. Addams, who became a friend of the Hitchcock family, even gets name-checked by Cary Grant in *North by Northwest* when his character, Roger Thornhill, acidly comments on seeing Eva Marie Saint, James Mason, and Martin Landau at an auction, "The three of you together. Now that's a picture only Charles Addams could draw."

A week prior to the filming at South Gate, Hitchcock phoned Patricia Highsmith to extend his personal invitation for her to come watch him film the Granger-Walker tennis-related scenes. The author declined the invitation and wrote about Hitchcock sourly in her diary, "He seems to be going . . . mad for my book." Would she have preferred indifference?

—

By the end of the day on November 4, Hitchcock was relieved that he finally wrapped the tennis scenes. Then, that same day, Jack Warner put Hitchcock on notice in a memo, warning him that he was officially one day behind schedule. The director refused to be perturbed. He'd soon be back where he was happiest, most efficient, and most in control—on the soundstage.

On his return to the studio soundstages, Hitchcock underscored to Robert Burks the specific way in which he wanted Walker to enter and exit scenes whenever possible. The director revived a device he had developed for Judith Anderson's scenes as the imperious, unsettling, and ghostly housekeeper in *Rebecca.* He learned that the more often he photographed Anderson's Mrs. Danvers unmoving and staring fixedly, the more unnerving her screen presence became. As he had also worked out with Anderson, cinematographer George Barnes, and editor W. Donn Hayes, rather than show Mrs. Danvers walking like other mere mortals, she would often simply materialize in a scene, as if out of nowhere. Explained Hitchcock, "You never know where she's going to be. She's always there. She just appears and to see her move from place to place would have been humanizing her." He wanted Walker's Bruno to emit a similarly unsettling sense of unpredictable omnipresence, so their idea was to omit showing him moving into a scene; instead he would appear and remain as motionless as possible. During filming of a particular take on location at the Jefferson Memorial, for instance, Walker had improvised a mocking wave at Guy in a particular take. "Too much movement–keep Bob Walker still," read Hitchcock's editing notes to William Ziegler. In the finished film, Bruno stands stock-still. No wave. The fullest and most effective and memorable expression of Hitchcock's edict to "keep Walker still" is, of course, Bruno sitting motionless, watching Guy play tennis while the heads of the spectators around him swivel from side to side.

In working with Robert Burks, Hitchcock reveled in having found a brilliant new collaborator uniquely attuned to the director's intention to make *Strangers on a Train* a visually compelling, almost baroque work, replete with such bravura visual exclamation points as a murder reflected in the fallen eyeglass lenses of the victim, a cigarette lighter's flame reflected in eyeglass lenses, and a carousel that spins out of control and collapses on itself. These and other visual flourishes required not only technical prowess but also the instincts of a visual poet who is well versed in surrealism. Said Burks, a low-key, mild-mannered man who became a close friend of Hitchcock's, "You never have any trouble

A light moment on set during a break from filming the opening train sequence, with Farley Granger (above) and art director Ted Haworth.

with him as long as you know your job and do it. Hitchcock insists on perfection. He has no patience with mediocrity on the set or at a dinner table. There can be no compromise in his work, his food or his wines." From the outset, Hitchcock and cinematographer Burks were a matched set. "Hitch knows exactly what he wants," said Burks, the adventuresome cinematographer who was instinctively drawn, as was Hitchcock, to dramatic lighting and moody ambience. Burks spent his first twenty-three years in the movie business at Warner Bros. before following Hitchcock to Paramount in the 1950s (winning an Oscar for *To Catch a Thief* [1955] and a nomination for *Rear Window*) and, finally, joining the director for two of his films at Universal in the 1960s.

Hitchcock referenced the work of several painters and illustrators to prepare Burks and other colleagues for their work on *Strangers on a Train*. Immediately following Hitchcock's initial preproduction conferences with Burks, art director Ted Haworth, and, earlier, screenwriters Whitfield Cook, Raymond Chandler, and Czenzi Ormonde, he dispatched the Warner Bros. research department to provide visual material to familiarize his colleagues with the work of American realist painter and printmaker Edward Hopper, a master of shadow and images of isolation and alienation. Hitchcock also had the studio share the work of Milton Caniff, known as "the Rembrandt of comic strips," particularly *Terry and the Pirates*, the cinema-influenced, high-adventure World War II strip that, at its height, enthralled 31 million newspaper subscribers daily and ran from 1934 to 1973. "My father and Mr. Hitchcock were well matched," said Sean Haworth, son of the late Ted Haworth and himself the art director of such films as *Avatar* (2009) and *Thor* (2011) and the production designer on *Deadpool* (2016). He continued,

> Mr. Hitchcock had a vision of what he wanted before he got to the set, communicated it clearly, so there was no mistaking his intention. He arrived fully prepared. He wanted a booth in the movie—I don't remember whether it was for the amusement park scene, a train station, or something else. Anyway, my father brought for his approval a sketch of a booth and it had three sides. Mr. Hitchcock: "Two sides. The audience will imagine the rest." He could see my dad working that out in his mind and not necessarily agreeing. Hitch reiterated, "Two sides." That's what he got and, of course, it worked great.

> Another time, Hitchcock asked my father how he thought they could highlight the important moment on the train when the toe of Farley Granger's shoe accidentally taps Robert Walker's shoe. Dad proposed they put the camera in a compartment under the floor. Hitchcock looked at him and said (my father loved imitating him), "Whose point of view would that be—a mole's?" My father worked with some of the very best—William Wyler, Billy Wilder, John Frankenheimer—and he made a lot of good director friends with others he worked with, like Don Siegel, Sam Peckinpah. But even in their presence, he would call Hitchcock the most precise and prepared director he ever worked with. He took what Hitchcock taught him right to the end of his career.

Hitchcock turned Haworth loose on a series of production design challenges and opportunities. Apart from the sleek train compartment interiors, the contrasting Gothic interiors of the Antony mansion, the more traditional Morton apartment, and Guy's brownstone apartment interior, Haworth got to design an entire amusement park midway, as well as paint several canvases meant to represent the hobbyist paintings of the dotty, troubled Mrs. Antony. For the latter, Hitchcock suggested Haworth use as his inspiration the brilliant-hued surrealistic and Expressionist paintings of American artist Abraham Rattner (1895–1978), who not only often painted religious subjects but also designed stained glass windows for prominent synagogues. Although only one of Haworth's paintings is seen in the finished film, it provides the punchline for the unforgettable reveal of the unhinged Mrs. Antony's latest monstrosity. Described in the shooting draft of the screenplay as "a horrible mess. Out of the violence of the pattern, a man's face can be discerned, wild-eyed and distorted," Bruno interprets the painting as a portrait of his father, while his mother claims she intended to

Art director Ted Haworth proposed Hitchcock set the camera below the train floor to visually punctuate the importance of the collision of Guy's and Bruno's shoes. Hitchcock chided, "Whose point of view would that be—a mole's?"

depict St. Francis. Haworth responded with a nightmarish image of a grimacing man displaying a clawlike hand. To complement Haworth's work, Dimitri Tiomkin composed a jarring, frisson-producing musical cue that perfectly punctuated the visual.

Walker told the press that he fully understood what it meant to get "the Hitchcock Treatment" when, in mid-November, he and Farley Granger shot the scene of Guy slipping into the brooding Antony mansion at night and finding Bruno hiding in his father's bed (could the Freudian implication be any more literal?). "So for this scene, I'm dressed in custom-made white tie and tails, something I don't own or wear in real life," said Walker. "Alfred Hitchcock wouldn't let me lie down in bed on the set until I was assured that the sheets were silk. Why silk? 'Because, dear boy,' says Mr. Hitchcock, 'Silk means no lint.' I've never felt more expensive in my life than taking a snooze in white tie between silk sheets. But then, this is my first time making a movie for Alfred Hitchcock."

The director spent much of November 7 on Stage 5 filming with Robert Walker the scene of Bruno desperately trying to retrieve Guy's incriminating cigarette lighter from the storm drain. Walker would experience the director laser-focused on the smallest details of his character. In preparation for the scene, Hitchcock personally selected the debris that the prop men placed at the bottom of the storm drain built on set. His choices included an orange peel, a chewing-gum wrapper, wet leaves, and crumpled bits of paper. Then, with the smallest possible crew, Hitchcock

Hitchcock calculatedly invited to the set the viperlike gossip columnist Hedda Hopper on a day when the entire focus was on her favorite Robert Walker, the emotionally turbulent star whom she championed.

precisely directed the movements of Walker's right hand and fingers struggling to capture the lighter from the storm drain. While on set, Hedda Hopper documented Hitchcock as he sat immediately beside the camera with cinematographer Burks, while Walker, on a platform above, reached into a deep shaft created expressly for the scene. First, they reviewed the choreography and intent of the scene, with Hitchcock explaining,

> We must be photographic about this, also realistic. I want you to clutch yet not clutch, if you get what I mean. We'll break the action into five or maybe six steps, Bob. First, you can't touch the lighter at all, you just can't reach it. We'll do a big close-up on your face straining, straining, straining. Then, a big close-up from under the grating. Your hand is groping but your fingers are a long way from the lighter. If you do touch it at all, this time it should be just a brush. Then, we're doing a low shot on you bent over the grating. We'll bring in the extras who will be seen as the legs and feet of onlookers behind you. Next we're going back on a big close-up of your face straining and panicking. From that, we'll go right away to a big close-up under the grating. Your fingers get near the lighter and you secure it. But in your groping, you lose it and knock it off the ledge onto the ledge even lower. Now you desperately fight to salvage it, so we're going to do an angle shooting through the grating. It will be a big close-up of your head and shoulder straining. We'll stay under the grating as you stretch and strain to reach the lighter still a few inches out of reach. You'll slowly . . . slowly . . . slowly close in on the lighter and manage to grasp it. [To cinematographer Robert Burks] What do you say we add a big close-up of Bob's fist holding the lighter as he triumphantly lifts it through the grate? [To

Walker] Okay, let's get through it and I'll show you what I want your hand and fingers to do, Bob.

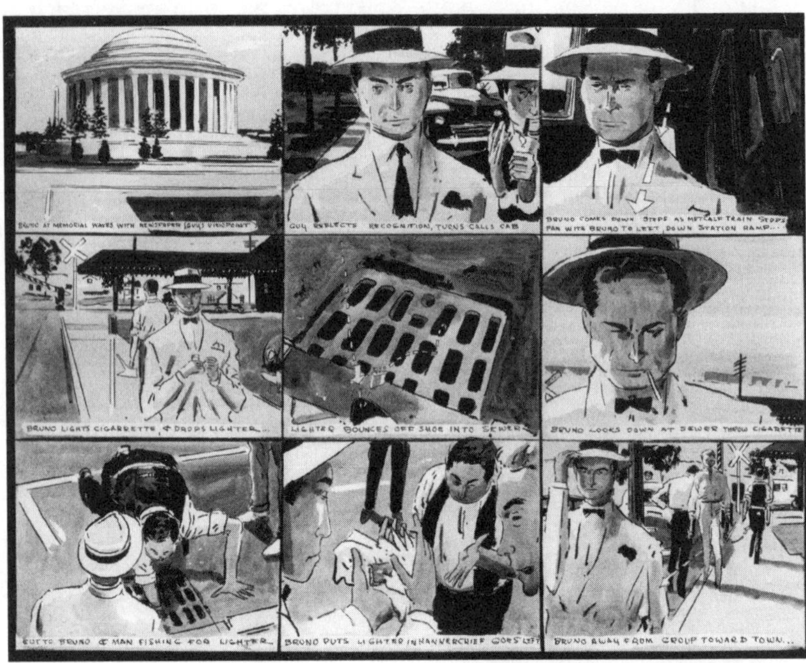

Alfred Hitchcock broke down into six steps Bruno's frenzied retrieval of Guy's incriminating cigarette lighter from a storm drain, personally selected the articles that appear in the drain, and spent four hours on set directing Robert Walker's right hand and fingers in that scene.

This was at 8:00 a.m. Four hours later, Hitchcock said, "Everybody, you can go eat now. Be back in an hour." Walker said, "Send my hand out to lunch. It's earned it. The rest of me is going to lie down and rest. It's also earned it."

"Is Hitchcock a taskmaster, Bob?" asked Hollywood's feared, powerful gossip columnist Hopper. After all, the director could have used another actor's hand and spared Walker the agony. Answered Walker, "For that one scene, he directed me down to the movements of my hands and fingers—and for hours. But it was for good reason. If that's being a taskmaster, I'll happily work with such a taskmaster on every picture from here on in." As an intelligent, committed actor, Walker understood that he must portray Bruno's struggle to reach the lighter as equal the intensity of Guy's frenzy to win the decisive tennis match. Said Marshall Schlom, a sought-after script supervisor for Hitchcock on his feature films and his TV series and, later, for William Wyler, John Huston, Stanley Kramer, Peter Bogdanovich, and Mike Nichols: "Mr. Hitchcock never had trouble with actors so long as they were smart, and prepared. He had no patience or respect for those who were not prepared or gave less than their best. He once told me that he gave Robert Walker the chance to opt out and Mr. H would shoot that scene with a 'hand actor.' Walker wouldn't have it and said something funny like, 'What and give up my hand's big Hollywood close-ups?' Now, I know that if Robert Walker had let another actor do the storm drain scene, Hitchcock would have thought less of him. But Walker was the kind of pro actor Mr. H. liked best—talented, prepared, intelligent, unpretentious, and funny."

ABOUT GUY'S CIGARETTE LIGHTER

Guy's cigarette lighter is not merely the McGuffin—that thing everyone's chasing in a Hitchcock movie, such as the organization of spies stealing wartime secrets in *The 39 Steps*, or the vital message encoded in a folk song in *The Lady Vanishes*, or the radioactive sand stored in magnums of champagne in the spy's wine cellar in *Notorious*. As Hitchcock put it, "The McGuffin is the thing that the spies, or what have you, are after but the audience doesn't care." The *Strangers on a Train* McGuffin is an all-timer. For starters, it holds symbolic power. After all, the lighter is a love token from the wealthy, worldly Anne to the working-class Guy. It is a chromium-plated totem of her privilege and her "heat" embodied in a sleek, mechanical, specially engraved ("A to G") lighter, custom decorated with crossed tennis rackets. For Bruno, who opportunistically pockets the lighter when Guy leaves it behind in his private train compartment, possessing Guy's lighter is a way to withhold an object that conveys sentimental and romantic meaning to and a means of wielding power over Guy if he hesitates to keep his end of the madman's "murder swap." When Bruno accidentally drops the lighter down a storm drain, forcing him to agonizingly struggle to pull it out of the urban underworld, viewers sweat, cry out, and worry for him. That's Hitchcock's way of holding up a mirror to show us exactly what we're made of—fully capable of rooting for a murderer to get away with his crime, just as Hitchcock dares us not to breathe a sigh of relief with Norman Bates when Marion's car sinks into the swamp in *Psycho* or when Rusk in *Frenzy* gruesomely pries his incriminating jeweled "R" monogrammed tie pin from the rigor-mortised fingers of the blameless barmaid he's strangled to death.

Although some have tried to locate the precious cinema artifact used in *Strangers on a Train*, many movie memorabilia collectors and aficionados of vintage cigarette lighters believe that no original lighter used in the film has resurfaced. Hitchcock's choice of lighter was a Ronson chromium-plated satin-finish Adonis model (fit for a Hollywood Adonis like Farley Granger). Operating out of Newark, New Jersey, the Ronson Company debuted the Adonis lighter in 1947 and produced upward of forty-five variations over the years. In 1950 the Adonis—advertised as "slim as a fine watch"—retailed for $10 (about $130 today); the jeweler's engraving and customizing of the lighter with the crossed tennis rackets would have significantly upped the cost.

How did this lighter end up as a plot engine in *Strangers on a Train*? In Patricia Highsmith's novel, there is a book (Plato's *Phaedrus*, containing speeches about love, inspiration, and madness) that serves a similar function, but Hitchcock obviously required something more dynamic and cinematic. The lighter appears in the first script treatment by Whitfield Cook. Successive writers who developed the screenplay—Chandler, Czenzi

Ormonde, Barbara Keon, and the two Hitchcocks—gave the lighter even more prominence and psychosexual cachet in their iterations of the narrative. Enter celebrity publicist–turned radio producer Gary Stevens, whose popular radio panel quiz show *Twenty Questions* was sponsored at the time by Ronson. When an executive of the company asked Stevens to use his show-business connections to persuade Hitchcock to insert a Ronson product into one of his films, the director told Stevens he would "work out something." Voilà! Hitchcock gave the lighter enough screen time to make it one of the most memorable visual elements of *Strangers on a Train*. It's practically a costar.

Says Michigan-based lifelong Hitchcock fan and vintage cigarette lighter aficionado Al Wurst, "I'm excited when any lighter shows up in a movie. If I see a model I don't own in a movie, it sets me on the hunt. But the holy grail of lighters used in movies is the one in *Strangers on a Train*. It's the petroleum-drenched wick of fate that burns all the way through one of Hitchcock's most thrilling plots." Wurst spent years vainly trying to find the original before deciding to make a replica. He hunted down an authentic Adonis model of the correct vintage, then searched high and low before finally unearthing a vintage sterling-silver pin exactly matching the style and size of the crossed tennis racket decoration as seen in the film. He even got a jeweler to precisely replicate the "A to G" engraving as seen in the film.

One of Hitchcock and Ziegler's biggest editing challenges of the entire production was sparked by the ingenious decision to cross-cut between Guy's frantic attempt to finish the tennis match with this moment of Bruno frenziedly trying to retrieve the lighter from the storm drain. Hitchcock realized too late that, in his quest for perfection and plenty of coverage, he had amassed over three hours of tennis footage, so much that there wasn't even enough time for him and his editor to view it all. That left Ziegler to struggle with an inconvenient truth that had plagued Raymond Chandler while he tried to write that sequence: logically, Guy's victory in the tennis match has little or nothing to do with Bruno's retrieval of the lighter. But, in Hitchcock's view, a dazzling film sequence could and should overcome something as plebian as mere logic. As the director described the two grafted-together sequences almost two decades later, "There we were playing with time, expanding and contracting time for the purposes of putting the audience through it." Intercutting the tennis and the storm drain sequence took him and Ziegler three weeks to perfect. It took Ziegler's editing (and the musical score) to truly sell Hitchcock's cinematic conceit. The sequence is a corker—sleek, tense, edge-of-your-seat filmmaking. Hitchcock and Ziegler so masterfully match Granger's and Walker's physical efforts that the audience buys it when Guy and Bruno "win" their separate matches at the same time. Often, they applaud the audacity of the sequence. The magic largely happened during the editing and scoring process.

SEEING DOUBLES

Even before Hitchcock began developing the screenplay, when he read Patricia Highsmith's novel he was convinced that *Strangers on a Train* could provide him a spectacular lens through which he could explore themes of intersecting identity, crisscrosses, double-crosses, and doubles. Throughout filming, Hitchcock kept his eye out for opportunities to reinforce the "doubles" motif, to the point of improvising on location by capturing shots of Granger and Roman standing under the engraved lettering that read, "And treat those two imposters just the same," quoting Rudyard

Kipling's poem "If." Because the poem also refers to "Triumph" and "Disaster" as "imposters," and because Hitchcock positioned Guy and Anne under those words, he invites us to read the quotation as a comment on the actors; the characters; their inequitable, shaky relationship; or even an allusion to the fateful link between those two imposters, Guy and Bruno. Other examples of doubles in the film include:

- A Diamond Cab pulls up at Pennsylvania station, a porter opens the cab door and removes the luggage, and Bruno Antony alights and pays the fare. Another Diamond Cab Company pulls up to the station entrance, a porter opens the cab door, Guy Haines exits, and the porter pulls out luggage and two tennis rackets. (Note how Walker lifts his right foot off his heel and slightly points his toe as he bends his knee inward while tipping, and compare that with feet-on-the-ground Guy. The movie's just begun and they're both delineating characters.)

- The two passengers cross the terminal at the same pace as if they are destined to collide.

- From the POV of a locomotive departing the station, a train heads toward an intersecting pair of tracks before veering right.

- On the train, Bruno introduces himself to tennis player Guy Haines and says, "I suppose you're going to Southampton for the doubles." (Note, too, the crisscross pattern of Farley Granger's necktie and the vertical stripes of Robert Walker's suit. Notice how the shadows of the window blinds cross Walker's face. Guy pulls out his cigarette lighter embossed with a pair of crossed tennis racquets. Bruno orders from the waiter Scotch and water, "a pair, doubles," he says. Both men display gifts from women: Guy carries his inscribed silver cigarette lighter from Anne, and Bruno wears his sterling silver "Bruno" tie pin from his overly doting mother.

- In Bruno's private train compartment, Bruno proposes to Guy a murder swap, "a perfect murder." Twice he calls it a "crisscross." He says, "Your wife. My father. Criss-cross." After Guy leaves the compartment to exit the train, Bruno mutters to himself, "Criss-cross."

- Guy and Bruno are shadows, doubles. To Guy, the lower-class, serially unfaithful Miriam is a painful reminder of who he once thought he was and what he once accepted for himself. Now, eager to level up, Miriam is an inconvenience. Bruno—who tells Guy, "I'm your friend. I like you. I'd do anything for you"—longs to be seen, accepted, maybe loved by Guy, a person who "does things." Bruno is a shadow aspect of Guy and becomes the agent, an instrument who acts on and manifests Guy's thinly veiled, suppressed desires to be rid of Miriam. Both men are deceivers. Guy pretends to be shocked by Bruno's casual talk of murder, yet the book he carries on the train is a murder mystery anthology.

- As Guy exits the train in Metcalf, Hitchcock scrambles aboard carrying a double bass.

- When we see bespectacled Pat Hitchcock for the first time playing Anne's younger sister, Barbara, we note her resemblance to her famous father. So, *Strangers on a Train* offers double Hitchcocks. Barbara and Anne are daughters of a distinguished, significantly older father, and Bruno's father is also significantly older.

- In Miller's Music Store, when Guy's estranged wife, Miriam, takes from Guy the cash meant for her lawyer, she enrages Guy by announcing she's going to spend it on new clothes for her move to Washington, as she has changed her mind about getting a divorce. Guy says, "Why, you little double-crosser." The same scene visually establishes that two young women provide customer service, and in the two listening booths behind the one in which Guy and Miriam argue, one is occupied by a young man and young woman and the other by an older couple.

- In a telephone booth near the train station, when telling his fiancée, Anne, about Miriam's change of heart, the heretofore mild, passive "hero" begins to reveal a violent streak like Bruno. In a moment of rage, he says, "Sure, I sound savage. I feel savage! I'd like to break her neck. I said I'd like to break her foul, poisonous, useless little neck! I said, 'I could strangle her!'" Guy's angry face dissolves into a close-up of Bruno's fingers flexing as though he is strangling someone; it is almost as if Bruno is acting out Guy's wish.

- Bruno, at home, calls Guy and learns that his meeting with Miriam went badly. Bruno says, "Oh, so she double-crossed you."

- Guy reads on a train and checks his wristwatch at the same time as Bruno, at the amusement park, checks his own watch: 9:30.

- At the amusement park, Bruno follows Miriam, who is accompanied by two young boyfriends.

• Bruno and Miriam are doubles, agents of chaos, childlike, hedonistic, and cases of arrested development. Bruno inserts himself into Guy's life—at the tennis club, at a swank party at the home of Senator Morton, at the art gallery where Guy and Anne are browsing. Although Bruno is amusingly eccentric, he is always an embarrassment and causes a scene. Miriam announces, "I'm coming to Washington to have my baby" and fantasizes about how she's going to spend money on pretty clothes, saying, "I wouldn't want you to be ashamed of me in Washington when we go to all those dinners and swanky parties," where, like Bruno, she too would be an embarrassment and undoubtedly cause a scene.

• After strangling Miriam on the island at the amusement park, Bruno meets Barbara Morton, who wears thick-lensed eyeglasses like Miriam and resembles the dead woman in ways that trigger Bruno's memories of murder. As we hear for the second time the carousel calliope playing "The Band Played On" and Bruno saying in his memory "Is your name Miriam?" Hitchcock triples the doubling by reflecting the image of the flame of Guy's lighter in Barbara's glasses. While staring at Barbara—Miriam's visual double—Bruno nearly strangles one of two wealthy matronly guests. Both women suggest bloodthirsty "perfect crimes" and both wear similar hairstyles.

• During the Metcalf section of the film, Guy encounters a familiar policeman twice.

• We see the train come around the curve, and Bruno disembarks the train in Metcalf. The same angle is used when Guy's train arrives in Metcalf.

- Bruno also enters a public telephone booth in Metcalf as we have seen Guy do earlier.

- Guy struggles to win an important tennis match quickly; at the same time, Bruno struggles to retrieve the cigarette lighter with which he intends to incriminate Guy in Miriam's murder. During the match, the umpire calls a "double fault."

- On the train to Metcalf, Guy lights a cigarette for a fellow passenger, and Guy also lit Bruno's cigarette in the film's opening.

- Guy, on the train, watches a passenger accidentally kick the shoe of a fellow passenger, as Guy did to Bruno in the opening moments of the movie.

- A cleric on the train asks Guy if he is Guy Haines, as Bruno did in the opening scene. This time, Guy and Anne change seats to avoid him.

Farley Granger faced his own days of challenging shoots. W. C. Fields once quipped, "Never work with children or animals," and Granger and Hitchcock might have agreed wholeheartedly after spending from November 15 to 18 filming scenes on Stage 14, where the set of the Antony house interior was located. Hitchcock made short work of the moments involving Ruth Roman, Marion Lorne, and Robert Walker, and all had gone comparatively smoothly. Yet shooting the moments of Farley Granger entering the shadowy mansion and being confronted by a massive Great Dane on the staircase landing was an entirely different matter. To prepare for filming the payoff of the scene—when the menacing, growling dog licks Guy's hand and lets him continue up the stairs–a large fawn Great Dane underwent weeks of training. But once it was time to shoot the scene, the dog observed Granger and ignored him as though he wasn't there. The nervous trainer dispatched an aide to the nearest pet store to buy an assortment of canned dog food to slather on Granger's hand to entice the dog. Meanwhile, Hitchcock, the gourmand and longtime dog lover, hatched an alternate strategy. He sent a production assistant to The Smoke House, the celebrity-haunt restaurant across the street from Warner Bros., to pick up a juicy porterhouse steak.

Hitchcock watched as the animal trainer dabbed Ken-L Ration dog food on Granger's hand. Hitchcock called "Action!" for a take, and the dog showed no interest at all. Then, another take, this time with Purina Dog Chow. Nothing. The finicky pup rejected three other brands and utterly refused to interact with Granger. Take after take got marked "N.G. – dog" (No good–dog). Finally, the porterhouse arrived from the chophouse. The dog happily licked Granger's hand–and on the very first take. But only briefly. As Hitchcock told Francois Truffaut, understating as usual, "I remember we went to a lot of trouble getting that dog to lick Farley Granger's hand." In postproduction, the moment needed to be slowed down and double-printed.

Hitchcock took special pains to film the record-store confrontation between Guy Haines and his conniving wife, Miriam, rehearsing it on November 20 and 21 on Stage 22. For Laura Elliott, who played the role of Miriam, the challenges were multiple, and the studio's daily production notes confirm the need for retakes. She recalled,

> Because of the glasses Mr. Hitchcock wanted me to wear, I could not see Farley Granger's face when I looked at him. In the record store, when I'm ringing up the cash register sale, I can't see the cash register. When I'm running after Farley saying something like, "You can't toss me aside

> like that!" as he's leaving the store, I could not see him or where I was going. Watch for my hand running along the counter—I did that because when my hand came to the end of the counter, I knew I had hit my mark, and that's where I stopped. I'd find out that objects that seemed a distance away were actually close—as I'd crash into them! I kept forever bumping into Farley. He'd be nearer than he was further or further than nearer or whatever I mean!

The solution came when Hitchcock rehearsed the actors for a solid hour without Eliott wearing glasses and another hour with Elliott wearing the glasses, then tried for a take. Said Elliott,

> Mr. Hitchcock and I would count out the number of steps to my various destinations in the scene. He also had a prop man nail small wood blocks to various spots on the floor so I'd know when I hit the right spot. We finally got there with the scene and I think it turned out pretty well! And Hitchcock insisted that I wear those glasses even in the long, long shots, outdoors, which was pretty strange considering we had pairs that would have allowed me to see but shouldn't have been noticed by the audience! So, basically, I did the picture blind. Robert Walker, who was just brilliant, was nearsighted and always wore thick glasses off-screen. But in this picture, he didn't wear glasses at all. So he said, "Well, this is the blind leading the blind." He told me he wanted to play Bruno wearing glasses.

Walker indeed asked Hitchcock if he, as Bruno, could wear glasses in the film, but Hitchcock wanted the actor to look the way his bobbysoxer fans expected him to look, the better to subvert their expectations about the character he was playing. Walker told journalist Patricia Clary, "Hollywood has typed the guy who wears glasses as a milquetoast. I'd like to undo that impression. I wear glasses and I'm not a milquetoast. I'd enjoy making a movie wearing glasses and helping to prove that girls do make passes at men who wear glasses, to paraphrase Dorothy Parker. Why, we're all men of action! Want me to prove it? I'd love to."

On November 24, Hitchcock filmed Granger scuttling down a fire escape outside of Guy's apartment building. The locale was a much-used stretch of the Warner backlot known as "Brownstone Street" (originally built in the 1930s) but fitted with a backdrop of the Capitol Dome in the far distance. Then, after a quick costume change for Granger, Hitchcock and Robert Burks photographed him against rear-projection screens on Stages 5 and 6. In the first shot, he stood staring into a store window fancily stenciled Miller's Music Shop. In the second scene, Granger stood in a phone booth, talking with Anne, backgrounded by rear-projection footage shot in Danbury, Connecticut. On November 25, with Stage 22 as the filming site, Hitchcock shot Roman, Granger, and—in the distance—Walker in front of a screen on which was projected the second-unit footage filmed on location in the West Gallery of the National Gallery of Art. Also filmed in front of the rear-projection screen was Granger backgrounded by a Pennsylvania Station ticket window.

Granger, who cited *Strangers on a Train* as "my happiest filmmaking experience," noted Hitchcock's uniqueness as a filmmaker. When Granger starred in *Rope* two years earlier, Hitchcock experimented with simulating real-time and continuous action by filming in ten or twelve camera set-ups with no apparent cutting away from the action. When making that picture, much of the emphasis had been on the technical—or, as Granger put it, with "Technicolor cameras the size of refrigerators, set walls, furniture, and props constantly being yanked out of the way on wheels, and actors focusing on hitting their marks

Art director Ted Haworth and Alfred Hitchcock atop a scaffold on a Warner Bros. soundstage (most likely Stage 14) to assess one of the film's high angle shots to take place in the Antony mansion.

on time and not getting run over while doing it." Making *Strangers on a Train*, Granger felt he finally experienced "the real Hitchcock," that rare director who arrived on set knowing exactly how he planned to film the scene and not only where to put the camera but also exactly which lens to use. Said Granger, who had worked under directors Lewis Milestone, Nicholas Ray, Mark Robson, and Anthony Mann,

> Hitchcock preplanned exactly what he was after and usually knew how to achieve it technically. He had an assistant art director [Ted Haworth, not an assistant] seated on a high stool next to the camera, who was in charge of a very thick binder that contained every setup and shot for the entire film. These were the drawings I had seen pinned to the walls of his office or that he'd shown me earlier at his home. After he finished a setup, he would walk to [Haworth] who would turn over a page. Hitch would look at it and simply say to the cinematographer, "The camera goes here, here, and there." Then he would relax while the crew got ready. They respected and trusted him because he was able to be so precise about what he wanted. He never had to peer through a lens finder to see how a shot looked. Since all his shots were so well-planned, his film was practically pre-edited.

As Haworth explained, in case the cinematographer failed to read the screenplay or missed the point—something he did not have to worry about with Robert Burks—Hitchcock came armed with storyboards. Burks said,

> There is no hit-and-miss with him. He makes a sketch continuity, story-board fashion, of the entire picture. And every morning on the set, he hands his cameraman a small folder with the day's scenes sketched out. Frequently, too, he makes a rapid-fire drawing in thirty seconds and asks if a certain scene can be done in that way. But he never nails you down to those sketches. If, after discussion, Hitch finds that we achieve better results in another way, he has no hesitancy in rewriting the action or the dialogue. Unlike

> many directors who set every scene as if for a legitimate stage production and then almost defy you to get a shot, Hitch thinks of the set in relation to the camera.

One late afternoon, Granger noted Hitchcock slouched in his director's chair while waiting for the crew to rest for the next shot. When the actor approached and asked whether he was all right, Hitchcock said, "Oh, I'm just bored." Granger said he realized the screenwriters, Hitchcock, and his team—composed of the cameraman, production designer, costume designer, and more—had collaborated with him on his creative vision for long months before, and he was now "merely transferring it from paper to film." Perhaps more comprehensive is the perspective of script supervisor Marshall Schlom, constantly at Hitchcock's side while he directed *Psycho* and 17 of the 267 episodes of his TV series *The Alfred Hitchcock Hour*. Said Schlom,

> Yes, Mr. H would doze off, but other times, he would close his eyes and listen to the actors and the dialogue. If he thought an actor was doing something fresh and exciting, he would certainly not be dozing or sleeping. Sometimes, he'd be leaning forward in his chair with his eyes closed, too. But his mind was so active that he tended to find it excruciating to have to wait for the crew to reset a shot. Those who knew him knew it was a good time to sit next to him because, in his boredom, he would tell the most amazing stories from the past or repeat one of his hilarious, unprintable jokes or limericks.

THE FALL OF THE HOUSE OF ANTONY

Hitchcock knew it was essential to find the right real-world residence to "play" the Antony house, and he pursued that house with as much care as he did the casting of his characters. He reviewed photographs of dozens of estates on both coasts before choosing the one that conveyed exactly what he was after: opulence and scale that suggested Old Money, conservatism, and a more-than-slight ambience of melancholy, menace, and entrapment. He found all those qualities when Jack Warner suggested a neighboring house to his own—the George and Gertrude Lewis house, known as Hill Grove, which dominated ten acres on the southeast corner of Angelo Drive and Hillgrove Drive in the Benedict Canyon section of Beverly Hills. Designed by noted San Francisco–based architect Albert Farr and associate J. Francis Ward and completed in 1925, the grand Gothic Revival mansion was built to the highest standards of the Lewises, both from wealthy and socially prominent San Francisco families. In the 1920s, George had bought San Francisco's premier jeweler, Shreve and Company.

With its majestic wrought-iron gates, brick gateposts, acres of impeccably manicured rolling green lawns, and impressive Gothic Revival architecture featuring leaded-glass windows, multiple chimneys, and soaring archways lined with stone, Hill Grove became one of the most admired and distinguished showplaces in all of Beverly Hills in an ultra-exclusive neighborhood. The famous early residents of Benedict Canyon included Oscar-winning screenwriter Frances Marion (*The Champ* [1932]) and her cowboy movie-star husband, Fred Thomson; legendary film idol and sex symbol Rudolph Valentino; and Carl Laemmle, cofounder and president of Universal Pictures. Although some residents of the enclave were inveterate party-givers, like Jack and Ann Warner, the thoroughly modern Lewises led separate lives and rarely spent time there together, nor did Gertrude spend much of any time at their majestic San Francisco residence. That was where George, a renowned bon vivant, mainly resided and was well known for keeping several beautiful mistresses in the high style and great luxury he could give them. Meanwhile, Gertrude often resided in Europe, sometimes for as long as years at a time. But Mrs. Lewis was also a movie fan, and beginning in the 1920s, she began renting out her landmark estate as a film location, always making certain she was present to watch the production and meet the stars, including Clara Bow and Eddie Cantor during the filming of *Kid Boots* (1926), Laurel and Hardy while making *Pack Up Your Troubles* (1932), Barbara Stanwyck and Henry Fonda during *You Belong to Me* (1941), and Cary Grant and Alexis Smith while shooting *Night and Day* (1946), as well as the creatives making the serial *Batman and Robin* (1949), for which Hill Grove served as Wayne Manor. Like too many Beverly Hills showplaces, Hill Grove was demolished, with its grounds subdivided in the 1960s.

On November 9 and 10, Hitchcock especially enjoyed filming at Hill Grove, with its abundance of such highly cinematic elements as its towering Italian cypress trees and its dramatic acres of meticulously manicured lawn cared for by the owners' team of gardeners. There, the film crew captured shots of Farley Granger (and his stand-in) as Guy Haines crossing the lawn in the dark of night to enter the Antony house so he can warn Bruno's father that his troubled son is spiraling out of control.

Hitchcock dubbed the house "a life-size Manderley," referring to the brooding Cornwall Coast manse imagined by novelist Daphne du Maurier and built in exacting miniature for Hitchcock's film version of *Rebecca*. The baronial Antony house interiors, designed by Ted Haworth and built on Stage 14 at Warner Bros., consisted of an entrance hall, drawing room, partial living room, staircase, and upstairs bedroom. Hitchcock's dark vision for these spaces inspired Haworth and cameraman Robert Burks to heighten their Gothic elements. The director wanted the interiors to suggest Bruno's sense of "imprisonment in the house of his father" and, in addition, to provide a backdrop for conveying the emergence of the darker aspects of Guy Haines's character when he goes to the house to warn Bruno's father. When filming, Burks supplied properly stylized melodramatic lighting as well as skewed Dutch (a.k.a. German) camera angles. Haworth created vast-looking yet claustrophobic interiors, suggesting a sad, loveless haunted house.

From November 16 to 18, Hitchcock completed the scenes set in the interior of the Antony mansion involving Farley Granger, Ruth Roman, Robert Walker, and Marion Lorne. At Hitchcock's insistence, all of Haworth's interiors—including the train cars—featured actual ceilings. "[Hitchcock] felt it was always best to play the actors against the simplest and most dramatic background," explained Haworth. "He always wanted to make it look like the actor's every move and gesture was clear and wasn't compounded by a busy background. Bob Burks and other cameramen moved just as fast if there was a ceiling or not."

—

Hitchcock enjoyed hosting select press members on the set when shooting was going smoothly. On December 10, 1950, Philip K. Scheuer of the *Los Angeles Times* visited during the rehearsal of a scene in the Morton living room involving Ruth Roman, Farley Granger, Leo G. Carroll, and Pat Hitchcock, who wore slacks and an "impudent grin." Hitchcock said, "Sit down, Barbara"—using her character's name—and told her to wipe the grin off her face, which she did. When the columnist remarked on

Hitchcock and cinematographer Robert Burks (behind camera, in jacket and tie) rehearse Pat Hitchcock for the party scene. Note the crew's respectful attire, a hallmark of Hitchcock's sets, and Hitchcock's subtle hand signal to Pat to deepen her naturally high-pitched speaking voice.

the crisp professionality and formality between father and daughter, said Pat, who made her first film appearance as an eight-year-old extra in a crowd scene in her father's 1936 British espionage thriller *Sabotage*,

> The only comment he ever made when I decided on a career—I never really thought of doing anything else—was, "If you're going to be an actress, be an intelligent one." He never helped me in anything till *Stage Fright*. Father came with the film company to the Royal Academy of Dramatic Art, in London, where I was studying, so he used me in a bit [part], as a fan of [Marlene] Dietrich's. With *Strangers on a Train*, my new agent [Edith Van Cleve, whose client list included Marlon Brando, Grace Kelly, and Montgomery Clift] had to suggest me for the part of Ruth Roman's wisecracking sister, just as my former agent Kay Brown had before she began to focus more exclusively on representing literary talents. Father never thought of me. When my father interviewed me for the role, it was the same way as he would any other actress. It was though we had no relationship. . . . I get no personal attention at all either on the set or after we leave the studio. On the set he gives direction as well as criticism, but as he would "Jane Jones" instead of Patricia. It doesn't occur to us on the set that we're father and daughter. Not that he's severe, impolite, or gruff but always patient and calm.

Reporters invited to the set noted that Hitchcock and his daughter would exchange looks at certain points, often punctuated by the director slightly lowering his hand. It was code. Said Pat, "When I began acting, my voice was very high-pitched, and he said, rightly, we needed to work on that. I worked very hard to lower the pitch of my voice. If I ever reverted, I appreciated that he'd let me know. In terms of acting, what I had as a child was instinct. The reason I went to the Royal Academy of Dramatic Art was to really learn the job of acting." After hearing her say this, Hitchcock took aside a *Los Angeles Times* reporter and stage-whispered, "I want to see if she learned anything at the Royal Academy—and if it was worth the money." When asked more seriously by syndicated columnist L. L. Stevenson about casting his daughter in a small but potentially scene-stealing role, Hitchcock answered,

> The question is, shall you, seeing embryonic talent, stand aside and not give it a helping hand because you are a parent? You have your choice of being realistic, emotional, or very circumspect about the matter. My position is that the parent should be realistic but if there is a glimmer there, isn't it far better to permit it to have its head and give it every assistance possible? The real problem arises when emotion enters into it, when you find yourself, through pure emotion, giving opportunities to the untalented. In such cases, you encounter that extremely ugly word, "nepotism."

Pat Hitchcock said, "All my life, it's been said to me, 'Oh, be amusing, Pat,' or 'You're so funny, Pat, you make me laugh.' I've quite got used to the idea of being 'the comedy relief,' so to speak. Let me tell you that any comedy ability I may have is inherited from my father. He has a great sense of humor and a gift of fun." But she also told reporters that her role in *Strangers on a Train* provided her "first opportunity to really develop a character." According to her, Hitchcock especially enjoyed it when she—as well as other actors—made him laugh because of some unexpected spin they put on a line of dialogue or gesture. "He showed that side with Marion Lorne, whom he found to be endlessly amusing in her scenes. She was marvelous."

THE GIRL FROM THE WRONG SIDE OF THE TRACKS

More than one Hitchcock collaborator has claimed that the director often exorcised his frustrations by scapegoating one actor per film, most commonly the best looking, least gifted, or both. During the filming of *Strangers on a Train*, the person who most bore the brunt of Hitchcock's displeasure was Ruth Roman, whose high self-estimation of her sex appeal and talent Hitchcock did not share. Hitchcock is quoted as saying he found her manner "bristling" and that he thought she "lacked sex appeal." One afternoon during filming, Hitchcock was seen looking highly amused after the film's publicist Ned Moss handed him a film fan magazine in which a gossip columnist cattily mentioned she had observed something rare while visiting the Warner Bros. lot: "Ruth Roman and Shelley Winters having lunch together and not talking about their favorite actress (themselves)." In a 1950 letter Pat Hitchcock wrote to a friend from the Royal Academy of Dramatic Art, the prolific and well-liked Welsh actor Peter Halliday, she opined, "The boys Farley [Granger] and Bob [Walker] are going to be just wonderful. I'm not so sure about Ruth Roman. She's the sexy type but terribly hard and by no means 'a lady.'" As production wore on, the usually highly circumspect Pat grew more frank, again writing to Halliday, "The picture is really a 'blood-and-sweat' toil. The front office at Warners is just impossible. Ruth [Roman] is turning out to be quite tough to get anything and Farley is just—well, Farley. Bob Walker is magnificent. It'll be his picture and I'm so glad." But Pat Hitchcock was more upbeat when asked about Roman for *Strangers on a Train: A Hitchcock Classic*, a Laurent Bouzereau–directed documentary short that was included as supplementary material on the 2004 Warner Home Video release. She said, "I got on very well with [Ruth Roman]. We became very good friends. We'd go down to Palm Springs on the weekend." According to national gossip columns dated November 9, she and Roman double-dated with, respectively, Paul Davis and Mortimer Hall and did, in fact, spend a weekend in the California desert when Roman, like Robert Walker and others, came down with a cold or the flu after filming several nights in cold, foggy weather at the amusement park location.

Roman, who described herself as "very independent, quick-tempered and all that," learned quickly that she and Hitchcock, who loathed overt conflict and rarely raised his voice on the set, were ill-matched. As the director would do throughout his career with actresses including Madeleine Carroll, Joan Fontaine, Grace Kelly, Vera Miles, Kim Novak, Eva Marie Saint, and Tippi Hedren—who were rarely, if ever, more beautifully costumed, photographed, or impressive onscreen—he attempted to coach and rebrand Roman in dress, comportment, and screen presence. He wanted Leah Rhodes's costumes to help imbue Roman, most often cast as sensual working-class tough cookies, with a sophistication and restraint consistent with her role as a US senator's daughter and socialite. To that end, he also wanted her to deliver her dialogue in the plummy tones of a Boston Brahmin, that strata of wealthy Bostonian society of whom is often joked, "The Cabots speak only to the Lodges and the Lodges speak only to God." When Roman told Hitchcock she was born in Lynn, Massachusetts, ten miles north of Boston, the elitist Hitchcock cattily replied, "Ah, yes, but Lynn may just as well be in another country from Boston."

Roman proved to be a reluctant Galatea, resisting the efforts of a speech, elocution, and dialect instructor whom Hitchcock persuaded Jack Warner to employ—with negligible results. Roman expressed concern that her old New England accent would return and be difficult to shake off once it did. Meanwhile, Hitchcock feigned patience while Roman attempted various accents. To the director, she sounded faux British, not Bostonian. So he coached her on pronunciation and even demonstrated how to move with chic hauteur and glamour. Finally, she said, "Mr. Hitchcock, it appears I can't give you the effect you're after." The director calmly walked toward cameraman Robert Burks and said, loudly enough for Roman to hear, "Miss Roman is quite fond of her short new haircut, Bob. Let's make sure we show off a lot of the back of her head in these scenes." Hitchcock loathed any overt display of temperament on the set. His usual modus operandi was more passive aggressive. He might have saved himself considerable frustration and effort had he listened to the screenwriter, who had dated Roman in the past and summed her up as "earthy, like Betty Hutton. She has too much ambition to be fenced in by a lot of social embroidery." How could Hitchcock not take it personally when Roman essentially told a United Press reporter she was not a fan of the type of intelligent, independent, resourceful, witty women Hitchcock idealized on film—and often hired as producers, costume designers, and writers—nor did she aspire to be perceived that way, either on screen or off. "I don't want to be one of those super-sophisticates," she told journalist Patricia Cary. "They call me corny but they're so jaded they've lost the tang of life. They're cynical, tired, and filled with ennui. I'm a sentimentalist. I cry at movies and laugh at puns. My first stop when I got to Hollywood was the footprints of the stars at Grauman's Theater."

While some found the actress refreshingly unpretentious, the more Hitchcock worked with Roman, the more her presence seemed to irk him. With the actress falling woefully short of the elegant, capable Anne Morton—the role for which he thought Grace Kelly would be ideal—Hitchcock reportedly declared, sotto voce, in front of several cast and crew members, "Never mind, Miss Roman. I'll simply hire an actress to dub some of your lines in postproduction." Magically, Roman's accent improved enough to persuade Hitchcock that she was—at least in the phrase he used privately—"trying but trying." As for her shorter hairdo, columnists reported that she and fellow Warner Bros. contract player Virginia Mayo (whose locks had been cropped for a Kirk Douglas western) were among those actresses against whom "studios have issued sharp orders against any further bobbing." Translation: too many male fans were having problems fantasizing about their love objects when they had chopped hair. Meanwhile, Roman often heard Pat Hitchcock tutoring Farley Granger during filming breaks in breathing, vocal exercises, and speeches designed to improve diction, pitch, and annunciation. As Roman heard Granger intoning the "Now is the winter of our discontent" speech from *Richard III*, she quipped, "That extra sound you hear is Shakespeare whirring in his grave."

Roman was miffed and scrappy enough to defend herself in the press, telling one reporter,

> Mr. Hitchcock is very careful to keep the accent Bostonian and not British. It would have been easy if I had been born on Beacon Hill, not Revere Beach. I come from what is usually called "the other side," meaning I never saw a Cabot or a Lodge let alone speak to one. So, a senator's daughter is what I am distinctly not. But I concentrate on the idea of what a senator's daughter ought to be like—with or without a Boston accent—and I only hope I will please Mr. Hitchcock.

Observed Farley Granger, with whom Roman played the lion's share of her scenes:

> Since they had to pay MGM to use Bob and Goldwyn to use me, Jack Warner insisted that Hitch use Ruth, who was really not right for the part. Hitch did not like his artistic wishes thwarted. As a result, he was cold and sometimes cruel to Ruth, which was unfair to her because as a contract player, she was just doing what her studio told her to do. But he was right, she was wrong for the part.

Roman refused to let Hitchcock's disappointment break her stride. Meanwhile, Granger did what he could to keep things light. During filming of the diplomatic reception party scene, Granger knew that his leading lady was anxious to impress Hitchcock and show him that she could convincingly handle all that the scene required of her—smoothly greeting friends and dignitaries; hiding her uneasiness and growing suspicious when Bruno crashes the dressy affair; taking charge and trying to minimize scandal when Bruno nearly strangles a society grand dame while staring at Barbara; monitoring the odd interactions between Guy and the even odder Bruno, whom he claims to barely know; and finally, confronting Guy about his role in Miriam's murder. To help ease Roman's jitters after a run-through, Granger made her laugh by saying, "Why, Ruth, you're a regular Perle Mesta," comparing her to the real-life socialite, legendary Washington political hostess, and US ambassador to Luxembourg. Granger amused Roman, who found his earnestness and speedy arrivals to and from the set hilarious. When she'd see him running frantically onto the set, she would announce, "Here comes Farley—like he's ten minutes late for an appointment with himself."

Off screen, Roman was also in the throes of a whirlwind romance that cushioned her reactions toward Hitchcock's resistance to her. She made her costars aware that she was being courted by a wealthy, socially prominent fiancé who wooed her with fur coats and expensive jewels, including a platinum ring with diamond baguettes that he designed for her. She repeatedly paraded her bounty before the cast and crew. "I can't think of a worse candidate for a wife," Roman said about herself to a prominent show-business reporter during a shooting break on Saturday, December 16. The reporter and Warner Bros. publicist Ned Moss concluded the interview certain that Roman was not about to tie the knot anytime soon. But just hours later Roman instructed Moss to make immediate hotel arrangements for her in Las Vegas. The flack called Wilbur Clark, owner of the Desert Inn: "Dust off the bridal suite, Wilbur, cool the champagne, and be ready to wake up a judge. We're going to have a wedding." Roman finished her day's work for Hitchcock that Saturday night, rushed off the studio lot, and—though mortally terrified of flying—flew to Vegas that same night with her twenty-six-year-old horseman and yachtsman fiancé, the CEO and president of radio station KLAC, Mortimer "Morty" Wadhams Hall (son of Dorothy Schiff, editor-in-chief and publisher of the *New York Post*). Arriving at 4 a.m. that Sunday, Roman and Hall checked into the Desert Inn and exchanged vows an hour later. The groom promised his bride a delayed honeymoon and gifted her a full-length Canadian wild mink coat. They arrived back at Hall's Hollywood home that same afternoon. The speedy marriage prompted Robert Walker to joke, "They ought to change the title of this picture to *Lovers on a Rocket*." By Monday, after showing off to her costars another wedding gift from Hall, a Mickey Mouse watch, Roman completed her role in *Strangers on a Train*. Or so she thought.

As an end-of-production, farewell thank-you gift and good-luck talisman, Roman presented to Pat Hitchcock a framed silhouette portrait of the renowned nineteenth-century Italian actress Eleonora Duse. After bidding a perfunctory goodbye and thanks to Hitchcock, Roman promptly reported to another Warner Bros. soundstage to play a dime-a-dance dame to volatile, childlike ex-con Steve Cochran (*White Heat*, *The Damned Don't Cry* [1950]) in the lovers-on-the-run crime drama *Tomorrow Is Another Day* [1951]). Far more appropriately cast in the hard-boiled melodrama directed by Felix Feist (*The Devil Thumbs a Ride* [1947]), she shot off erotic sparks with the ferociously macho Cochran. Jack Warner gave her top billing. She earned it. Meanwhile, the press gave Roman and Hall's new marriage slim hope of surviving. According to one columnist, "[Roman] came up the hard way and those rich guys can never understand them. . . . With Ruth, her friends will tell you that her career comes first." The marriage to Hall ended in divorce six years later.

Still, she seemed to believe in romance—at least for others. One day, while *Strangers on a Train* was still shooting, Roman paid a visit to Pat Hitchcock on the set, bringing along her two-fisted notorious womanizer and bad-boy costar Cochran and introducing the two. Warner Bros. publicist Ned Moss immediately pumped out breathless press releases announcing a budding romance between the highly unlikely duo as "a steady twosome," even hinting that Pat was considering canceling an upcoming European trip with her mother to spend more time with Cochran. Considering Cochran's hair-raising record of run-ins with the law, let alone the long list of actresses he purportedly bedded—Mae West, Jayne Mansfield, Mamie Van Doren, Barbara Payton, Merle Oberon, among scores of others—his "romance" with Pat Hitchcock smacks of pure press agent spin. (She married businessman Joseph O'Connell in 1952.)

To appease Jack Warner's constant complaints of wanting more of Ruth Roman in *Strangers on a Train*, Hitchcock called her back, and on a break from *Tomorrow Is Another Day*, he restaged a scene in which Roman's character and her sister anxiously await a crucial phone call from Guy to let them know he is no longer a murder suspect. He had originally blocked the scene with Roman in the foreground, Pat in the middle distance reading a paperback novel, and Leo G. Carroll in the far distance sitting in a Morris chair. Hitchcock knew he had to play the scene off Roman's tension and eventual relief. But having learned that underplaying was not Roman's strong suit, he devised a quintessentially Hitchcockian way of appearing to appease Warner and giving the scene a visual lift while also taking some pressure off Roman's performance. He chose to make the phone call itself the star of the scene by positioning the telephone to dominate the frame. Even for such a gifted cinematographer as Burks, depth of field could pose challenges for camera lenses in the 1950s. Hitchcock instead ordered the studio prop department to construct a giant phone. On set, he placed that phone in the foreground of the frame so Burks's camera could push in on Roman. When the phone rang, the large phone moved out of frame. As Roman reached for the handset, an unseen grip placed a standard-sized phone on the table so Roman simply picked up that handset and played the scene. It was so simple, elegant, and effective that Hitchcock would later crow, "I did that in one take." And the effect proved so memorable that the Zucker brothers parodied it in their 1984 spy spoof *Top Secret*.

Ted Haworth's stunning and atmospheric production sketch for the moments at the amusement park entrance when Bruno begins slowly stalking Guy Haines's bespectacled, flirtatious wife Miriam. Haworth designed the film's carnival midway, built at the Rowland V. Lee Ranch in Chatsworth, California.

CHAPTER SEVEN

BEFORE THE *PSYCHO* SHOWER SCENE: SO LONG AT THE FAIR

The *Strangers on a Train* amusement park sequences—two of them, fittingly—deserve to be celebrated among the great set pieces of Hitchcock's fifty-three-movie career. Having been impressed as a youth by such German silent films as *The Cabinet of Dr. Caligari* (1920) and *The Man Who Laughs* (1928), Hitchcock was especially excited about exploring a small-town amusement park as a backdrop for nightmarish events. It wasn't his first time at the fair, cinematically speaking, but it certainly proved to be his most indelible and most perfectly realized. After all, the best moment in Hitchcock's uneasy 1941 foray into romantic screwball comedy, *Mr. and Mrs. Smith*, traps Carole Lombard and her suitor, Gene Raymond, atop an amusement park Ferris wheel when a rainstorm erupts. One of the eeriest, best-remembered episodes of *The Alfred Hitchcock Hour*, based on Ray Bradbury's 1944 short story "The Jar," presents memorably haunting carnival imagery. And in 1961, *Blind Man*, an original idea by *North by Northwest* screenwriter Ernest Lehman, would have featured an extended suspense chase sequence across Disneyland—had the project not been throttled by the mutiny of James Stewart (its intended star), the chronic insecurities of Lehman, and Walt Disney's refusal to permit the maker of the "disgusting" *Psycho* to sully his shiny, happy wonderland by filming there.

The first of *Strangers on a Train*'s two amusement park sequences—a stalking and seduction scene—occurs roughly thirty minutes into the film. Hitchcock entrusted production designer Ted Haworth to work out both sequences according to the director's preliminary sketches and the formative camera setups and moves that he and Robert Burks preplanned. Hitchcock also had Haworth storyboard the scene from start to finish and envisioned the slow, steady stalking ending in the quick, cruel murder of Miriam Joyce Haines as one of the most memorable of his film's six "showstoppers."

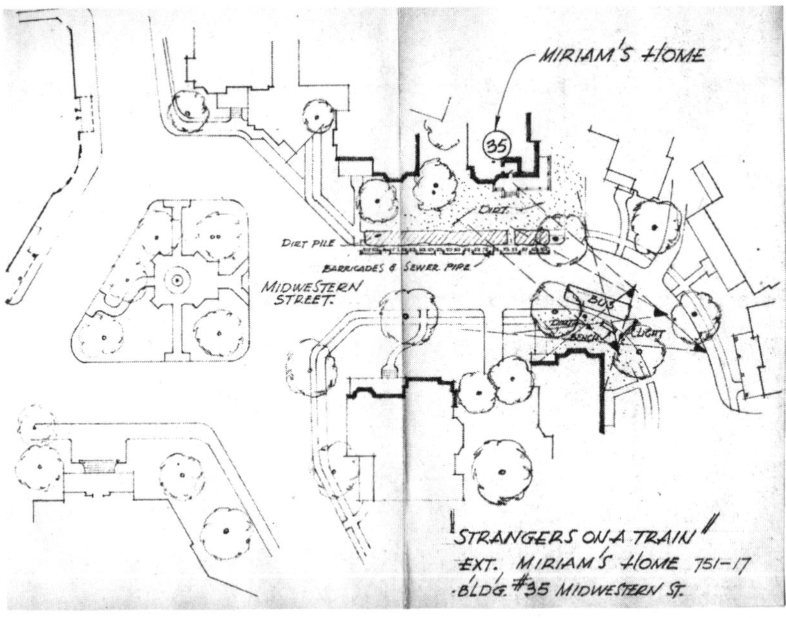

Art director Ted Haworth's choice for the weatherbeaten home of Miriam Haines and her mother was on Warner Bros.' expansive Midwestern Street, built in 1939 for *Four Wives* and subsequently used for *Rebel Without a Cause*, *The Music Man*, and *Bonnie and Clyde*. It is still in use today.

Ted Haworth's evocative storyboard production sketches detail every step of an early screenplay's depiction of Bruno shadowing Miriam Haines to the amusement park. Hitchcock simplified the sequence during the filming and editing processes but retained most of the significant elements.

As scripted in the October 18, 1950, draft and as boarded, the sequence begins at nightfall in Metcalf, with an overhead god's-eye camera angle finding Bruno sitting on a bus-stop bench, shielding his face behind a newspaper while monitoring Miriam's house. Sitting in a rocking chair on the front porch is Miriam's white-haired mother, Mrs. Joyce (played by veteran Edna Holland [*Gentleman's Agreement* (1947), *The Snake Pit* (1948), *Criss Cross* (1949)]; Hitchcock substantially whittled down Holland's role during the final editing when he thought the picture was running too long).

Hitchcock shot but cut the following dialogue exchange from the film:

WOMAN

(calls out as she passes)

Hello, Mrs. Joyce. Warm, ain't it?

MRS. JOYCE

That it is.

WOMAN

I've been reading where your son-in-law's been coming right along at tennis.

MRS. JOYCE

(sourly) We don't have any interest in tennis anymore.

After that dialogue, Hitchcock planned on filming an image that intrigued him for decades: "At this moment, the front door swings open, emitting a long streak of bright light, and we see the silhouette of a woman (Miriam) emerge."

Although he dropped that visual flourish from *Strangers on a Train*, two films later he would utilize it for the lead-in to an attempted strangulation of the heroine in *Dial M for Murder* and, in 1960, the prelude to the stabbing of the smug private detective in *Psycho*.

The scene continues as Miriam is followed by two men, who are laughing and joking as they see the bus pull up in front of Bruno's view, "cutting off the sight of his quarry." And soon Bruno follows the three on the bus to the amusement park.

Of filming the scene, Laura Elliott recalled,

> Again I was basically working blind because I was wearing those very thick lenses. Watch the sequence and from the time we left the house and get on the bus, one of the boys always gives me his hand because I didn't know where the steps were and they were always there to help and make it look like we were just holding hands and having fun. The

> same thing happened when I had to run toward the carousel and jump onto it while it was moving. That was tricky. But they always offered their hands, or I took their hands because I couldn't see anything in front of me at all!

Miriam and her dates disembark, and Bruno begins his slow pursuit, with Miriam goading him on with hungry glances and lascivious licks on an ice cream cone. She declares she wants a hot dog to satisfy her "craving." "Craving for what?" shoots back one of her boyfriends. "I never saw a girl eat so much in my life," says the fair-haired boyfriend (actor Roland Morris), who adds, "How're we going to neck with a mouth full of popcorn?"

Laura Elliott (as Miriam Haines) finds her stalker Bruno Antony more intriguing than her amorous young boyfriends (left, Tommy Farrell; right, Roland Morris).

Said Elliott of filming the amusement park sequence,

> We improvised a lot. Not in the written dialogue, that was done as written. But from the time the two young men picked me up at my house and we went out to go to the carnival, that was all improv. It was just, "Hi, come on," "Let's go do this," and "Did you see that?" It was whatever would bubble up at the moment.

In the finished film, what "bubbled up at the moment" is tossed off and sometimes half-heard, but it was risqué and boundary-pushing enough to make one wonder how the Breen Office censors weren't all over it.

The slow amusement park pursuit of Miriam by Bruno was mapped out in meticulous detail by art director Ted Haworth in close consultation with Hitchcock.

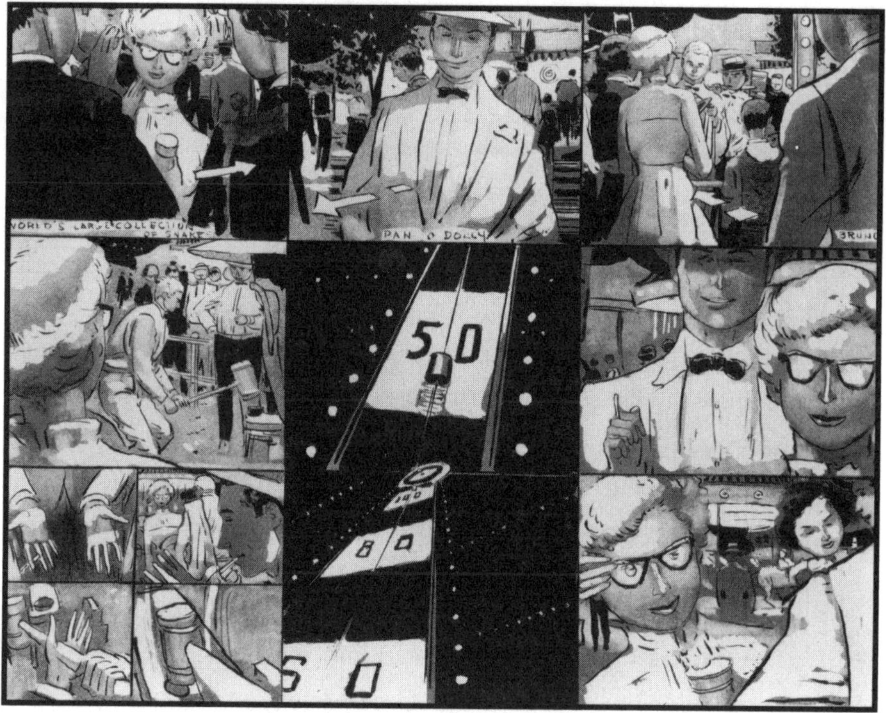

Bruno's flirtatious seduction of Miriam at the amusement park has him showing off his strength at the strongman game (also known as the high striker). Note how Haworth depicted Miriam as blond.

A little boy in a Hopalong Cassidy outfit points his toy gun at Bruno. Bruno pops the kid's balloon with his cigarette. The boy is mystified. Bruno is pleased with himself. The original plan, as shown in the production sketches, would have costumed the boy in a "Yale 1970" sweater, a throwback to Bruno telling Guy he was expelled from Harvard, Yale's most famed rival. The studio's legal department warned against Hitchcock referencing actual school names—hence the costume change.

Miriam's two boyfriends fail to impress her at the sledgehammer concession. Bruno steps up, swings the hammer, and hits the 100-pound mark, ringing the bell. After making the bell clang, Bruno does a little strongman flex and waggles his eyebrows at Miriam. "Hitchcock loved whenever Bob Walker threw in little things like that," recalled Robert Burks, adding,

> We shot several takes of Bob when Bruno puffs a cigar, waiting on the bench watching the two boys and Miriam run out of her house and toward the bus. It's that moment when Bruno sees Miriam for the first time. In editing, Bill Ziegler and I chose what we thought was a great take. Almost any take of Walker was great, though. Anyway, we showed it to Hitchcock, who made a face like we had disappointed him. He said, "Wrong one, boys. Find the one where he shows what he thinks of Miriam." *What?* Well, we came back a couple of times thinking we had it, but no. Finally, Hitchcock told us the exact number of the take he wanted. When we watched it, darned if Walker doesn't show a subtle bit of disdain, "*This* is the woman Guy married?" We missed it. But not Hitchcock and that's just one of the kinds of things that set him apart.

Miriam is intrigued, aroused by Bruno's prowess with the sledgehammer, though her oblivious boyfriends lead her away. Bruno casually follows them toward the merry-go-round, hopping on when the ride starts moving. Miriam smiles coyly at Bruno, who mounts a carousel horse directly behind hers. Bruno, on his horse, pretends to be chasing Miriam. He laughs.

Miriam and her boyfriends begin singing the (unspecified in the script) song being played on the merry-go-round's calliope. Miriam glances back to Bruno, who joins in the singing. (Note: Hitchcock filmed this sequence in three different ways. When Bruno joins in the singing of "The Band Played On," it was meant to be shown from his point of view, with Miriam riding on the horse ahead of him. Instead, Hitchcock

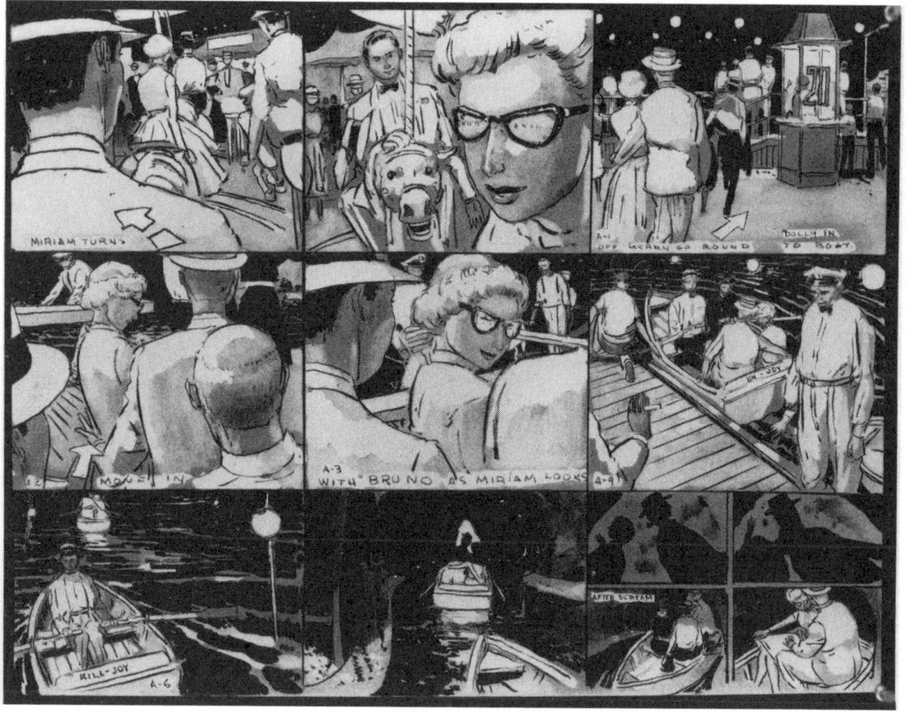

Laid out with all the care of Saul Bass's montage for the *Psycho* shower murder, these storyboards suggest how the killing of Miriam was planned as a visual tour de force.

filmed it in one shot close on the teeth of Miriam's horse, Miriam riding behind, and Bruno behind her. He also shot the scene with incidental dialogue and no singing, and a third time without dialogue and only the music of the calliope. In the end, he dictated to editor William H. Ziegler a list of ten shots, paring the sequence down in the impactful way we know from the finished film.)

In the scene, the painted horses fill the screen as the music and velocity of the spinning merry-go-round increase in tempo. Miriam and her companions enter a shot of an artificial lake and small wooded "Magic Isle" with a "Tunnel of Love." They approach the boat concession, and her face in close-up shows coy satisfaction when she sees Bruno also approach the pay box.

Hitchcock was so impressed by Ted Haworth's talents, temperament, and detailed schematics for the amusement park murder sequence that he handed off the climactic merry-go-round-gone-wild scene to the art director.

The ride attendant escorts the threesome to a small motorboat. They climb in, and the boat chugs away from the landing. Then Bruno climbs into the next boat, which gets swallowed by the darkness. Miriam's boat enters the tunnel as she glances over her shoulder. Bruno's boat comes into the shot and also enters the tunnel.

In the tunnel, the silhouettes of Miriam and her two handsy boyfriends are reflected on the tunnel wall, lit by the light coming from the tunnel exit. Bruno's shadow looms over the other three, and the silhouettes almost converge.

At the tunnel exit, a piercing scream breaks the silence, followed by protestations and giggling as Miriam's boat emerges into the light. She pushes one of the boys away, saying, "George, stop it, I tell you!" (cut from film). The boat moves out of frame, toward the island. Bruno's boat "comes smilingly forward," then moves out of the picture.

When the trio arrives at the lover's island shore, actor Morris helps Miriam out of the boat. As they scramble onto the island, he shouts, "Let's not break a leg—we got use for it later." Shadowy glimpses of couples sprawled out on the grass make the reference and the ambience of the locale unambiguous. Later in the film, Leo G. Carroll, as the staid Senator Morton, describes the amusement park as a "sordid atmosphere"—into which the trio now disappears. Bruno's boat reaches the island, and he lifts the prow onto the shore and follows them.

A long shot of the island reveals the lights of the park beyond the lake, with the trees and foliage in the foreground. The silhouetted figures of Miriam and her companions move from right to left. Miriam half-protests: "George, no!" She backs away and goes in another direction, losing George while he calls out her name.

Miriam backs out of the bushes until the back of her head is in close-up in the foreground of the shot. Hearing footsteps behind her, she turns her head toward the camera, and her face changes as she recognizes someone off-scene.

MIRIAM
Oh!

The camera pulls back to reveal the head and shoulders of Bruno between Miriam and the camera. His hand holds Guy's lighter, which he flicks on as he raises it above Miriam's face. We only see the back of Bruno's head and shoulders.

BRUNO
Is your name Miriam?
MIRIAM
(with surprise) Why, yes. How did you—?

Hitchcock's bold, uncompromising vision for the murder sequence required Laura Elliott to not only be a fine actor but also a contortionist, bending her body until she appeared to literally float backward to the ground.

Bruno's gloved hands grasp Miriam's throat. The lighter falls out of shot. As Bruno's hands grip Miriam's throat, his head moves slightly to blot out Miriam's face. His head moves further until Miriam's face is nearly covered at the other side of the screen. Her glasses fall off and hit the ground. The shadows of their struggling figures cover the shot.

In a close-up, the screen is filled with one of the lenses of the glasses. They are of the diminishing type. Against the moonlit sky we see reflected the elongated struggling figures as though we were shooting up at them. Suddenly one of the figures falls forward. Miriam's head drops into the picture beside the glasses. Bruno's hand comes into the picture and picks up the glasses. Miriam's fall broke one of the lenses. As we see Bruno's sports shoes move away, the camera moves past Miriam's hair until it arrives at Guy's lighter pressed into the earth.

Bruno glances back over his shoulder. He looks down and goes backward one or two steps. In close-up, his hands retrieve the lighter from the ground.

In a long shot, we see the full view of the island again, with the amusement park beyond. The faint noise of the calliope continues in the distance. Bruno has been lost to view. We hear faint voices in the distance, calling, "Miriam! Miriam! Where are you?"

Bruno comes to the shore where his boat is moored. He gets in and quickly chugs away. He moves calmly, matter-of-factly.

In long shot, Bruno's boat throbs its way across the landing stage. We hear a loud call from the island. Someone has found Miriam. The voices continue, "Hey, here she is! What's the matter with her? Has she fainted?"

More shouts from the island cause the people at the landing stage to look back. This also attracts the boatman's attention. As Bruno disembarks from the boat, a loud scream erupts from the island. One voice says, "She is dead." Another cries, "Help! Help!"

Bruno, now on the landing stage, looks back with the other people as if to see what's wrong on the island. As Bruno moves away, the boatman turns and glances at him but quickly returns his attention to the disturbance across on the island. Bruno moves forward and jumps into one of the boats with other male passengers. The boatman calls to an assistant, "Get a cop!"

Bruno calmly threads his way along the midway. Above the noise of the various concessions, a shrill police whistle is heard in the distance. Policemen run from the direction of the main entrance past Bruno, who glances at them over his shoulder and strolls toward the main park entrance.

The sequence ends with one of the more perverse jokes in all of Hitchcock's work: Bruno, fresh after the kill, solicitously helps an elderly blind gentleman cross a street as he exits the amusement park. The blind man thanks him. Bruno moves on, glances back toward the park, and glances at his wristwatch: 9:30. The moment was a vestige of two ideas from earlier screenplay drafts. In one, in which Bruno's father would have been blind, Bruno would have shoved his father malevolently into traffic before rescuing him at the last minute. In the second abandoned idea, Bruno aiding a random blind man across the street would have been played as a suspense sequence, in which the audience would have been on edge, fearing Bruno might turn his anger on the innocent blind man. Hitchcock decided against complicating the moment, letting it remain a character quirk as well as a bit of shared fun with the visually impaired Walker, who said, "You know, Hitch, I could easily play both roles. I've had a lifetime of practice."

The screenplay sets up the sequence to run approximately twelve minutes or more.

During the ten nights spent filming the amusement park sequence, Pat Hitchcock rode out to the Chatsworth location to visit her father, Robert Walker, and Farley Granger. "It was freezing cold," she recalled. "I went out that night to visit them and I rode all the rides like the Whip Ride and the Ferris Wheel. The still photograph man [Durward

Ted Haworth and a freezing cold Hitchcock on the frigid nighttime amusement park location with an actor who plays a carnival worker.

"Bud" Graybill] got me stuck–with the two boys who go round with Miriam–on the top of the Ferris wheel, and he took some publicity stills." Hitchcock biographer Donald Spoto interpreted in his own way this mildly amusing publicity story, which Warner Bros. planted in newspapers nationwide to promote the film. In Spoto's hands, an innocuous press release meant to highlight Hitchcock's sense of humor became yet further proof of Hitchcock's alleged sadism toward women. He reported that Pat

> begged for a ride on the Ferris wheel. And when she reached the topmost point of the ride, Hitchcock–practicing what Spoto characterized as "a special kind of harassment"–ordered the machine stopped and all the lights extinguished. With the area in total darkness, he left to direct another scene in a far corner of the park while she became hysterical with fear. An hour passed before he ordered the carriage lowered and his trembling daughter released.

When an interviewer asked Pat in 1993 about the incident, no wonder she scoffed, saying, "I wasn't working in the scene, but I was visiting the set that night, and [my father] asked me, 'How much would you want to go up on that Ferris wheel?' And I said, 'You know I'm petrified of heights!' So he said, 'Well, seriously, how much would you want?' And I said, 'Well, I'd want $100.' [About $1,300 today.] He said, 'OK.'"

So she, Tommy Farrell, and Roland Morris–who played Miriam's boyfriends in the midway sequence–climbed into a Ferris wheel gondola and posed and waved for photographer Graybill.

Pat continued, "The operator threw the switch. When we reached the very top of the ride, the wheel stopped for I would say maybe three minutes, at the outside, pretending like they were all going away to film something else. But then they came right back, turned the lights on, and we came down. The only sadistic part about it was that I didn't get the $100."

Who could possibly seriously entertain the idea that any professional of Hitchcock's caliber–under the major production pressures (and insurance strictures) of a night shoot on location–would risk potential calamity by switching off the lights for five seconds, let alone for any longer while his stars and crew, as well as hundreds of adult and child extra players, milled around a Ferris wheel, other working rides, and multiple food concession booths immediately nearby? All for the sake of a sadistic practical joke? Also, based on Ted Haworth's schematics of the set, in the unlikely event that Hitchcock had wanted to plunge the area into darkness, he would have had to turn off not only the lights on the Ferris wheel but also two equidistant lighting towers, which would have obscured the entire front half of the park, including the entrances and exits. Foolishness.

Interestingly, newspaper stories of the day identify *Strangers on a Train* screenwriter and intimate family friend Whitfield Cook as the person with whom Pat Hitchcock purportedly "hooted and hollered for help" while "trapped atop the Ferris Wheel with the lights doused." Somewhere in these differing narratives is the truth, and more than likely that truth is closer to Pat's 1993 account.

"IS YOUR NAME MIRIAM?"

From his first reading of Highsmith's novel, the director envisioned the stalking and strangling of Miriam Joyce Haines as one of what he subsequently called the film's "six showstoppers." The scene was entirely storyboarded by production designer Ted Haworth, pre-choreographed with cameraman Robert Burks, and thoroughly discussed with Robert Walker. Laura Elliott was the last to know anything. She recalled,

> *Of course, we shot all the exterior things out at the park, with everyone wearing warm coats and me in just a little silk dress. Remember when Miriam is choked and her glasses fall to the ground? That was all done probably a week later,*

on an empty soundstage at Warner Bros. First, Mr. Hitchcock said, "Now, Laura, I want you to float to the floor. Float backwards to the floor." I mean, I'm not a gymnast or anything, but I turned around and started floating down. He said, "Arch your back like you're doing the Lindy. Just float to the floor." And I said, "Yes, Mr. Hitchcock." "Okay, roll 'em,'" he said, and I started leaning back and back and back. But you can only get so far until, suddenly, thunk—you drop two feet to this concrete floor! He'd say, "Cut! Laura . . . float to the floor." "Yes, Mr. Hitchcock." And we'd do it again, and I'd get just-so-far and go thunk onto the cement floor. Seven takes—but on the seventh take, I literally floated all the way to the floor. And he said, "Cut. Next shot." That was it! I don't know how I did it, and I've never tried it since! But it shows what you can do when somebody insists—you can do things that you had no idea you could. As I was doing all this "floating," sinking lower, lower, lower, that was all in reflection because I had my back toward this big, round, two-and-a-half, three-foot diameter, concave-type mirror sitting on the concrete floor Hitchcock had on the soundstage. The camera was on one side, shooting straight down at the mirror. That shot is studied in the film schools at UCLA and USC, and I don't have an explanation for how he did it. I should go to school and find out how it was shot [laughs]. Mr. Hitchcock had a wry sense of humor, and you never wanted to cross him or to be a smart-ass, 'cause he could just cut you down. So you were pretty respectful of him.

As Hitchcock explained the shot, "That involved a double printing job. We took a large concave mirror and we photographed the murder in it. Next, we photographed the glasses as they lay on the grass. Then the image filmed in the concave mirror was diminished and printed into the frames of the glasses." Hitchcock indicated, in postproduction, to double-print several frames, giving the scene a slightly surreal aspect, rendering Walker's looming and Elliott's floating backward like a tragic, languid, slow-motion Grand Guignol dance distorted in a funhouse mirror.

Did Hitchcock provide Elliott with any special direction for that now-classic murder scene? She recalled,

I must say he really didn't give me a lot of directorial stuff about the character at all, just "Play her as you played it in the audition" and "Walk here" and "Go there." That was pretty much it. Robert Walker and Farley Granger and the two actors who played my boyfriends were really the only actors I really worked with in the whole movie. I adored Robert Walker. He was very quiet, very much a gentleman, and very talented. He was just brilliant.

Laughing, she added,

Farley Granger was . . . handsome. He was an 8x10 glossy, you know what I mean? But he did fine. He was in a couple of Hitchcock films—you can't be all bad and be in a Hitchcock film, you know. You didn't want to cross Mr. Hitchcock. He could just cut a performer down if he was unhappy with them. He could do it with a smile. And his wit was just rapier sharp. He was brilliant—he did some wonderful, wonderful things. I'm just so thrilled that I was lucky enough to be in one of his films.

On November 10, Hitchcock rehearsed Farley Granger and Robert Walker in their tense scene after Miriam's murder, when Bruno emerges from the shadows behind an iron grate to seduce Guy into keeping his end of the bargain. The studio's daily production reports indicate the actors were going at a fever pitch when an especially good take got ruined. Apparently, Ruth Roman, while standing on the sidelines, announced—much louder than she probably intended—how hungry she was. Spotting Hitchcock's wince in reaction to Roman's intrusion, the gallant Walker rushed to the rescue, quipping, "Here's your chance for a toasted sandwich, Ruth." Roman looked confused. Said Walker, "Well, here's two hams working against a grate." Even Hitchcock laughed. Tension dissipated.

On the same day, national newspapers reported that "expert tennis player" Pat Hitchcock was not only assisting Granger off-hours with his diction and projection but also helping him perfect his tennis serve. Was there nothing this girl couldn't do?

On November 19, 1950, the nationally syndicated Sidney Skolsky's "Hollywood Is My Beat" column took the journalist to Warner Bros.,

The sprawling set drew many celebrity visitors, despite the plummeting temperature.

where Hitchcock invited him to visit while Walker and Elliott rehearsed and shot a part of the strangulation scene. Reported Skolsky,

> Alfred Hitchcock is directing and therefore the main attraction on the set is Hitchcock. He gives the show. The performers listen to Hitchcock and they watch him demonstrate how a scene should be played—because Hitchcock loves to perform. It is no secret that Alfred Hitchcock has no special fondness for actors, yet he always contrives to be an actor. Director Hitchcock always manages to play a bit in every picture he directs and this is no exception: Alfred Hitchcock will play a librarian.

He initially considered making his cameo appearance in the scene of Bruno barging in on Guy and Anne at the National Gallery. Although he had already filmed his cameo with Granger at the Danville train station, after returning to Los Angeles from his location filming, Hitchcock told publicist Ned Moss that he remained unsure which cameo would be the most fun but least disruptive to the narrative. He shot the National Gallery cameo but told Moss, "It's such a small bit, I'm just likely to do another one before the film is finished." And he did. Still, if one looks very, very closely, Hitchcock can be glimpsed (barely) behind Bruno in the fuzzy rear-projection shot captured in the National Gallery's West Wing.

For yet another alternative cameo, Hitchcock pondered appearing as a character he called "The Slumbering Man," a gentleman dozing in a car and remaining oblivious when a police car with a screeching siren zooms off to chase Guy as he heads to the amusement park. In the end, Hitchcock preferred the cameo he did with Farley Granger disembarking from the train and himself boarding it with his own "double"—the double bass.

CHAPTER EIGHT

ON A CAROUSEL

As November drew to a close, the company was set to film the amusement park sequence finale. The production schedule was set for filming at least seven nights on 11 of the 214 acres of the Canoga Park, California, ranch in the San Fernando Valley, bought in 1935 by film director-writer-producer Rowland V. Lee (*Son of Frankenstein* [1939], *The Bridge of San Luis Rey* [1944]). Although Lee named the spread Farm Lake Ranch, among movie people it has always been known as the Rowland V. Lee Ranch. Until 1940, the director raised cattle and alfalfa there. After the drowning deaths of two young women in a lake on the property while Lee was away, he devoted a section of the acreage exclusively to renting it out as a filming location. At the time when Hitchcock and Warner Bros.' location manager Bill Guthrie was choosing the Lee Ranch as the locale for the amusement park sequences, the property offered all that they required, including two small lakes and rolling hills of barley chaff, eucalyptus, and olive trees. Best of all, there was more than sufficient flat acreage on which to construct the fully functioning midway set mapped out by production designer Ted Haworth to match Hitchcock's narrative requirements. The story and background demands included midway attractions; ticket booths; games of chance; manned concession stands offering popcorn, ice cream, and cotton candy; a Ferris wheel; boats passing through a tunnel of love leading to a "Magic Isle"; and of course, a merry-go-round. Another major bonus was the ranch's proximity to the Warner Bros. lot: in the event of bad weather, the crew could—theoretically, anyway—relocate to the studio one hour away.

On November 22, the studio's call for 150 extras willing to film from dusk to dawn attracted over five hundred hopefuls. During the run-up to the start of the amusement park filming—to control looky-loos, manage crowds, and prevent traffic jams in and out of then-bucolic Fallbrook Avenue—the studio issued this directive to the cast and crew: "Do not, under any condition, invite any visitors to the Hitchcock set at the Rowland V. Lee Ranch while the company is getting there! The police officers at the gate have been instructed not to admit any visitors without passes. This includes everybody." Exceptions were made, however, for Hitchcock, Granger, and Walker.

Granger had just moved into a rented home in Laurel Canyon and, after a long night in Chatsworth, was looking forward to his first night in his new digs. He got there and realized he had not arranged to have the electricity turned on. "I am not practical-minded," he told Pat Hitchcock when relating the story days later, adding, "Why haven't I, as a supposedly able housekeeper, heard of this thing known as electric lights?"

The night of November 25, with Ted Haworth's remarkable amusement park set completed, Hitchcock and his production team inspected every inch, with the director dictating to Haworth last-minute changes before officially beginning filming. Hitchcock later took a second reconnoiter with Granger and Walker, where they dutifully stopped to pose aboard rides for Bud Graybill's publicity photos. Meanwhile, Hitchcock gave his stars first dibs on locations for their dressing rooms. Given Walker's and Hitchcock's penchant for dark, self-effacing humor, no wonder the star amused his director by proposing that his and Granger's dressing rooms should be in the sideshow area devoted to "biological rarities." Walker chose the room behind a baroque painted sign that read, "International Oddities–Electronic Marvel." The hirsute Granger chose the room behind the sign that read, "See Rondo, The Ape Boy." However, Granger's rationale was less playful and predictably practical: "We moved into the freak show because we heard that the rooms would be the warmest on those cold nights."

Despite the embargo on set visitors, celebrities flocked to the location. Ruth Roman was required to be on hand; although her character had been written out of those scenes, she had to be immediately available and ready to work in case weather conditions or technical issues forced the crew to film close-ups or scenes set in other locations. Others who dropped by included Robert Cummings (who appeared in Hitchcock's *Saboteur* and *Dial M for Murder*), the omnipresent and possessive Shelley Winters, and actress-director-producer Ida Lupino, whom Walker, according to such Hollywood gossip harpies as Hedda Hopper and Louella Parsons, had recently "been seeing a lot of" and to whom he was "making phone calls between scenes." The emotionally volatile Lupino, who married actor Howard Duff in October 1951, insisted that she and Walker were only "good friends" and that their conversations largely revolved around her wanting to star opposite him in a (never made) love story with a car racing backdrop titled *As Long as I Have You*. On an earlier visit to the soundstage, at Lupino's request, Walker had brokered an introduction to Farley Granger, whom Lupino hoped to direct in a drama called *The Man* for her production company, The Filmmakers. That one never happened either.

While on location, Hitchcock chose for Robert Walker to either ride or always be filmed fighting near a tan merry-go-round horse decorated with flourishes of silver and bright green. "As it's the most ostentatious horse on the merry-go-round, that's the one Bruno would choose for himself," Hitchcock explained. Walker agreed, saying,

> That's the thing about Hitchcock. Of course, we weren't filming in color so you can't really see how showy that horse was, but Hitchcock thinks about everything and he has reasons for why you ride this or that horse or why you wear that bright blue suit he put me in or whether you order lamb chops, potatoes, and ice cream—as Bruno, I mean, not as Bob Walker. But that night of filming was rough. We were on that carousel so long, I got so dizzy. I told Hitch, "If only some fans knew how actors make their living—the hard way."

That same night, Walker and Hitchcock also faced some challenges while working with six-year-old actor Louis Lettieri, who played the wonderfully obnoxious little boy in Hopalong Cassidy cowboy garb whose balloon Bruno bursts with his lit cigarette. To capture the boy's surprised reaction on the first take, Hitchcock didn't tell little Lettieri what Walker would do with the cigarette. Hitchcock was dissatisfied with the first take, but the young actor's flinch and anticipation of the balloon's pop spoiled his reactions in successive attempts. The director tried various means of eliciting another spontaneous reaction from Lettieri, but nothing worked. Then the director huddled with Robert Walker and assistant director Mel Dellar, the latter of whom stepped away and returned shortly after, his hand hidden behind his back. While Robert Burks pretended to reset the cameras, Hitchcock assured his pint-sized actor, "Mr. Walker is not going to break the balloon." Hitchcock whispered "Action" and ordered Burks to keep the cameras rolling while Walker and Lettieri "rehearsed" the scene several times with no popping of the balloon. The boy relaxed. On the next take, on signal from Hitchcock, Dellar fired a gun into the air. The boy reacted so perfectly—looking back in annoyed bewilderment at the still-inflated balloon—that Hitchcock told him, "Exactly what I wanted, Mr. Lettieri."

The moment was wrapped, and Lettieri got to spend the rest of his evening riding the Ferris wheel and snacking with Robert Walker's young sons, Bob and Mike, who visited their doting father frequently, rode all the rides, and were welcome to raid the concession stands for popcorn, hot dogs, and soft drinks.

A reporter asked little Robert Walker Jr. what he thought of the excitement going on around him, and he said, "Gee, Dad's work is a lot of fun." His father said, "I think Bob's going to become an actor." The Walker boys could not have been better behaved. But what could not be controlled was the weather. At least twice previously, such heavy fog blanketed Chatsworth that it forced the company to cancel the location filming for the night and remain in Burbank, filming on the soundstage.

Weather conditions grew so bad on November 29 that the company was forced to quit filming entirely. Earlier in the evening, waiting for the fog to lift as the weather reports had predicted, Hitchcock and crew shot speed tests of the merry-go-round. But this night, the fog worsened suddenly and so dramatically that Hitchcock dismissed the entire company before midnight. Ida Lupino had been visiting Robert Walker again on that evening, bringing along her aunt, the British actress and film producer Nell Emerald. Because of Walker's poor eyesight, Lupino attempted to drive Walker and her sixty-eight-year-old aunt home, but the fog grew so intense that they got hopelessly lost. Pulling over to the roadside, hoping to wait things out, Lupino's car stalled and the engine wouldn't turn over. The trio spent two uneasy hours, fearing they'd be stranded until daybreak, but Hitchcock, being driven in a limo in the bumper-to-bumper caravan of Movieland pilgrims trying to get back safely to Burbank, spotted and rescued them. They spent over three hours navigating a trip that usually took only one hour.

After remaining on the Lee Ranch site for one month, the entirety of "Craft's 20 Big Shows" got relocated to the parking lot of Oakland Auditorium in Oakland, where it became the centerpiece of the city's

Fourth of July celebration. After the film's release, the attraction toured the state and was promoted as "the carnival presented in the picture *Strangers on a Train* starring Farley Granger and Ruth Roman, now playing at the Paramount." (A spectacular 3,046-seat, Art Deco–knockout built in 1931, the Paramount today is a meticulously preserved premiere concert and event venue.)

Back on the studio lot, Hitchcock devoted the entire afternoon of December 8 on Stage 22 to filming close-ups and isolated action involving Laura Elliott at the amusement park and on Magic Isle. On December 11, Hitchcock sent a second-unit crew, headed by Hans F. Koenekamp and Haworth, to film additional process photography background plates at a number of locales, including sunset views from the Los Angeles–Santa Barbara train as it traveled through Camarillo, about fifty miles from Warner Bros. Hitchcock earmarked the footage to be projected outside the cutout train built on the soundstage, specifically as the train rumbles toward day's end. Said Haworth, "We built everything for the interior of the train in the studio and [those scenes were] all photographed against a process screen. . . Since Hitch had picked all of the setups and angles, they weren't malleable; they were tenacious and fixed. Koenekamp and I knew that and so there was no room for saying, 'Well, maybe it ought to be a little freer and looser.'"

Dead ahead lay Hitchcock's biggest scene—the last of his "showstoppers," the one meant to top them all.

CHAPTER NINE

WHOSE SCENE IS IT ANYWAY?

The carousel sequence is one of the greatest sequences of Hitchcock's oeuvre, a technical and emotional tour de force equal to the airplane crash in *Foreign Correspondent*, the assassination in Albert Hall in *The Man Who Knew Too Much*, the *North by Northwest* crop-duster attack, the *Psycho* shower murder, and the birds'-eye-view aerial attack on the town of Bodega Bay in *The Birds* (1963). The runaway carousel sequence does not exist in the source novel; in fact, Highsmith's dénouement is lamentably convoluted and uncinematic. In the novel, a private detective ferrets out the connection between Bruno and Guy, but he lets the case drop. Then, while on a sailing cruise, Guy can't rescue Bruno when he topples overboard. Later, wracked by guilt, Guy confesses everything to Miriam's lover and, overheard by the detective, then surrenders to his arrest.

So what was the source of the out-of-control carousel sequence in the film *Strangers on a Train*, which combines a chase, a fistfight, and a finale worthy of a disaster movie? The merry-go-round's inclusion in the film dates from Raymond Chandler's involvement in Hitchcock's screenplay development process. But it would be a stretch to ascribe authorship—let alone *auteur*ship—to Chandler, or to any of the subsequent screenwriters. Or even to Hitchcock, as it turns out. After all, the carousel run amok plays pretty much like a direct lift from *The Moving Toyshop*, Edmund Crispin's delightfully tongue-in-cheek 1946 detective novel.

Considering Hitchcock's relentless search for potential film material, it would be difficult to believe that he could be completely unaware of the book by novelist-screenwriter–film score composer Crispin (real name Robert Bruce Montgomery). Why, even the set-up of *The Moving Toyshop* feels distinctly Hitchcockian: In the dead of night in the picturesque university city of Oxford, England, after a trouble-plagued train trip, restless, caustic poet Richard Cadogan is on holiday but has misplaced the address of his place of lodging. Wandering the deserted High Street, he spies the open door of a toyshop and, his curiosity piqued, wanders through the eerily empty shop and is shocked to find a dead woman with a wire wrapped tightly around her neck. Cadogan suddenly gets conked on the head and locked overnight in a storage closet. Escaping the following morning, Cadogan leads the police back to the site. But the corpse has vanished. So has the toy shop. A grocer's stands in its place. What's more, Cadogan gets accused of trespassing and stealing food. The character's inability to convince the police he isn't crazy, drunk, or a killer leads to him teaming up with eccentric old university chum and literature professor Gervase Fen (who appears in nine of Crispin's novels), resulting in much witty banter, many plot twists, and breakneck chases. The best of the action sequences involves Fen pursuing the villain to a fairground, where both men trade punches aboard a carousel. The ride attendant gets shot accidentally, the merry-go-round spins out of control, and Cadogan and a fairground worker risk their lives by crawling underneath the whirling mechanism to try to stop it.

There are too many similarities between Crispin's work and the famous finale of *Strangers on a Train* to chalk things up to mere coincidence. Yet in the extensive files pertaining to Hitchcock and

Strangers on a Train donated in 1977 by Warner Bros. to the School of Cinematic Arts at the University of Southern California, one finds no mention of *The Moving Toyshop* nor of Crispin lodging a complaint, let alone the hint of a lawsuit, apology, or payoff for his creation.

The possible inspiration for the sequence aside, fleshing it out and achieving it so spectacularly on film—with the carousel spinning crazily and hurling gondolas, wooden horses, and riders into the air—required a high level of technical expertise and intricate planning. There had to be a fully working carousel, plus a miniature version, rear projection, and a seamless marriage of astute direction, acting, production design, special effects, editing, cinematography, and an unusually powerful montage of visual elements to convey chaos, panic, dark comedy, and symbolism—sometimes all in a single shot. If any one sequence should have cemented the award worthiness of the screenplay, the work of editor William H. Ziegler, cameraman Robert Burks, and production

The impact of the collapsing carousel sequence required the close collaboration of Hitchcock, art director Ted Haworth, cinematographer Robert Burks, editor William H. Ziegler, the actors, composer Dimitri Tiomkin, and the audience's willing suspension of disbelief.

designer Ted Haworth, this should have been the one. But what about the work of Hitchcock himself? That topic deserves its own close-up.

While on location at the amusement park set at the Rowland V. Lee Ranch, Hitchcock filmed Farley Granger pursuing Robert Walker right up to the moment they leap aboard the carousel. There, the director also shot the white-knuckle section of the sequence when the carnival worker wriggles under the merry-go-round platform to shut down its out-of-control spinning. But the rest of the sequence and its pyrotechnical finale were to be filmed on Stage 15 at Warner Bros. The back wall of that soundstage was equipped with a giant screen on which the dizzying moving background footage was projected, with Granger and Walker, plus dozens of extras, emoting on and in front of the carousel. Hitchcock tapped Ted Haworth to play a significant role in filming the climactic sequence. As the date loomed to begin shooting the make-or-break sequence, Hitchcock was well over a week behind schedule, sending Jack Warner and other studio executives into another uproar. Hitchcock needed to finish his work with the actors and determined that he should hand off to the gifted Haworth the responsibility of directing and filming the second-unit merry-go-round showdown and climax. "The degree of trust Hitchcock had in my father was justified, but it was also thrilling and inspiring to Dad," said Sean Haworth.

As Haworth told author Vincent LoBrutto, *Strangers on a Train* had him working closely with special effects ace and cameraman Hans F. Koenekamp. Haworth said Koenekamp was "a pleasure to work with," as well as an acknowledged master in the fields of optical, process, and blue-screen work. Together, the duo had filmed all the process plates Hitchcock required for the train travel and the carousel sequences that were captured on location. With Jack Warner threatening Hitchcock with potential consequences–including assigning a new director to film the merry-go-round sequence and, perhaps, complete the entire film–the director put his foot down with the studio brass. In a memo to Jack Warner he wrote, "I've long since determined that Mr. Haworth will do the second unit. Nobody is to interfere with that. Mr. Koenekamp will be the cameraman." Hitchcock informed Haworth that when he finished filming a scene with Granger and Walker on Stage 1, the actors would change costumes and then walk across the street to film with Haworth on Stage 15. Haworth said,

> [Hitchcock] told me I had to do it. I said, "Hitch, why do you have this faith in me? I'm not a member of the Directors Guild anymore. I let my dues go." He said, "I shall oblige you on that. When you're ready to shoot, I'll stand by the stage door. I won't interfere at all with a thing you've been doing. I'll just say "Roll 'em" and "Action." When you're done you can say "Cut" or hold your hand up and I'll say "Cut!"

Haworth recalled how Hitchcock had "painstakingly laid out" the sequence during preproduction, breaking it down into 90 to 110 separate shots. Haworth not only "knew all the details that went into it" but also devised a means to tilt the merry-go-round off its axis and accomplish that feat in a single shot. Again, Hitchcock had already directed and shot on the Lee Ranch location "everything from the guy climbing underneath the speeding merry-go-round up to the merry-go-round breaking down and collapsing." As for that gentleman who crawled underneath the actual merry-go-round, Hitchcock told interviewers that a real-life carnival worker, not an actor, volunteered to do the stunt with no special effects or trickery involved whatsoever. "If the man had raised his head even slightly," Hitchcock admitted, "it would have gone from being a suspense film into a horror film." Which is true. But Harry Hines, who bravely performed the dangerous scene, appeared

Ted Haworth's production storyboards illustrate how Hitchcock, during preproduction, envisioned the shots and details leading into the out-of-control carousel sequence; the director broke the latter into 90–110 separate shots.

in almost eighty movies and on twenty television series, including two episodes of *The Alfred Hitchcock Hour* in the 1960s.

Picking up from what Hitchcock had filmed previously, said Haworth, "I did that sequence all by myself; they were his sketches—his determination of what I should shoot—but I did it." Haworth's work entailed directing Granger and Walker duking it out on the carousel (at times on several nonmoving carousel sections built for the sequence) "against all of the fast background movement on the process screen." Cinematographer and special effects maestro Koenekamp undercranked the camera to achieve that vertiginous effect. In postproduction, by speeding up the film, the velocity of the editing, and the process photography projected on the screen behind the actors, they were able to

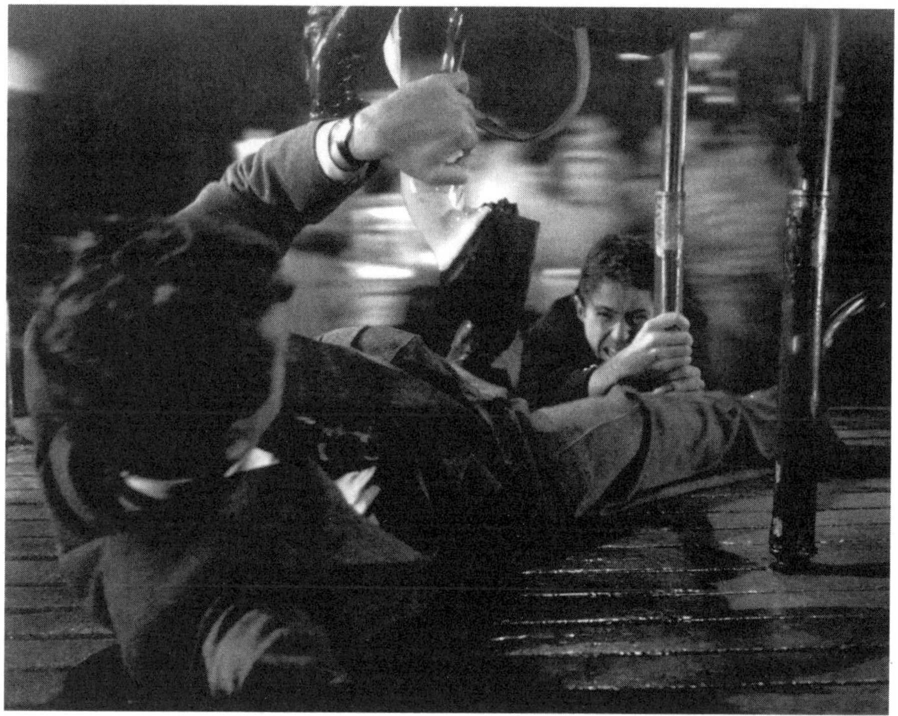

To create the illusion of Farley Granger's body appearing to hang in space as he gripped the brass rail, Ted Haworth built a platform that hung under the carousel's floor; wind machines and film footage projected behind the actor intensified the effect.

convey the impression that the carousel was spinning uncontrollably faster and faster. The trick is made more convincing by simple strategic placement of several remotely controlled Ritter fans that were modulated to blow around the actors' hair and their clothing according to what the moment required.

The production designer did "exactly what Hitchcock asked me to do: the horses' hooves coming down on the actor's faces, the madness of the points of view." To convince audiences that, at one point in the sequence, Farley Granger was hanging for dear life from a brass rail of the merry-go-round, with his outstretched body flying parallel to the ground, Haworth revealed, "I had a platform that went in and just hung underneath the carousel floor. The carousel that collapsed and broke was a miniature that we built and demolished with controlled explosives." Koenekamp was challenged to create a convincing breakdown and disintegration of the amusement park carousel. As Hitchcock explained of arguably his biggest and most technically audacious sequences since the harrowing plane crash depicted from the points of view of the passengers and crew in *Foreign Correspondent*,

> This was a most complicated sequence. For rear projection shooting, there was a screen and behind it an enormous projector throwing an image on the screen. On the studio floor there was a narrow white line right in line with the projector lens, and the lens of the camera had to be right on that white line. The camera was not photographing the screen and what was on it, it was photographing the light in certain colors. Therefore, the camera lens had to be level and in line with the projector lens. The big difficulty with that scene was that the screen had to be angled differently for each shot. We had to move the projector every time the angle changed because many of the shots of the merry-go-round were low camera setups. The projector had to be put up on a high platform looking down. We spent a lot of time setting the screen in line with the camera lens. For the carousel breakdown we used a miniature blown up on a big screen and put live people in front of the screen.

With the climatic amusement park sequence completed, a few final key details awaited Hitchcock's attention.

On December 13, on the train's observation car set built on Stage 5, Hitchcock restaged and reshot several moments involving Farley Granger's encounter with the tipsy Professor Collier (actor John Brown). From December 19 through 21, Hitchcock worked nonstop.

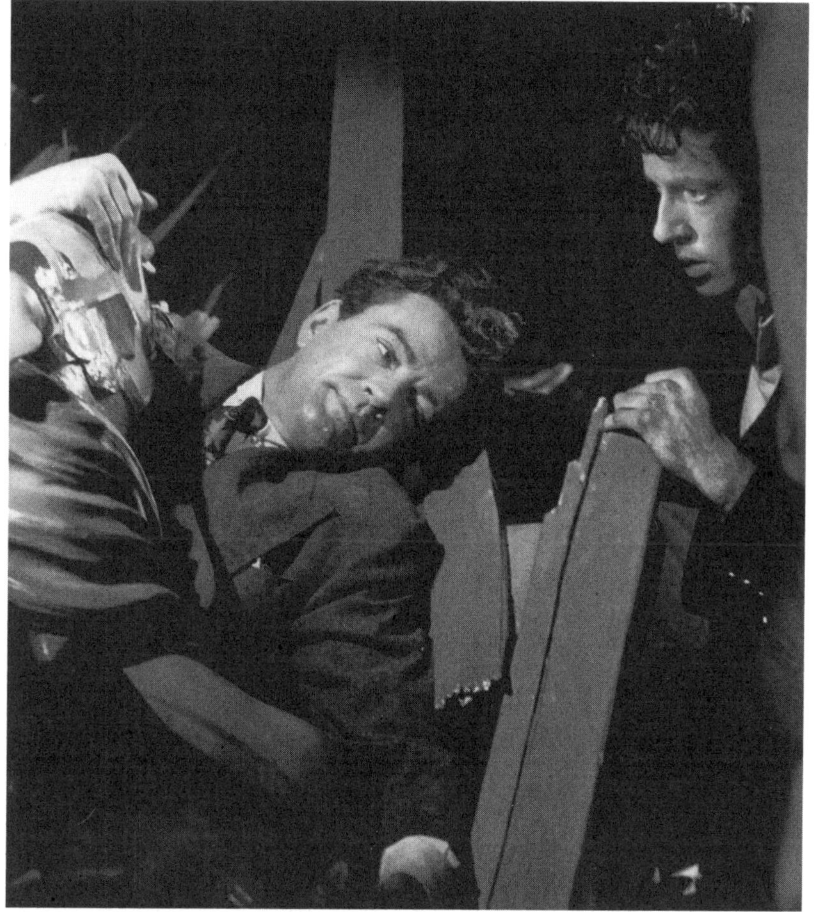

When Robert Walker (seen here with Granger) died before completing his next film, *My Son John*, director Leo McCarey got Hitchcock's permission to borrow a tiny piece of Walker's *Strangers* death scene to complete his film.

First up was the additional work needed on the Morton house party scene filmed on Stage 18; Hitchcock shot retakes and additions to the scene that required the services of Ruth Roman, Farley Granger, Pat Hitchcock, and Norma Varden. On Stage 22, from 9:00 a.m. to 6:15 p.m., Hitchcock filmed additional moments with Laura Elliott, Tommy Farrell, and Roland Morris (as well as extras), as the trio approached and rode the carousel. Filming got delayed several times when the carousel required repair after malfunctioning. Hitchcock also supervised recording sessions on Stage 8, where two voice actors recorded arrival and departure announcements to be used in the Metcalf train station scenes filmed on location in Connecticut and on studio soundstages. Even with this amount of work, Hitchcock was able to send everyone home by 6:00 p.m. or 6:15 at the latest. On December 21, Ted Haworth and two dozen extras worked on Stage 22 capturing the final medium shots and close-ups of the reactions of various merry-go-round riders as well as crowds running in panic when the carousel (the miniature, projected on a large screen at the rear of the stage) comes to a sudden forced stop and then buckles, sparks, and explodes. That same day Haworth shot close-up inserts of the merry-go-round pulleys, drive belt, and the motor malfunctioning.

The censors warned Hitchcock against showing any suggestion of blood on Farley Granger's hands as Robert Walker stomped on them on the spinning carousel. Hitchcock ignored them.

Hitchcock wrapped principal photography on December 23. Budgeted at $1.25 million and shot on a sixty-day production schedule, the film ran seven days over schedule—but under budget. On that final shooting day Hitchcock filmed alternative tag endings with Ruth Roman and Farley Granger—though not entirely willingly. He preferred to end the action on the amusement park midway, immediately after Bruno's death. After Guy is cleared of suspicion, a policeman would ask about Bruno, "Who was he?" Guy's answer: "Bruno. Bruno Antony. A very clever fellow." Fade-out.

Except Jack Warner wouldn't have it. He insisted the audience would want to see Guy and Anne reunited, restoring at all costs that all-American heteronormative order—although in this case, an emotionally arid and oppressive order. The better of the two tag endings, written and submitted by Czenzi Ormonde on December 16, put Guy and Anne together aboard the train and pointedly moving away when a clergyman (apparently innocently) asks whether he is Guy Haines. Because of the Breen Office's warning against conveying any impression of the minister being satirized or ridiculed—and the scene somehow potentially triggering the censor's wrath—Hitchcock covered his bases by filming a second alternate tag. It depicted the chief of police clearing Guy of Miriam's murder, leaving our hero and Anne to canoodle outside the policeman's office door. Even Jack Warner rejected that groaner, exactly as Hitchcock shot it, fully expecting that Warner would.

What Hitchcock absolutely refused to film was the following penultimate scene between Anne and Barbara (with a bit of Senator Morton), set in the study of the Morton house, occurring just after Anne puts down the phone, having heard from Guy that he has been cleared of suspicion:

ANNE

Guy'll be back tomorrow.

(Overcome with emotion, she has difficulty speaking)

He wants me to take him some things.

With a sob, Barbara flings herself into Anne's arms. As she cries, Anne strokes her head comfortingly. Then, with a half-choked sob, Anne too begins to cry. She speaks through her tears, looking over Barbara's shoulder to her father, who has just walked in.

ANNE *(cont'd)*

He says he looks silly in his tennis clothes.

SENATOR

I presume from all these tears that you have some good news.

The Hitchcocks left town on December 27 to spend the holidays at their beloved two-hundred-acre Scotts Valley ranch near Santa Cruz, California, situated high and among redwoods overlooking Monterey Bay. Refreshed and reenergized, on his return to the studio the director enthusiastically announced to his editor and postproduction team, "At last, we actually get to make this picture."

CHAPTER TEN

TIOMKIN: MUSIC, MAESTRO, PLEASE

During the holidays, national newspapers ran a studio press release announcing—once again!—that Max Steiner had been "assigned" to compose the musical score for *Strangers on a Train*. Hitchcock immediately called Jack Warner to make certain the news was incorrect, and it was. Jack Warner's handpicked choice of composer for the film's musical score was the masterful fifty-seven-year-old Russian American Dimitri Tiomkin. The studio officially announced the five-time Oscar nominee's signing on February 12, 1951. Hitchcock and Tiomkin had not collaborated since *Shadow of a Doubt* eight years earlier, but they picked up as though there had been no interruption. They were well matched. Like Hitchcock, Tiomkin loved fine food and drink and hosting lavish parties. Unlike Hitchcock, Tiomkin was ebullient and highly sociable. Tiomkin worked on *Strangers on a Train* during what has come to be called his "golden period," which began in 1937 when Frank Capra championed him to write the score for *Lost Horizon* (1937). That fruitful relationship continued with *You Can't Take It with You* (1938), *Mr. Smith Goes to Washington* (1939), *Meet John*

Doe (1941), and *It's a Wonderful Life* (1947). At the time of Tiomkin's getting hired for *Strangers on a Train*, he had most recently completed scoring Fred Zinnemann's powerful *The Men* (1950), in which Marlon Brando made his film debut as a paralyzed World War II veteran struggling to adjust to civilian life. Tiomkin, one of the few film composers who insisted on working at home rather than at the studio, told Hitchcock and Jack Warner that he wanted to score *Strangers on a Train* in just that way: "Where else can you be at your best to create new music, but when you're surrounded by the symphony of quietude you understand so well?"

Tiomkin began by meeting with Hitchcock, who, as was his custom, had already written tentative notes describing where he thought specific sounds and music cues might begin and end. These were dated October 9, 1950, but withheld until the composer was given the screenplay. Hitchcock's notes (titled "Music Suggestions") contained such detailed observations as:

> *Music Shop Scene (Guy and Miriam)*
>
> *As Guy enters,* THE SOUND OF A PIANO BEING TUNED *is heard from the back of the store. In one [glass listening cubicle], a* CUSTOMER *is playing* SYMPHONIC MUSIC RECORDS, *in a second glass cubicle, a customer is listening to* POPULAR MUSIC *and a third cubicle is empty. As Guy and Miriam talk, piano tuning is still heard but less stridently. Through the glass partition, we see Guy and Miriam* QUARRELING *until Miriam's* VOICE *grows louder, Guy exits and they continue arguing outside their cubicles.* OTHER CUSTOMERS *simultaneously throw open the doors of their listening cubicles. All the sound comes flying out from the different booths—a* LOUD CACOPHONY OF NOISE—A BIG [TCHAIKOVSKY] SYMPHONY, LOUD HOT BOOGIE-WOOGIE, *and the* PIANO TUNER.

> ALL OF THIS OVER MIRIAM'S ANGRY TIRADE.
>
> *Long Shot of Island with Amusement Park with* FAINT NOISE OF THE CALLIOPE *in the distance.*
>
> *On the train, the Drunk fuzzily eyes Guy up and down and bursts suddenly into a* MAUDLIN SONG.
>
> *[As Guy and Bruno trade punches on the merry-go-round]*
>
> *The Calliope has little figures and these figures beat away on their cymbals almost as though they are applauding what's going on.*
>
> *The calliope music carries on, even after the carousel is wrecked and in a heap.*

When Tiomkin asked about Hitchcock's special interest in the music shop scene, Hitchcock reiterated one of his key moviemaking tenets: "Dialogue and image should counterpoint each other. With that scene, the whole idea is to help the characterizations through sound. I think of it as cinematic use of sound or, if you will, sound turned to dramatic account." Tiomkin understood implicitly. "The impression of the abnormal is so necessary to the story," he observed, citing, for instance, Hitchcock's note of wanting the counterpoint of jaunty calliope music to continue playing while the images on the screen evoke horror, violence, and the smoking wreckage of the carousel. "If our music is to help explain these characters, it must be carefully written and played. Mr. Hitchcock understands music and knows just about what it can do to establish character and set the mood of a scene. He agrees that music must be an integral part of the whole production—not just a frame around it." Hitchcock told Tiomkin he wanted his music to suggest "calculation and inspiration on the part of the characters playing out the story." Tiomkin's response was, "It makes a big order but it also makes good sense."

As noted by Joseph Stefano, the *Psycho* screenwriter who had formerly been a songwriter and singer,

> People always talk about how Hitchcock saw his movies in his mind—and that would happen long before you'd be sitting in his office talking with him about that movie. You'd start working together and he'd repeat the story to you not only in words but also in terms of sounds and images. He trusted himself. He made it clear that he trusted you. That's a marvelous and rare way to work.

Tiomkin read the *Strangers on a Train* screenplay several times to assure his grasp on the characters, setting, tone, and action. He also viewed the current cut of the picture in a Warner Bros. screening room before beginning to work. Tiomkin immediately understood that Hitchcock, just as he had in *Shadow of a Doubt*, was continuing his fascination with doubles, malaise beneath a veneer of normalcy, and the transference of guilt. Just as clearly, the movie was to be an exclamation point—a supremely confident, visually bold, and resounding reclamation of Hitchcock's mastery of the medium and a triumphant reconnection with his audience. The director had abandoned the emotionally cool experimentation of *Rope*, *Under Capricorn*, and to a lesser extent, *Stage Fright*. Said Tiomkin, "Robert Walker, our central character, portrays a madman; Farley Granger, on the other hand, stars as a normal, pleasant, stable young man who may be tempted by Walker's plan to exchange murders. Ruth Roman, the girl who loves Farley, shares in the suspense and terror with these two men. The music must explain these three people."

For the film's title sequence, Tiomkin drew immediate inspiration from the visually dynamic introduction of Guy and Bruno exiting their respective vehicles and heading into the railway station as two contrasting and converging pairs of men's shoes—one tasteful but conservative, the other sporty and showy. Creating and then artfully juxtaposing the separate themes, "Strangers" (brassy, vivid, and bombastic, with echoes of Gershwin and Leonard Bernstein for Bruno) and "Walking" (whimsical, playfully ambiguous for Guy), Tiomkin's opening would establish an atmosphere of brio, bombast, and eccentricity. The music celebrates and undergirds Hitchcock's world-building, helps define character, and announces the film's unconventional brand of storytelling. Tiomkin shrewdly conspires with Hitchcock to temporarily conceal that *Strangers on a Train* will be the director's darkest, most troubling, and nihilistic movie since *Shadow of a Doubt*. Instead, Tiomkin's score beguiles us into believing that we're only in for a rousing good time.

To Jack Warner's credit, the studio boss did not skimp when he approved Tiomkin to score, George Parrish to arrange, and Ray Heindorf to orchestrate the sequence with a sizable orchestra—saxes (alto, tenor, and baritone), three clarinets, four horns, three pianos, several violins, and a novachord, the electronic musical instrument adept at producing an otherworldly ambience, as heard in Max Steiner's *Gone with the Wind* entr'acte music and Franz Waxman's score for Hitchcock's *Rebecca*. Tiomkin laid down themes that recur throughout the running time—discordant and troubling motifs for Bruno; sentimental, neurotic violins for Guy and Anne; and an ambiguous theme for the initially malleable, often inscrutable but eventually decisive Guy. As the narrative progresses to Guy's do-or-die tennis match and, especially, his and Bruno's amusement park showdown, Tiomkin responds by accelerating the tempi and orchestrating the themes in a satisfying, if conventionally heroic, style.

Despite the minimalist approach suggested by Hitchcock's original cue sheet, *Strangers* offers lots of scoring and reveals Tiomkin unabashedly flaunting his virtuosity at every turn. He composes with complete understanding of the film's themes and character arcs.

Fittingly, dueling themes mark the entire musical score. Tiomkin gives Bruno the full treatment–neurosis, rage, deception, and turmoil conveyed through complex, growling basslines, unsettling chord combinations, weird strings, and eerie flute riffs that help suggest not only his troubled inner life but also convey the sense of unease he evokes in others. A character as rich as Bruno demanded motifs and an overarching theme. In Tiomkin and Hitchcock's ruminations on the character, things inexorably led back to the surreal, seedy, and sexually charged backdrop of a carnival midway. Calling Hitchcock a director with whom he saw "eye to eye" and "ear to ear," Tiomkin prepared to write for Bruno by accompanying Hitchcock on tours of amusement parks in and around Los Angeles, including Ocean Park Pier in Santa Monica, the Pike Amusement Park in Long Beach, and Beverly Park in Beverly Hills. Aside from soaking up ambience, their specific objective was to discover which tunes were most frequently played on carousel organs and decide which of those might best serve their film, in which calliope music would repeatedly remind the audience of Bruno's capacity for trancelike fugue states and bursts of homicidal violence. Director and composer compared the challenge to how Tiomkin adapted and distorted Franz Lehar's "The Merry Widow" waltz as a theme for the inner life of the debonair, worldly, but desperately sick Uncle Charlie, secretly the notorious "Merry Widow Murderer" in *Shadow of a Doubt*. With Bruno as Hitchcock's most complex and multifaceted villain since Uncle Charlie in *Shadow*, Tiomkin's musical evocations of Bruno parallel those for Uncle Charlie, only even more florid and bombastic.

Tiomkin especially excels in the scene when Guy unfurls a gun while penetrating the Antony house and bleeds those twisty, macabre chords previously reserved for Bruno into Guy's theme. Crisscross, indeed. From there, Robert Burks's skewed Dutch angles on Guy, augmented by Tiomkin's musical cue, fuse the so-called hero and his nemesis in our

Art director Ted Haworth's sly billboard for a nonexistent but plausible product aligns with Hitchcock's and composer Tiomkin's commentary on the film's "sick" characters.

minds. The sequence is more redolent of Orson Welles–style baroque Gothicism than anything Hitchcock previously attempted, even at his most Gothic in *Rebecca*.

Recording sessions for the score began on April 27, 1951. Studio documents indicate that the score was rehearsed, played, and recorded in the precise order of its use in the film. Thus, the first session, for Reel 1 of the film, kicked off with Tiomkin's opening musical theme, "Strangers," to be heard over the credits and "Walking" to accompany Guy and Bruno's feet arriving at and crossing through the train station. Reel 2's scene between Guy and Miriam in the record shop required a mélange of music: the sound of a piano tuning; Ray Heindorf's ebullient arrangement of the Scherzo from Mendelssohn's "A Midsummer Night's Dream" featuring airborne strings and conversational woodwinds; the jazzy J. P. Johnson and Josef Myrow tune "Keep Cool, Fool" (with its lyric warning, "Keep cool, fool 'cause you don't know what you're doin' . . . Or else you're gonna bring somebody down") mingled with more of the Scherzo; and concluding with the bluesy Johnson-Bernie-Unger number "Don't Cry Baby" (with its plea, "You know I didn't mean to ever treat you so mean. C'mon, sweetheart, let's try it over again"). Reel 2 ends with the blaring discord of Tiomkin's "Mother and Bruno: St. Francis," which is horrific enough that it could have been used in Tiomkin's score for *The Thing from Another World* (1951).

Reels 3 and 4 were largely devoted to the amusement park midway and the merry-go-round. The calliope was played throughout by no less than Buddy Cole, the jazz pianist, organist, and orchestra leader who worked closely with singers Bing Crosby and Rosemary Clooney, whom Henry Mancini chose as the organist for the television series *Mr. Lucky* (1959–1960) and who would go on to be heard during the wedding processional on the soundtrack for *The Sound of Music* (1965). Nothing but the best for Tiomkin and Hitchcock. For *Strangers on a Train*, Cole recorded on the calliope the popular old-time tunes:

"Ain't She Sweet?"–the roaring twenties hit with lyrics by Jack Yellen and music by Milton Ager.

"Carolina in the Morning"–introduced in the bawdy Broadway musical revue *The Passing Show of 1922*, with lyrics by Gus Kahn and music by Walter Donaldson, Warner Bros. repeatedly used the song in such films as *Jolson Sings Again* (1949), *Young Man with a Horn* (1950), and *I'll See You in My Dreams* (1952).

"Baby Face"–a 1926 number-one hit, with lyrics by Benny Davis and music by Harry Akst, it was a signature tune for popular singer Al Jolson and was used in such films as the delightfully ribald 1933 Warner Bros. film of the same name starring Barbara Stanwyck.

The ditties were recorded in their entirety, complete with refrains, verses, and choruses. During the same session, Buddy Colo also recorded a medley, blending the tunes "The Band Played On" and "Oh, You Beautiful Doll." Also recorded during this session were Tiomkin's music cues, including "The Meeting" and "Guy and Anne."

The recording sessions for Reels 5 and 6 found the orchestra mostly returning to Tiomkin themes, including "Worry," "The Senator's Home," "Lincoln Memorial," and "Jefferson Memorial," followed by a medley of "Barbara" and "The Band Played On" to be played during Bruno's strangulation demonstration at the party. Reels 7 and 8 involved recording Tiomkin's compositions of a medley of "The Band Played On" and "Strangling," then back to "The Band Played On" and "Glasses" for flashback images of Miriam's murder. Other cues included "Hennessey," "Guy Agrees," and "Menace." The recording sessions covering Reels 9 and 10 encompassed the off-balance themes in "Anne Visits Mother" as well as in the witty, sepulchral bass notes of "Cigarette Lighter." Recording sessions for Reels 11 and 12 focused on intercutting between Guy racing to get to the amusement park before nightfall and Bruno arriving way ahead of him; these scenes required the orchestra to intersperse the "Train" theme with "Ain't She Sweet?," "Baby Face," "Ain't We Got Fun?," "Oh, You Beautiful Doll," and "The Band Played On," then spilling onto the fistfight on the carousel and, finally, shifting to the "Happy Ending" theme, on which Jack Warner insisted for Guy and Anne. (Warner thought Buddy Cole's renditions of the merry-go-round music were so impressive that Warner Bros. reused them for the studio's *East of Eden* [1955], starring James Dean, and for the semi-biographical 1952 Doris Day–Ronald Reagan baseball drama *The Winning Team*, triggering residual payments for Cole.)

Although Hitchcock considered Tiomkin's choices for the merry-go-round, including "The Sidewalks of New York," "The Man on the Flying Trapeze," and "Oh, You Beautiful Doll," in the end Tiomkin chose what Warner Bros. referred to internally as "the 'theme' for the picture"—the perennially popular waltz tune "The Band Played On." As an internal studio memo and, later, a press release described it, "The Band Played On" "has become so much a part of the American scene, at least in amusement parks, along the beaches, and wherever carnival music is wanted, that it is, according to the Warner music masters, a 'must' for this picture."

Written in 1895 by Charles B. Ward (music) and John F. Palmer (lyrics), "The Band Played On" became an immediate hit thanks to impresario, performer, and theater owner Antonio "Tony" Pastor. Known as the "Dean of Vaudeville" for his role in sanitizing risqué vaudeville variety acts at Tony Pastor's Opera House at 201 Bowery in New York City, he made a fortune by cleaning up the entertainment form for the middle-class family trade, expanding his audience beyond the male-only clientele that usually frequented the bawdier vaudeville shows. At Pastor's shows, he and others performed "The Band Played On," complete with its verses in 2/4 time and its refrain as a waltz in 3/4 time:

VERSE 1

Matt Casey formed a social club
That beat the town for style,
And hired for a meeting place a hall.
When payday came around each week
They greased the floor with wax.
And danced with noise and vigor at the ball.

Each Saturday you'd see them
Dressed up in Sunday clothes,
Each lad would have his sweetheart by his side.
When Casey led the first grand march

They all would fall in line.
Behind the man who was their joy and pride. For . . .

CHORUS

Casey would waltz with a strawberry blonde,
And the band played on.
He'd glide 'cross the floor with the girl he adored,
And the band played on.
But his brain was so loaded it nearly exploded,
The poor girl would shake with alarm.
He'd ne'er leave the girl with the strawberry curls,
And the band played on.

VERSE 2

Such kissing in the corner
And such whisp'ring in the hall,
And telling tales of love behind the stairs.
As Casey was the favorite and he that ran the ball,
Of kissing and lovemaking did his share,
At twelve o'clock exactly they all would fall in line,
Then march down to the dining hall to eat.
But Casey would not join them although everything was fine,
But he stayed upstairs and exercised his feet. For . . .

CHORUS

Casey would waltz with a strawberry blonde,
And the band played on.
He'd glide 'cross the floor with the girl he adored,
And the band played on.
But his brain was so loaded it nearly exploded,
The poor girl would shake with alarm.
He'd ne'er leave the girl with the strawberry curls,
And the band played on.

VERSE 3

Now when the dance was over and the band played home sweet home,
They played a tune at Casey's own request.
He thank'd them very kindly for the favors they had shown,
Then he'd waltz once with the girl that he loved best.
Most all the friends are married that Casey used to know,
And Casey too has taken him a wife.
The blonde he used to waltz and glide with on the ballroom floor,
Is happy Missis Casey now for life. For . . .

CHORUS

Casey would waltz with a strawberry blonde,
And the band played on.
He'd glide 'cross the floor with the girl he adored,
And the band played on.
But his brain was so loaded it nearly exploded,
The poor girl would shake with alarm.
He'd ne'er leave the girl with the strawberry curls,
And the band played on.

Recorded and performed repeatedly over the succeeding decades, the song's earworm of a refrain became its best-known section. A decade before *Strangers on a Train*, "The Band Played On" won renewed popularity thanks to a 1941 Billboard chart–topping recorded version by Guy Lombardo and His Royal Canadians, the release of which was timed to promote Warner Bros.' theatrical release of the Raoul Walsh–directed *The Strawberry Blonde* (1941). That song was prominently featured in the film—a sizable hit for stars James Cagney and Olivia de Havilland and an attention-getter for newcomer Rita Hayworth, who starred in the title role. The lovely and lively melody aside, Hitchcock and Tiomkin also liked the lyrics' references to a man "whose brain was so loaded it nearly exploded" (like Bruno's, especially with alcohol or some psychosexual trigger) and the coincidence that actress Laura Elliott (playing "the poor girl" who would "shake with alarm") happened to be a natural strawberry blonde. But what they found most irresistible was how, over time, the phrase "And the band played on" had become synonymous with the phenomenon of authority figures deliberately ignoring or discrediting disaster by keeping the orchestra playing loudly and as long as possible—such as, so legend goes, on the sinking *Titanic.* (Decades later the song took on new significance when Randy Shilts used it as the title of his 1987 book about how the Reagan administration's political gamesmanship, incompetence, hatred, and apathy toward the gay community allowed AIDS to destroy thousands of lives.)

Hitchcock highlighted the importance of the song by filming one version of the scene with Laura Elliott and her ménage à trois partners, Tommy Farrell and Roland Morris, breaking out in a rousing rendition that turns chilling when Walker's Bruno quietly sings along on the carousel horse behind them. Elliott knew the song lyrics by heart, but the Warner Bros. casting department asked the studio's music department's Joe McLaughlin to supply Farrell and Morris with lyric sheets. How perfect and cruel it is that Miriam, unknowingly about to go to her doom, spends some of her last moments on Earth singing a lyric like "the poor girl would shake with alarm"? To provide himself with editing options, however, Hitchcock filmed an alternate version of the scene, in which Elliott and the boys do not sing at all. But in the end Hitchcock could not let go of a carefully calculated reprise of the song when, at the Washington society party, Pat Hitchcock's owlish gaze fascinates Bruno as he pretends to strangle a society matron. As Barbara's coke-bottle lenses reflect a cigarette lighter's flame, "The Band Played On" floats to the surface as if from a half-remembered nightmare. Hitchcock earmarked the moment in one version of the screenplay:

> *From Bruno's viewpoint, as Barbara speaks, CAMERA MOVES IN CLOSER until the faintest impression of the merry-go-round fills the screen with the effect of whirling around Barbara's head. Her glasses seem to glint until her eyes are obliterated by the glare. All talk dies out as all eyes turn to Bruno, who is staring at Barbara. Except Anne's who is saying to Bruno: This is my sister Barbara. Barbara, this is Mr. Antony.*
>
> *CLOSEUP BRUNO. He does not acknowledge the introduction immediately. He is still staring at Barbara. Then he nods abstractly.*
>
> *CLOSEUP ANNE. She is looking at Bruno, wondering what mystery lies behind this strange individual and why he and Guy have disclaimed any previous acquaintance.*
>
> *(Barbara's glasses glint in the light. . . . Bruno is now transfixed. His breathing becomes heavy. A strange expression comes over his face. He still stares off at Barbara. Medium shot Barbara. We see the whirling merry-go-round spinning around her head. . . . [Bruno] now seems to have gone into a trance. Over the shot we begin to hear a strangled cry.)*

Instead of the potentially unintentionally funny visual of a merry-go-round spinning around Barbara's head, Hitchcock let the acting, the reflection of the cigarette lighter flame, and the reprise of "The

Band Played On" carry the scene. The music morphs from the carousel calliope version to a full orchestral rendition.

Primarily, though, Tiomkin thought the melody would work especially effectively when the merry-go-round spins out of control and the carousel organ speeds up frenetically. As Tiomkin explained, "The music keeps going. It's 'way up here' and it continues an impression of the unusual, which is so necessary to the story." He explained to a *Press-Telegram* interviewer in a story published March 31, 1951, how he planned on using "The Band Played On" as a starter for his theme music for the film and his "real task [would entail] bridging the beginning to the climax with the integral musical lapses fitting into the mood of the lead characters throughout the picture."

One of Tiomkin's most impressive choices comes during the intercutting between Guy's do-or-die tennis match (building from a tense to a frantic pizzicato) and Bruno's desperate attempts to retrieve Guy's cigarette lighter that had fallen into a street grate (rumbling brass that wittily suggests creatures of the oceanic deep). The music volleys from one man's theme music to the other's, effectively joining them as one in the audience's minds. The same level of virtuosic know-how can be heard in the music store scene, which blends the sound of a piano being tuned, a bit of Mendelssohn's "A Midsummer Night's Dream," and Great American Songbook material like "Keep Cool, Fool" (which Guy, pointedly, does not) and "Don't Cry Baby" (which hardened Miriam does not), first popularized in the late 1920s by Bessie Smith.

Hitchcock and Tiomkin also wanted to give the tipsy college professor (whom Guy encounters on the train) a signature nonsense song to sing. Hitchcock proposed the traditional 1925 ditty first recorded in May of that year by New Princes' Toronto Band and written by the English songwriting team Jimmy Campbell and Reg Connelly, "Show Me the Way to Go Home."

Ted Haworth's design for the train's observation car made an elegant backdrop for Guy's chance meeting with a professor on sabbatical, who could have helped prove Guy's innocence, if he hadn't been so drunk.

Instead, though, they made up their minds to use "The Goat," known also as "Old Bill Grogan's Goat," "Old Hiram's Goat," or "And When I Die." It is one of several traditional 1920s "echo" (or "call-and-response") songs, such as the familiar "How Dry I Am." The lyrics to "The Goat," each of which is repeated, became especially popular as summer-camp songs among boy and girl scouting organizations.

Hitchcock favored the song not only for its whimsical lyrics but also for its mention of trains and tracks. Although he and Tiomkin assumed the song was in the public domain, Warner Bros.' legal department could not risk the potential of a lawsuit, so dozens of studio memos (printed with "Verbal messages cause misunderstandings and delays. Put them in writing") flew back and forth between the legal department and Hitchcock's office. After searching obscure compendiums of traditional songs, the studio advisers were unable to affirm the actual copyright holder. With time running out, an unhappy Hitchcock proposed instead a tune familiar to him from his twenties, "How Dry I Am," which is the best-known section of the song "The Near Future," written by Irving Berlin for *The Ziegfeld Follies of 1919* and used frequently in movies and animated short cartoons. However, those Berlin lyrics did not delight Hitchcock, nor did he think they were as amusing for the professor to sing as those whimsical ones for "The Goat." As it turned out, they decided to have the tipsy professor sing an abbreviated version of "The Goat."

In a late change of plans, Hitchcock elected to use a section of Beverly Park, the popular children's amusement park situated on the corner of Beverly Boulevard and La Cienega Boulevard in Beverly Hills—particularly its spectacular Parker carousel, with its colorful derby horses and animal-shaped seats and cars—as one of several shooting locations for the spectacular midway showdown between Guy and Bruno. This footage would be blended seamlessly with filming done at the Rowland V. Lee Ranch in the San Fernando Valley and the studio soundstage. Hitchcock would also hire the park's owner and operator, David Bradley, as technical advisor for the Parker carousel that became a virtual costar of the sequence. In this sequence, Tiomkin returns to the crosscutting of Guy's musical cue (the frenzied, jangly "Train") with Bruno's carnival cacophony of Gus Kahn's 1921 hit "Ain't We Got Fun," Ayer and Yellen's 1929 peppy standard "Ain't She Sweet?," and "The Band Played On."

Through his use of chimes and elegantly funereal chords, Tiomkin gives "Bruno's Death" a kind of ironic nobility, as the antagonist, even with his crushed body pinned by the merry-go-round wreckage, relentlessly refuses to clear Guy of Miriam's murder. In the final summation of the love theme, apparently meant to send us off with the cozy feeling that the oddly paired Anne and Guy will be just fine after all, Tiomkin lets loose with a swoony, fully romantic waltz. We may not buy it for a second, but we never feel that Tiomkin is pandering nor that he is cynical in his intention to sweep us up in the romantic moment. When he completed the score, Tiomkin and Warner Bros. musical director Ray Heindorf spotted the film for twenty-five music cues. Of those, the majority were original Tiomkin compositions. The sole exceptions were the music store background music, the carousel calliope medley heard and sung on the midway, "The Goat," and the organ music that played during Bruno and Guy's final showdown. Licensing these vintage tunes added the equivalent of roughly $30,000 to the film's budget.

Hitchcock and Tiomkin made beautiful music together. According to Tiomkin's wife, Olivia, the composer appreciated how the excited and reinvigorated Hitchcock told the composer what he wanted and then "allowed him to do his own thing." What is more, Tiomkin, as a sentimental gentleman who "liked families," appreciated the Morton family aspect of the story and the fact that Hitchcock's daughter was part of the film. *I Confess* and *Dial M for Murder* were next on Hitchcock and Tiomkin's agendas and, like the *Strangers on the Train* musical score, to date none has been sufficiently celebrated nor recorded in its entirety. Certainly, none has become revered the way the Hitchcock–Bernard Herrmann collaborations of the 1950s and 1960s have been, nor do they seem likely to be. In 2007, Varese Sarabande released a CD of Charles Ketcham conducting the Utah Symphony Orchestra as it performed selections from the score, including the main theme and other selections, including "The Tennis Game/The Cigarette Lighter" and "Bruno's Death and Finale." That disc—also containing selections from Franz Waxman's *Suspicion* score, Roy Webb's music for *Notorious*, and the end-credit music for *Family Plot* (1976) by John Williams—has long been out of print.

Tiomkin told his wife that he did not worry about acclaim or adulation. He compared himself to the pop pianist-showman Liberace—mocked for excess, wildly popular, and laughing all the way to the bank.

Tiomkin lavished three months on the score, and on its completion, he graciously telegraphed Jack Warner on April 2:

> *DEAR MR WARNER MY HEART GIVES THANKS FOR GIVING ME THE OPPORTUNITY TO WRITE THE SCORE ON STRANGERS ON A TRAIN IT WAS A VERY HAPPY EXPERIENCE FOR ME TO WORK IN YOUR GREAT STUDIO DIMITRI TIOMKIN.*

Jack Warner sent an appreciative response, ending in a vague "hope you will be with us again real soon."

TRAILING THE TRAIN

On Monday, February 19, 1951, Hitchcock convened Robert Walker to postrecord dialogue in Projection Room 14 on the studio lot. Later that same day, he held a dubbing session with Warner Bros. contract actors Phil Carey (*Operation Pacific* [1951], but eventually best known for his almost three decades on the soap *One Life to Live*) and Paul Picerni (*Inside the Walls of Folsom Prison* [1951]) as they synchronized the scripted comments made by the two announcers at the Forest Hills tennis match during the footage shot on location. In May, Hitchcock oversaw the production of the theatrical trailer, revision of the copy, and selection of choices of clips. The trailer, with an approximate run time of 2:36, features various themes from Dimitri Tiomkin's musical score and footage from the film, some of it alternate takes. Also heard as narrator is Frank Lovejoy—the tough, no-nonsense actor who enjoyed an extensive career starring on tough-guy radio shows and had recently appeared in the Warner Bros. film *Starlift* (1951) and had the starring role and narrator in *I Was a Communist for the F.B.I.*

The copy, written in classic vintage trailer hard-sell style, begins,

A speeding train . . . A chance meeting . . . A strange toast . . . With these fibers of fate Alfred Hitchcock weaves the startling adventure . . . That marked one man's conscience with another man's evil! . . .

Over various shots from the film, some of which are alternate takes, the raspy, hard-edged voice of actor Frank Lovejoy narrates,

Fantastic, isn't it? You didn't know when Bruno proposed this pact that he was serious—dead serious! You would make the mistake of speaking to a stranger on a train. . . . And now, wherever you go, whatever you do, you'll find yourself dominated by his evil presence. And you, Bruno, to you, killing was the answer. Murder without proof, without motive. The perfect crime! Too perfect. And Anne. Life looked very attractive to you—until the love in your heart became gripped by a terror that drew you deeper and deeper into this vortex of conspiracy! With three striking personalities on an exciting journey into suspense!

STRANGER than any fiction you ever read! STRANGER than any picture you ever saw!

You'll talk to your friends about it. But you'll never talk to . . .

STRANGERS ON A TRAIN!

And with the completion of the trailer, production on *Strangers on a Train* ended, not with a bang but a whimper. But the big bang awaited just around the corner.

CHAPTER ELEVEN

PREVIEWING, FINESSING, AND SELLING THE PICTURE

With the film being finalized for release, the Motion Picture Association cleared it with no restrictions. But a cautionary note was struck by the National Legion of Decency, a Catholic organization that rated films "A," "B," and "C" (for *Condemned*). The Legion slapped a "B" rating on the film, indicating the film was "morally objectionable" to the devout because it "Reflects the acceptability of divorce." However, unlike Warner's *A Streetcar Named Desire*, from which the studio cut four minutes to avoid the specter of Legion of Decency–led protests and boycotts, *Strangers on a Train* looked as though it might remain relatively unscathed. But that hardly guaranteed the movie would escape the wrath of the local decency warriors who lay in wait for it.

Warner Bros. chose the Mirror Theater at 1615 Vine Street in Hollywood for a low-key March secret preview of *Strangers on a Train*. The 1,200-seat theater—the first in Los Angeles designed specifically as a

This moody promotional photograph features Ruth Roman, Robert Walker, and that cigarette lighter. Of course, there is no such scene in the film. What's being sold here is the sizzle, not the steak.

Broadway-style house—usually played host to the star-studded live productions of the radio anthology series *Lux Radio Theater*, broadcast for over twenty years. In 1931, the Mirror was converted to a movie theater. (Today it is the Ricardo Montalbán Theater.) The preview version shown was two minutes and eight seconds longer than the print known to most audiences who saw it during its original release to theaters as well as in theatrical reissues (1957), television showings, and first issues on home video. Around 1991, this different, longer print—erroneously labeled "British Version"—was unearthed in a private collection.

—

Following that March screening, Jack Warner insisted on taking another look at his choices of tag endings. The mogul's memo to Hitchcock dismissed the director's unwavering preference for ending the movie with Guy talking about Bruno after his death on the merry-go-round: "I assure you that audiences will want more of Ruth Roman in the picture. Moreover, so does Warner Bros." With a proverbial gun to his head, Hitchcock added the tag ending of Guy and Anne canoodling on the train and slipping away from the clergyman. It feels as tonally false and tacked on as when Joel McCrea and Laraine Day played a similar scene at the end of Hitchcock's *Foreign Correspondent* in 1940 and even more so in 1966 when the Universal front office demanded Hitchcock film the equally ill-matched Paul Newman and Julie Andrews warming themselves under a blanket after escaping gunfire from Russian agents and icy waters while hiding in wicker baskets in the director's fiftieth feature, *Torn Curtain* (1966).

On April 26, 1951, with much more fanfare, Warner Bros. previewed *Strangers on a Train* to the public at the palatial Huntington Park Warner Theater in Huntington Park, California, seven miles outside of Los Angeles. The VIP attendees included the three Hitchcocks, writers Barbara Keon and Whitfield Cook, Jack Warner, Steve Trilling (Warner's second in command), Dimitri Tiomkin, and arranger-conductor Ray Heindorf. Invitees Raymond Chandler and Czenzi Ormonde each had responded that they would be "out of town." Ida Lupino accompanied Robert Walker, who, on his way into the 1,468-seat Art Deco–style theater, answered a reporter who asked whether he was as excited to see his performance as Jack Warner, Alfred Hitchcock, and others said he should be, "I'm always the last one to like my work. I'm such a

The theatrical poster for the film's successful release in Italy, where it was titled *The Other Man*. In 1961, after *Psycho* made Hitchcock an even bigger name internationally, Warner Bros. re-released the film retitled as *Delitto per Delitto* (*Crime for Crime*).

wonderful audience for the performances of others that it would give me a thrill to turn in a job that would excite me as a member of the audience." Lupino revealed later that Walker had confided in her, "I know you will understand what I mean. I am thrilled about my work in *Strangers on a Train* and *My Son John* [1952] with Helen Hayes. My career has never been as stimulating. I think this is going to be my best year." After the preview, Hitchcock and the studio brass reviewed the responses and comments of the audience on the preview cards, which ranged from mixed/positive to highly positive. The lion's share of the plaudits went to Walker for delivering "startlingly unexpected villainy" and to Hitchcock for his directorial "touches," particularly in the amusement park murder, the tennis match, and the carousel finale.

All involved had good reason to feel celebratory. In response to several complaints about the film's pacing, Hitchcock and William Ziegler made some last-minute changes before the release prints were struck. They include the omission of a shot of several detective novels with lurid dust jackets strewn around Bruno's private train compartment, as well as this trimmed dialogue between Bruno and Guy:

BRUNO
Sure, I went to college. Three of them. Every time they kicked me out, my father threw me back in.
(bitterly)
He finally gave up. He thinks I'm awfully small fry, not worth the bait.
(wistfully)
You're my friend, Guy?
GUY
Sure. I'm your friend, Bruno.
BRUNO
(woozy)
No, you're not. Nobody thinks I'm anything special. Only my mother.
(empties the liquor bottle into his glass)
My father hates me.

(Guy smiles this off as nonsense.)

GUY

You must be imagining things.

BRUNO

(hitting the bottom of the bottle for the last drop)

And I hate him.

GUY

What do you want to do?

BRUNO

You mean before or after I kill him?

GUY

(chuckling)

Before, of course.

BRUNO

(leaning forward eagerly)

I want to do everything.

[and, later, speaking of Miriam]

BRUNO

Played around a lot, I suppose?

GUY

Let's not talk about it anymore.

BRUNO

(almost hopefully)

Maybe she'll make more trouble for you.

Also axed: Just after the murder, Bruno eases into the shot. Backgrounded by the Ferris wheel, he casually cleans those recently manicured fingernails. (Twenty-two years later, Robert Rusk, the "Necktie Murderer" in Hitchcock's 1972 shocker *Frenzy*, strangles a woman, then takes a bite of the apple she'd been eating on her lunch break, then callously picks his teeth with an ostentatious jeweled necktie pin in the shape of an "R.")

And with those cuts, *Strangers on a Train* was ready to meet critics and audiences worldwide. Warner Bros. tied the publicity campaign for *Strangers on a Train* to its Silver Anniversary celebration of "Warners Talking Pictures." In a series of "Look Forward! Go Forward! With Warner Bros." ads targeting the film industry and the paying public, the studio heavily featured the July 3 wide release of Hitchcock's latest thriller. On May 31 and June 1 in New York and then on June 12 and 13 in thirty-one cities nationwide, Jack Warner and the studio's vice president and general sales manager Benjamin Kalmenson oversaw luncheons, pep talks, and national screenings of its upcoming releases *Strangers on a Train, A Streetcar Named Desire, Captain Horatio Hornblower*, and *Jim Thorpe–All American*. The studio extended invitations to 2,500 theater owners, managers, and bookers across the country. Enthusiasm ran high. In Manhattan alone, on the morning of June 1, 1951, Warner Bros. hosted 500 film theater insiders to the first private screenings of *Strangers on a Train*, with Kalmenson cheerleading the crowd with a pep talk that began, "If ever the times call for exhibitors in this business to look forward and go forward, that time is now. If we look forward we can't help but go forward."

It was music to Jack Warner's ears when Hitchcock announced he would personally promote the movie–and meant it. In the best of times, Robert Walker never liked doing interviews–and these were not the best of times for him. The Warner publicity department worried that the press would focus less on Bruno Antony's personality kinks and more on Walker's ongoing anguish aggravated by his loss of Jennifer Jones.

As Walker preferred, he would be kept from the press, except in rare instances; however, contract players Farley Granger and Ruth Roman had no choice but to be fed to the fan magazine contingent–not that either was exactly shy when it came to self-promotion. Meanwhile,

Hitchcock and his daughter would focus on touting the film to newspapers and radio reporters. "Every picture's opening should be an event," Hitchcock would tell reporters, adding, "Every picture should have some sort of personal appearance in its promotion." But when he tried proposing novel (and expensive) promotional gambits, Warner slammed on the brakes, such as when the director suggested holding special screenings aboard trains for top critics and opinion makers. The idea had been first tried out in 1922 when Paramount showed the Sam Wood production *My American Wife*, starring Gloria Swanson, in the observation car aboard a Pennsylvania Railroad trip from New York to Chicago and again when Paramount previewed Cecil B. DeMille's *Adam's Rib* on a 1923 trip from Chicago to Los Angeles. Because of its title and certain scenes, *Strangers on a Train* presented far more obvious train-related promotional tie-in opportunities. But Jack Warner wouldn't go for it.

Strangers on a Train

Warner Bros.' publicity department got the film promoted in such bestselling film fan magazines as *Photoplay*, *Modern Screen*, and *Screen Stories*.

An estimated 5.2 million readers got a glimpse of *Strangers on a Train* via a splashy three-page spread in *Life* magazine's July 9, 1951, issue.

On June 15, Hitchcock, accompanied by Graham Wahn of Warner's publicity department, began a twelve-city publicity swing in support of the movie. Warner publicity head Morton Blumenstock arranged the tour, making certain that the director met only with the leading newspaper, magazine, and radio reporters in such top urban markets as Boston, Philadelphia, Pittsburgh, Cincinnati, Cleveland, Detroit, Chicago, Kansas City, and Los Angeles. Newspapers reported "full-force turnouts for the suspense director." But Hitchcock, the consummate showman, was disappointed that few to none of the whistle-stops provided publicity stunts appropriate for the movie. In Philadelphia, for instance, the director was met by "Thomas Jefferson" and "Betsy Ross" commemorating the signing of the Declaration of Independence in City Hall. Knowing his publicity department had missed a beat, Jack

Warner called them on it when he noted the United Artists publicists generating big word of mouth by concocting cigarette cases to promote—of all movies—their *Cyrano de Bergerac* (1950) starring Mel Ferrer. In a series of internal memos and telegrams, Warner blasted his publicity team for failing to arrange a tie-in with Ronson cigarette lighters to promote *Strangers on a Train*: "How was this opportunity overlooked? The lighter is a character almost as important as Farley Granger and Robert Walker." A good question, as the Ronson Company heavily promoted the Adonis model lighter—as seen in the film—in many of the day's biggest-selling magazines. In 1950 alone, Ronson sold thousands of the standard version of the Adonis model lighter and Guy Haines's rarer deluxe version in brushed sterling silver and 14K gold, though it wasn't personalized with crossed tennis rackets and an engraved inscription.

Meanwhile, Pat Hitchcock also hit the publicity trail hard throughout the northeast, including recording a Boston, Massachusetts, radio interview, excerpts from which were broadcast in the region thirty times a day for two weeks. She appeared at City Hall with Boston Mayor John B. Hynes, and she met with local movie critics and Sunday supplement newspaper feature writers at a big press reception at the posh Copley Square Hotel. Traveling to Cape Cod, she got crowned Queen of Cape Clam Bakes. On July 3, she attended the grand opening of the new 2,750-seat Warner Theater at Broadway and 47th Street in Manhattan (the former Strand, refurbished and renamed for the late Sam Warner) when *Strangers on a Train* premiered as part of the celebration of Warner's twenty-fifth anniversary of talking pictures. The newspaper ads promised "The first public glimpse of a thrilling suspense shocker on our giant motion picture screen!" Pat Hitchcock, along with actor Dennis Morgan and comic Danny Thomas, both with Warner Bros. movies of their own to hawk, also participated in a closed-circuit special telecast live from NBC Studios, marking the first-ever instantaneous broadcast from a TV studio directly to a Broadway theater screen. The program included clips from twenty-five of the studio's most famous films—including, of course, *Strangers on a Train.*

Not surprisingly, the studio's publicity department worked overtime to generate personal publicity for Hitchcock's daughter. Few days went by without Pat being mentioned for a new role, such as playing a nurse on Broadway in *The High Ground* with future *Vertigo* (1958) player Tom Helmore and Ruth McDevitt, who would one day play a fussy pet shop saleswoman in *The Birds.* Newspapers also ran stories about how Pat's recent long trip through Italy and Switzerland with her mother had interrupted that "steady twosome" of Pat and Steve Cochran. If the public was buying Ms. Hitchcock as a footloose gal about town, Hollywood certainly wasn't. One film trade insider magazine, clinically assessing the appeal of the under-thirty crop of actors, cruelly sized her up this way: "Nice, intelligent, hardworking girl but unfortunately rather plain."

Warner Bros.' hyperbolic newspaper ads promised the film "begins with the shriek of a train whistle and ends with shrieking excitement!" and that audiences would "be in the grip of love's strangest trip!" because "It's off the beaten track!"

Meanwhile, the studio's publicity department had engineered the magazine and newspaper ads for the film itself, peppered with hard-sell taglines. "The Thriller-Chiller of the Year." "A film with the punch of a locomotive." "This will leave you limp with excitement." For those left limp, Ruth Roman came to the rescue by agreeing to pose for a busty portrait while swinging a tennis racket and wearing a tight sweater and come-hither smile. That photo, accompanied by the text "Ruth Roman costars in *Strangers on a Train*," served as the focal point of a national campaign titled "Let's Play Tennis for Better Health and Recreation." The actress promoted her softer side in a purportedly self-written *Photoplay* piece "Miracle in Boston" about a local physician who helped pull her through a serious childhood illness. She also served as the focus of a Lustre-Crème shampoo magazine campaign—"one of the top twelve selected by *Modern Screen* magazine and famed hair stylists as having the world's most beautiful hair"—that prominently mentioned her costarring role for Hitchcock and appeared in leading magazines and Sunday newspaper supplements reaching 62 million readers. A color publicity photo of Roman and Farley Granger embracing served as the May 1951 cover of *Screen Stories* magazine. Between takes of *Starlift*, her latest Warner Bros. effort, Roman also did more than her share of promotions for the film by sitting for interviews with over fifty radio, television, and print journalists.

Even publicity-wary Robert Walker enthusiastically talked up *Strangers on a Train*. He told reporters,

> It's got the stuff. It's keyed to a high pitch. In other words, it's a killer and I don't mean to pun. Doing this role in this movie is the ideal thing, the thing I've always wanted to do. I've served my apprenticeship as "the young American male" type. It was fine while it lasted and I'm grateful for the success it brought me. But I'm ready for the charac-

Farley Granger and Ruth Roman flashed their pearly whites to promote their pairing in the Hitchcock thriller.

> terizations which challenge me as an actor. As long as my face is up there on the screen, I want it to be the face of an accomplished character performer. That's what my role is in this Hitchcock picture and that's what I'm moving toward.

Although Farley Granger had hoped for career-changing reviews and perhaps even an award nomination or two, his good reviews did little to offset his standard "teen heartthrob" publicity. To salute his role in the Hitchcock film, *Photoplay* limited the actor to a full-page color portrait with this deep purple copy: "Youth on a mental fling . . . a dreamer in gaudy sports shirts . . . Don Quixote, tilting at life . . . a dark flame fed by a romantic puzzle. Farley's next is *Strangers on a Train*." Attempting to counteract the standard fan magazine nonsense, Granger allegedly penned a feature story titled "What Ails Me" for *Photoplay*, illustrated with beefcake pretty-boy images of the actor as Guy Haines. It was subtitled "What is happening with Granger? A great deal, according to this story. You will find the truth more amazing than any rumors." However, the only amazing thing about it is how much of a spoiled lightweight Granger makes himself sound. To bolster Granger's tennis bona fides, the studio arranged to have him pose for photos with "Gorgeous Gussie" Moran before one of the tennis star's matches at Madison Square Garden. Long before Granger ever knew he'd one day be playing a tennis ace, he had taken tennis lessons with no less than "Big Bill" Tilden, who in his 1930s heyday had led the US Tennis team to seven consecutive Davis Cup wins and is to this day ranked as one of the all-time greatest tennis players alongside Don Budge and Jack Kramer. However, Tilden's superstar career in sports, let alone his writing career and appearances in films, came crashing down in 1946 when Los Angeles police arrested and jailed him for soliciting an underage male prostitute. After a second arrest on a similar offense three years later, Tilden's income dwindled, and he was banned from teaching at clubs and public courts. Granger became one of the celebrities Charlie Chaplin encouraged to take lessons from Tilden at Chaplin's home tennis court. Chaplin, who knew what it was like to be shunned by America because of scandal, had befriended and provided financial support to Moran and Tilden when both were down on their luck. Granger had only good experiences with Tilden, whom he had first met through playwright and screenwriter Arthur Laurents. But Jack Warner refused to let Granger be photographed with Tilden.

Despite the hard work and practice Granger put into his tennis scenes in the film, his publicity inevitably veered into sex-symbol ter-

Movie theater lobbies displayed promotional photos such as these to lure undecided ticket buyers and to sell the fantasy of the stars as love matches on screen and off.

ritory, incited by the studio sending out masses of prerelease publicity photos of a tanned, leggy Granger in tennis gear. Granger's bare limbs in tennis shorts became—at least according to the nationally syndicated Hollywood columnists, who dutifully regurgitated Warner Bros. press releases—"the cause for female heart palpitations, challenging the curly hair of Tony Curtis and Kirk Douglas's chest. They're becoming the most famous pair of legs since Betty Grable's." But wasn't there something different about the cut of his tennis shorts, the press (purportedly, anyway) wanted to know? Said Granger, "I can't understand it. They're just like any other tennis player's shorts. Maybe they're just tailored a little better." And maybe that was because Leah Rhodes designed those white duck shorts to be briefer than "any other tennis player's shorts" and specifically tailored them to flatter Granger's contours. Still, Granger resisted when a sportswear company wanted to rush to the market a line of tennis clothes copying his in the film—so long as the screen heartthrob would model and personally endorse them.

Screenland magazine for October 1951 featured a sultry photograph of Laura Elliott sitting atop a conga drum with the squib "Laura Elliott, former secretary, gets her big break in *Strangers on a Train*." To help promote the movie and tout their silver anniversary, Warner Bros. sent Elliott and several other second-string players via bus on a press-junket tour through small towns across the United States. In each stop at theaters and other venues, an emcee would introduce the performers. Recalling these personal appearances, Elliott, billed as "Kasey Rogers" once she left Paramount in the later 1950s, said in conversation with author Tom Weaver,

> [The emcee would] introduce [me] and everybody would give me a very polite little "who-the-heck-is-she?" round of applause. Finally, I said to the emcee, "You know, I've got a picture out right now." He said, "Oh? What is it? Let me announce it." I told him, and he said, "Oh my God!" and so the next time he announced me, he said, "This is Laura Elliott, who is in *Strangers on a Train* as . . . Miriam." And everybody gave out these big gasps! They all recognized the character, and they'd look at me with these wide eyes, like, "Oh, you horrible girl!" and then great applause, a wonderful reaction! It was funny. My little niece Harlene was turning 16 and she

> was taking a bunch of her girlfriends to see her auntie in this film, *Strangers on a Train.* They're all sitting there in the dark theater watching the movie and I come on, being the "sweet" person I was in that picture. And they were all asking Harlene, "Is that your aunt?" But Harlene told 'em, "No–no, I–I don't know that woman! I've never seen her before!" She would not admit to it but oh, I loved playing Miriam.

Once the reviews from critics and opinion-makers began streaming in, it proved that Jack Warner needn't have worried so much whether *Strangers on a Train* would make a splash. Influential columnist Walter Winchell wrote, "Alfred Hitchcock's latest *Strangers on a Train* proves again he is spine-strumming virtuoso. Good to the Last Gasp." *Variety* hailed the film as:

> An imaginative, thrilling suspense melodrama gifted with Alfred Hitchcock's knack for getting shock on the screen. A sock meller [melodrama] pointed for a strong reaction at the box-office. . . . [Highsmith's] novel was a swell setup for murder and gains in punch through the adaptation by Whitfield Cook and the screenplay by Raymond Chandler and Czenzi Ormonde. Hitchcock started with a good story and developed and embroidered the production with artful suspense that never grows obvious. . . . Robert Walker as the neurotic playboy has the more colorful role and he socks it to a fare-thee-well. A gripping, palm-sweating thriller of the kind that has been absent for some time. It is by far the best of [Hitchcock's] recent pictures.

The Hollywood Reporter rated Robert Walker "outstanding," Farley Granger as "splendid," and cited Laura Elliott for being "brilliant in an exacting role in an enormously entertaining show." Wood Soanes for the *Oakland Tribune* opined, "For some time now, Hitchcock has been experimenting with forms other than the one in which he first found fame, that is the suspense drama. The results have not been spectacular. In *Strangers on a Train*, he has returned to first principles with consequent kudos. It finds him in top form. It's not precisely a horror film although it achieves spine-chilling peaks."

The era's popular movie fan magazine *Photoplay* saluted it as one of the three best movies of the month (along with *Show Boat* and *Jim Thorpe–All-American*) and rated the performances of Farley Granger and Robert Walker the month's best, alongside Burt Lancaster's as Jim Thorpe. Per *Photoplay*'s movie reviewer, "Hitchcock, at his eerie, frightening best has all but outdone himself" and declared that the movie's "interspersal of the normal and the 'awful' are enough to send customers out of the theater with large economy-sized breakdowns. . . . How scared can you get and still keep your hair on?" *The Exhibitor* proclaimed, "Alfred Hitchcock is back in the groove." The review in *Harrison's Report* was more mixed, calling it "an unpleasant subject," with Robert Walker "as the psychopath . . . realistic in the extreme." The film's action "is rather slow" except for a "highly thrilling and exciting struggle aboard a merry-go-round." A reviewer for the trade paper *The Film* assessed the movie as "top-drawer Hitchcock . . . a provocatively interesting version of a good novel with first rate [performances] given by the leads." Praising Tiomkin's musical score and William Ziegler's editing, the critic chided Hitchcock, who "indulges himself leisurely for about halfway through the tale and then increases his narrative speed to where it hits high-velocity development," ending in a "wildly exciting climax"–in which the spoilsport reviewer then revealed the secrets of the finale and the death of a major character. A *Visalia-Times Delta* critic singled out Walker as "the movie's knockout. His boyish appeal has won him many fans among the femme moviegoers . . . [but he]

does a complete turnabout as Bruno, the sinister playboy who uses a disarming smile to disguise a paranoiac personality."

Motion Picture Daily opined:

> The story itself is even more leisurely than most Hitchcock narratives but the accomplished hand of the director in charging every scene with dramatic current more than compensates for this slight flaw. Acting honors, however, go to Robert Walker whose superb playing of a maniacal killer is brilliant. Hitchcock's knowing direction extracts exciting values from the situations at hand and is clearly reflected in the caliber of the performances. Walker is, perhaps, at an all-time best in a sadistic and savage role and, in many aspects, stands out and away from the others in the cast.

Motion Picture Daily was also among the many sources to praise the work of Raymond Chandler, "who himself knows a thing or two about suspense." How such reviews must have irked Hitchcock and Czenzi Ormonde. Most notably, the daily magazine predicted that the "excellent" Hitchcock suspense drama would fare best "in metropolis first runs, deluxe houses, and spots catering to sophisticated audiences. Elsewhere, its effete tone, psychopathic overtones and other subtleties will probably be lost." The choice of the terms "effete tone" and "psychopathic overtones" is telling. After all, a man was and is considered "effete" if he displays or adopts traits generally regarded as affected, overly refined, or, more to the point, feminine. Surely, the reviewer was referring to Bruno as portrayed by Walker. Also, at the time of *Strangers on a Train*, homosexuality was included in a large group of "psychopathic personalities" and "sexual perversions" in the mental health practitioner's bible *Statistical Manual for the Use of Hospitals of Mental Disease*, the precursor of the industry standard *Diagnostic Statical Manual*.

One of the few critics of the era to outright mention Bruno's sexuality, Manny Farber, wrote in *The Nation*: "The movie . . . is built around the travestied homosexuality of the murderer." *The Oakland Tribune* called out one particular performance, saying, "Walker is delightful as the daffy-dill ["daffodil" has been derogatory slang for a gay man since the days of Queen Victoria] who is not annoyed by murder." But overall, the movie's notices were astute, even in the usually deadpan journals written strictly for theater owners and managers. In *Exhibitor*, the critic wrote, "Topflight Hitchcock. A good cast and only an interesting script have been molded into a thrilling, engrossing melodrama by the genius of Alfred Hitchcock. Building suspense from the very outset, this works up to an emotional pitch. Turning in one of his best performances, Walker is completely convincing as the insane killer and the highlight of the film is the wild merry-go-round battle. With a cast that has plenty of pull, this should be good news at the box-office."

William Hogan of the *San Francisco Chronicle* cited the movie as one of "Hitchcock's best to date . . . imaginative, taut, enormously entertaining" and featuring a finale with "some of the most effective moviemaking we've seen in years." Walker and Granger, wrote Hogan, were "unusually effective . . . [and] all down the cast sheet there isn't an actor who isn't participating fully in this fine piece of entertainment." Although critic John Rosenfield of the *Dallas Morning News* thought the storyline "highly improbable because there is no time in the adventure when Granger could not have cleared up the whole thing without prejudice by merely telling the police," he nevertheless thought it was "one of the English dramatist's [*sic*] most successful thrillers."

Washingtonians, according to one rather sour Jay Carmody, the critic for the *Evening Star*, "will not exactly preen themselves on what Alfred Hitchcock says happens here in *Strangers on a Train*. Come to think of it, neither will Hitchcock," whom he describes as "a chef who made a beautiful icing but forgot to bake the cake," creating scenes that "do not seem to bear any notable relation to each other, or particularly to the story being told." And so on. No mention of the quality of the performances of the actors playing "the demented playboy" and "the not too bright tennis player." But Carmody spilled lots of ink detailing Hitchcock's grievous assaults to logic and to Washington, DC, leaving audiences "likely to find themselves exasperated and unconvinced." Why, he puzzled, is a trip between DC and New York shot instead "oddly enough on the New York, New Haven, and Hartford Railroad [*sic*]?" And what about "that moment when the tennis player is rushing to Union Station by driving west across Memorial Bridge[?] Whoever took that shot out of the library for Hitchcock should have read the label more carefully."

With the film opening simultaneously on June 29 on the West Coast at Warner's Hollywood, Warner's Downton, and the Wiltern Theaters, longtime *Los Angeles Times* film and drama critic Edwin Schallert sounded embarrassed to admit he enjoyed the film he called "one of his best," referring to Hitchcock as a "specialist in weirdly contrived thrillers." He carped that the movie "may test credulity, particularly at the start and finish [but] it glosses over even this weakness with its slick, sleight-of hand effects, of which Hitchcock is a master," even if "some of the most suspenseful scenes are at the same time genuinely laughable." After all, the "super wild" merry-go-round climax although "terrific in its cyclone of effects" and an indicator "of the razzle-dazzle of which the director is capable" but looks as if Hitchcock "were 'throwing the book at his audience.'" He thought the director "evokes from Walker a fascinating performance as the lunatic-at-large" and that the "very good" Roman, the "particularly fine" Marion Lorne, and even the "excellent Laura Elliott as the tramp wife" were probably bested by Pat Hitchcock, "who all but runs away with the feminine honors."

Once the good reviews rolled in, Warner Bros. suddenly began encouraging America's theater owners to hype *Strangers on a Train* with showy publicity gimmicks. Ticket buyers at the RKO Palace Theater in Rochester, New York, for instance, were greeted by an impressive model train display with photos depicting actual scene locales from the film. Warner Bros. suggested tie-ins with local sporting goods stores, tennis associations, and country clubs. In Connecticut, travel agencies launched essay contests relating to locations in the film.

Hitchcock had to be floating on air. His new film was receiving a level of critical approval he had not experienced in five long years.

CHAPTER TWELVE

STRANGERS MEETS THE PUBLIC

The previous year, when Hitchcock's *Stage Fright* was being publicized, to help safeguard its twist ending, Warner Bros. had offered theaters lobby-display posters announcing, "No One Will Be Seated During the Last Few Minutes of *Stage Fright*." But this was not done with *Strangers on a Train*. Nonetheless, one usherette took matters into her own hands when Hitchcock's latest was the big attraction at the nearly 2,800-seat Warner Theater on Hollywood Boulevard. "Our theater manager was nuts," said comic legend Carol Burnett of her stint as an usherette at the lavish theater decorated in a Moorish-Rococo style, suggesting a Spanish garden:

> He wouldn't talk to us, he would only line up the usherettes in the lobby and signal where he was assigning us that shift—candy counter, box-office, aisle two, aisle three, balcony. I was on aisle two one night and this couple came in and wanted to be seated during the last five minutes of *Strangers on a Train*. In those days, people would just walk into a movie anytime they pleased. They'd sit and watch the movie until they'd say, "This is where I came in," then leave. Well, I'm

> Miss Movie Buff. I was barring them from entering the theater. I mean it was right at the point where Farley Granger and Robert Walker were fighting it out on the merry-go-round! I love Robert Walker and in *Strangers on a Train* was he sensational! I saw that movie fifty-seven times because I was ushering for it. It has the most hair-raising murder scene and so many other chilling scenes. When Robert Walker died, I didn't want to go to school that day. I didn't want to leave the house. I loved him. I loved his work. I didn't know the man, I never met him, I must say. But I felt for him. It was as if a relative had died. And so I said to those people who arrived so late, "Oh, please, can't you just go get some popcorn and a drink because it will spoil it for you if you see the end of the movie." I mean, the movie was going to start again in just fifteen minutes. They said, "We want to sit!" and I said, "Oh, please wait. It's such a good movie." The manager came up and, as usherettes, we wore insane harem pants with fez hats and epaulettes. He asked, "What is the matter?" and the woman said, "She won't let us sit down!" I said, "It will spoil the movie for you." The manager ripped the epaulettes off my shoulders. I was fired on the spot! The beautiful retribution for me was when, about twenty-five years later, the Hollywood Chamber of Commerce asked me, "Where do you want your star on Hollywood Boulevard?" "Right in front of that theater!"

As predicted, the movie earned robust if not record-breaking box-office returns during what trade papers called "the mid-summer box office doldrums." Yet *Variety* still trotted out such superlatives as "booming," "propulsive," and "excellent" to describe ticket sales in such markets as Manhattan; Boston; Philadelphia; Washington, DC; Chicago; and Los Angeles, while across the rest of the country, business was mostly "excellent" and "above average." In its first week in Manhattan, the movie made $50,000, $30,000 in its second, and was solid enough in its third at $18,000 when Warner Bros. replaced it with the nostalgic Doris Day–Gordon MacRae crooner *On Moonlight Bay*. But to put in perspective the moviegoing tastes of the 1950s, according to such sources as the *Motion Picture Herald*, the box-office takings for Hitchcock's latest paled in comparison to that year's bigger crowd-pleasers, such as MGM's lavish musical *Show Boat* or Warner Bros.' aforementioned *On Moonlight Bay*, let alone such fare as *Ma & Pa Kettle Back on the Farm*, the Dean Martin–Jerry Lewis comedy *That's My Boy*, Bob Hope's *The Lemon Drop Kid*, and *The Thing from Another World* from director-producer Howard Hawks. Even so, internal studio records indicate that *Strangers on a Train* earned a healthy $1,788,000 domestically, plus $1,144,000 in the rest of the world—or, today, roughly $35,597,186. The film sold 13,207,547 tickets, just under the ticket sales for Disney's *Alice in Wonderland*

HITCHCOCK DEVISES NEW SUSPENSE MAGIC

BY EDWIN SCHALLERT

Eliminate a motive and the result may be a "perfect crime." Let two men exchange places as murderers and it is possible that neither will be suspect.

With this as a thesis, Director Alfred Hitchcock, a specialist in weirdly contrived thrillers, has managed to make "Strangers on a Train" one of his best.

His picture is showing at Warners Hollywood, Downtown and Wiltern Theaters and, amazingly, some of its most suspenseful scenes are at the same time the most genuinely laughable.

Slick Tricks

The production as a whole keeps up a great pace and though it may test credulity, particularly at the start and finish, it glosses over even this weakness with its slick, sleight-of-hand effects, of which Hitchcock is a master.

The picture only becomes a little bit thick at the end, with the runaway merry-go-round and the long fight on this contraption between the two principal male characters. It looks somewhat as if its director were "throwing the book" at his audience.

Hitchcock resorts to his old aide, the psychopathic killer, for his villain. His hero is a tennis champion, much in the public eye.

Good Advice

The picture suggests that it is not always wise to converse with "strangers on a train."

Farley Granger as the tennis star finds this out. Robert Walker is the stranger, a rich man's mentally deranged son—a very persistent and at the same time persuasive chap.

Walker knows that Granger has been unhappy with his wife, a promiscuous little tramp. He knows too from the gossip columns that a divorce is impending, but that Granger's wife doesn't want to give it to him; so he can marry a Senator's daughter.

Murder Plans

Walker hates his father. His mother is mentally weak, and his father wants him to be sent to an institution. Walker would like to see him dead, but he doesn't want to kill him.

Therefore he proposes to Granger that he (Walker) kill Granger's wife, while Granger disposes of his (Walker's) detested parent. No motive could be attached to either for this criss-cross killing.

Naturally Granger won't hearken to such a fantastic proposal. But Walker goes ahead with his part of the so-called "bargain."

From then on the picture is one to be seen rather than to be talked about, because that might spoil the very interesting unravelment on the screen. This unravelment reaches a great pitch during the tennis match, when Walker is attempting to plant evidence against Granger.

Here the Hitchcock suspense is at its height. Very skillfully contrived, indeed, is this whole line of action.

Wild Impact

The climax is terrific in its cyclone of effects. It indicates the razzle-dazzle of which the director is capable, though there will be arguments on whether or not there is too much.

It's hard to conceive how he might have wound the picture up otherwise to top what has gone before.

The net impact is super wild. Even the innocent bystander (so to speak) who operates the merry-go-round is the victim of a shot.

Hitchcock evokes from Walker a fascinating performance as the lunatic-at-large, and Walker qualifies all the way in the difficult role.

Granger also has his share of psychology to convey as the troubled second party to the alleged (by Walker) agreement. His problem is that he does not feel he can say anything about the Walker crime and scheme, even though he is innocent.

While Ruth Roman is the feminine lead, and very good, it is Patricia Hitchcock who all but runs away with the feminine honors in helping to express, like a Greek chorus, ideas about the situation.

Laura Elliot does an excellent job as the tramp wife, while Marion Lorne is particularly fine as the mother. Leo G. Carroll rates commendation and Jonathan Hale registers briefly and well. Howard St. John, Robert Gist, John Doucette, John Brown and Norma Varden are others to be noted.

Hitchcock Present

Raymond Chandler and Czenzi Ormonde wrote the script from the novel by Patricia Highsmith and adaptation by Whitfield Cook and a line of credit belongs to Dimitri Tiomkin for the music and Robert Burks for the photography. There is a glimpse of Hitchcock himself with big bull fiddle as a signature.

Reissue of a Larry Semon comedy with sound and narration is productive of so much hilarity that Gordon Hollingshead, producer, seems to have struck a new rich vein of entertainment in this kind of short exhibit.

Although the opinion of the influential drama editor of the *Los Angeles Times* (dubbed "the dean of West Coast critics") mattered to Hitchcock, the director often considered film critics "humorless."

(13,577,358) and *A Streetcar Named Desire*, ranking it the seventh-most popular film in a year dominated by big-budget, widescreen spectacles as *David and Bathsheba* and grand adventures like *The African Queen. Variety*'s list of Top Grossers of 1951 put *Strangers on a Train* at number 55 out of 131, just under such other classics as *The Thing from Another World* and *The Day the Earth Stood Still*. It also made the cut on the top-ten list of the National Board of Review Awards alongside *A Place in the Sun, Red Badge of Courage, An American in Paris, Death of a Salesman, Detective Story, A Streetcar Named Desire, Quo Vadis*, and *Fourteen Hours*.

The movie held less appeal to small-town and other less cosmopolitan audiences. "A good mystery with some thrills for the kids," reported one exhibitor in Paonia, Colorado, adding, "Small town average business." However, a Pennsylvania exhibitor took a sanguine view: "this will draw [audiences]–early or late. Startling action drama. Maybe that's why the show had realism and does business." A Loxley, Alabama, theater owner opined, "While I don't think the screen is the place for murder or idiot killers, this picture is more of a classic–a remarkable piece of work from every standpoint. A picture well worth playing in any situation. We did average business midweek doubled with [Leo Gorcey and the Bowery Boys in *Blues Busters*]."

In some locales, the movie hit speed bumps that may have made a dent in its profitability. While the Breen Office finally passed the film with no significant warnings, various local organizations and state censorship boards saw things differently. The US Department of the Navy requested that the following line be cut from all prints shown to service members:

BARBARA

Oh daddy doesn't mind a little scandal. He's a senator.

Going many steps farther, Jack Warner ordered the "He's a senator" wisecrack excised from all prints intended for all service branch members, as well as from negatives and prints intended for all foreign markets.

Ohio's censorship board demanded the removal of the following lines of dialogue:

In the record shop scene between Guy and Miriam:

GUY
Aw, skip it, Miriam. It's pretty late to start flirting with a discarded husband—especially when you're going to have another man's baby.

During the Washington party scene:

BRUNO
You're not going to tell me there hasn't been a time that you didn't want to dispose of someone. Your husband, for instance.
MRS. CUNNINGHAM
You know, I read of a case once . . .

Ohio's Board of Censors also demanded the axing of Barbara's line, "I still think it would be wonderful to have a man love you so much, he'd kill for you." Additionally, the board also insisted that there be no moaning from Mrs. Cunningham as Bruno strangles her, and they ordered the deletion of all footage depicting Miriam's reflection in her fallen eyeglasses as she is being strangled.

Similarly, Milwaukee, Wisconsin, censors refused to permit the film to be shown unless the strangulation reflected in Miriam's glasses be eliminated. Meanwhile, the Massachusetts Board of Censors insisted on cutting Guy's record shop scene line about "another man's baby" and Barbara's comment about Miriam, "She was a tramp."

It isn't known exactly when Patricia Highsmith saw the movie or what she thought of it at the time, although Hitchcock invited her to the premiere. But in 1986, Highsmith, at sixty-six, surprised many by agreeing to leave Europe to promote her new novel *Found in the Street* and appeared as a guest panelist at the Toronto Film Festival. There, she commented to Gerald Peary about *Strangers*, "They keep playing it on American TV, ancient as it is. A few years ago, there were requests to me, 'Can we make this?' I said that I have no rights. Contact the Hitchcock estate, which won't release it for a remake." (She clearly didn't know that Hitchcock had sold off the rights to Warner Bros. decades earlier.) Her strongest reaction to the movie was reserved for Robert Walker: "He was excellent. He had elegance and humor and the proper fondness for his mother." As for Ruth Roman, "She should be much warmer." She made no comments about Farley Granger but disapproved of Hitchcock's decision to make him a tennis pro, adding, "I thought it was ludicrous that he's aspiring to be a politician and that he's supposed to be in love with that stone angel." On another occasion, Highsmith said about the film that she was "pleased in general. Especially with Bruno, who held the movie together as he did the book."

Success should breed opportunity in Hollywood. Farley Granger mentioned in his 2007 autobiography that the movie vaulted him onto the A-list of young Hollywood leading men. But aside from being paired with glamorous fellow Hitchcock and *The Third Man* (1949) star Alida Valli in the ravishing costume epic *Senso* (1954, planned by director Luchino Visconti for Ingrid Bergman and Marlon Brando), little in Granger's subsequent film résumé suggests a major career bump. After buying out his contract from Samuel Goldwyn, he interspersed television work in the 1950s and 1960s with low-budget Italian sex-horror movies. By the 1980s he was a regular on the daytime soap

As the World Turns. He and his husband of forty-three years, Robert Calhoun, orchestrated a sold-out "Evening with Farley Granger" at Greenwich Village's venerable Film Forum Theater in 2007 to coincide with the release of his autobiography. Similarly, Ruth Roman might have hoped for wider horizons from starring in a Hitchcock thriller, but by the end of the decade and into the 1960s and 1970s, she found her best opportunities in episodic television series, low-budget exploitation horror movies, successful stage tours, and summer-stock appearances.

Considering the outstanding notices Laura Elliott garnered for her performance as Miriam, it is understandable that she told author Tom Weaver,

> I must say I was a little disappointed. It didn't change my career. I think it should have. I had brilliant writeups in the *Hollywood Reporter*, *Variety*, and things. But because it was a loan-out to Warner Bros. from Paramount, I had the feeling that no one at Paramount watched the film. It would have been nice if somebody had been a little bit impressed, or something! But I just think they didn't even see the film. Therefore, you have nobody "pushing" you publicity-wise or putting blurbs in the trades or anything of that sort. I didn't go to the front office and say, "Hey, did you look at that picture?" Didn't happen. I remember the first thing I did after shooting the film, as a contract player, I went back to Paramount and they had me holding up color swatches so the camera crew could test color. I don't mind. But I really thought *Strangers on a Train* might make some difference. But I've been very lucky. That turned out to be a classic. *Peyton Place* I was on 252 episodes. That was a classic television series and then to go right on to

> *Bewitched*, which was another Top Ten. Those are three classic things that I enjoyed and was able to participate in.

Robert Walker's career should have and could have soared after his work in *Strangers on a Train*. When the positive advance word about the movie proved true, Walker told Farley Granger that he hoped the film's acclaim and financial success would propel him to an Oscar nomination and some creatively challenging career options. Maurice Evans wanted to direct him in a New York City Center revival of the prizefighter drama *Golden Boy* by Clifford Odets. Not only did Walker field movie offers from major directors, but he was also in the process of searching for a screenwriter to develop a movie in which he would have played the man he described as "the haunted Branwell Brontë," the tragically drug- and alcohol-addicted brother of writers Charlotte, Anne, and Emily (whom Ida Lupino played in the highly fanciful 1946 Brontë "biographical" film *Devotion*). But immediately after finishing his work for Hitchcock, Walker was most enthusiastic about two things involving his sons. First, he wanted to show his sons, whom the terms of his divorce only allowed him custody of three months of the year, how he had converted his home's old riding stables into a knotty pine–paneled house of their own, lined with books he loved as a child. He had also booked for the three of them surfing lessons and a voyage to Honolulu, Hawaii, via freighter, to give them a taste of the experience he had as a seaman, sailing between ports all over South America.

Instead, he died in his Pacific Palisades home on August 28, 1951, after Dr. Frederick Hacker treated him with sodium amytal to calm what the physician told the press was "a recurrence of his old troubles." Reacting violently to the drug he should never have been given, he died of respiratory failure at age thirty-two, just weeks after the Hitchcock film's release. He had not completed work for director Leo McCarey on the shrilly anti-Red *My Son John* opposite Helen Hayes and Van Heflin, so the film required rewriting, employed doubles for Walker, and borrowed footage from *Strangers on a Train* for his character's death scene.

Granger recalled, "We ran into each other a few weeks after *Strangers on a Train* came out. He was very glad to see me. He said, 'Let's get together.' And I said, 'Let's, I'd love to.' He said, 'I'll call you.' And then, a week later, he died. I was very sad because he was a wonderful, wonderful actor and I respected him highly." Yet Walker was not among the Best Actor Oscar nominees when the roll call included such other worthies as Humphrey Bogart (*The African Queen*), Marlon Brando (*A Streetcar Named Desire*), Montgomery Clift (*A Place in the Sun*), Arthur Kennedy (*Bright Victory*), and Fredric March (*Death of a Salesman*). Some believed Warner Bros. should have championed Walker in the Best Supporting Actor category, which might have bumped out one of the other nominees: Leo Genn (*Quo Vadis*), Kevin McCarthy (*Death of a Salesman*), Karl Malden (*A Streetcar Named Desire*), Peter Ustinov (*Quo Vadis*), or Gig Young (*Come Fill the Cup*). Regardless, Walker's death shocked and saddened many in Hollywood. Even malicious gossip columnist Louella Parsons, who frequently took potshots at him for his emotional volatility and drinking, wrote:

> Poor Robert Walker. His death was one of the saddest deaths of this year. He tried so hard to get over the emotional upsets in his life. In the old days Bob felt that many things were written about him that were upsetting and he wrote me several caustic notes. He said he felt his personal life was his own business but all of us tried to help him after he left the Menninger sanitarium and started a new life. He seemed completely changed. Poor Bob—such talent and so much really to live for. He was one of the most popular actors and was much in demand at all the studios after he changed his way of living. I had many fan letters after

> Bob appeared in *Strangers on a Train*. He had the sympathy of the whole world in his fight.

Released to generally good reviews and box office in Britain in the late summer and early fall of 1951, *Strangers* won approval from the critic for the *Times*, who opined,

> The film contains some of Mr. Hitchcock's most brilliant experiments in time; perhaps the most remarkable is a scene where, very slowly, a hand reaches down to rescue an all-important clue which has been dropped through a grating in the street while, in the background, very rapidly and with great precision, a game of professional tennis is being played. If Mr. Hitchcock's timing has a fault, it is that he is sometimes so conscious of his own talent for nourishing suspense that he in fact keeps it alive a little too long; an instance is the final scene where the murderer is pursued on a roundabout which is made to whirl far too many times before he is caught.

Which sounds a bit like Emperor Joseph II telling Mozart in *Amadeus* (1984) that his work has "too many notes."

French audiences saw the film in 1952 (*L'inconnu du Nord-Express*), then it was released successively in West Germany (*Der Fremde im Zug*), then Norway (*Farlig reisefølge*), Argentina (*Pacto siniestro*), Italy (*L'altro uomo; Delitto per Delitto*), Spain (*Extraños en un tren*), the Netherlands (*Der maniak*), Denmark (*Farligt møde*), Austria (*Der Fremde im Zug*), Portugal (*O Desconhecido de Norte-Expresso*), and Peru (*Pacto siniestro*). In the international market, the film was well received and found financial success.

On October 3, 1951, the Screen Directors Guild awarded Hitchcock their first quarterly directing award for *Strangers on a Train*. The Directors Guild of America nominated Hitchcock for Outstanding Director–Feature Film, although it was George Stevens who took home the prize for *A Place in the Sun*. The Academy of Motion Picture Arts and Science's twenty-fourth year of Oscar nominations included Robert Burks for Best Cinematography–Black and White for *Strangers on a Train*. But in what *The American Cinematographer* termed "very close voting" at the ceremonies held on March 20, 1952, the award–presented by dancer Vera-Ellen–went to William C. Mellor for *A Place in the Sun*.

And in 2021, the National Film Preservation Board of the Library of Congress selected *Strangers on a Train* among its twenty-five "culturally historically or aesthetically significant films . . . showcasing the range and diversity of American film heritage to increase awareness for its preservation." Other Hitchcock-directed films so honored include (in order of induction) *Vertigo*, *Shadow of a Doubt*, *Psycho*, *North by Northwest*, *Rebecca*, *Rear Window*, *The Birds*, and *Notorious*.

With all the film's success, Hitchcock would never overcome his conviction that the film fell short of the mark–and for very specific reasons. In 1962, he agreed to sit for a now-famous series of interviews with a devotee of his work, François Truffaut, who had lots to say and ask about *Strangers on a Train*. As did Hitchcock, although not all of which survived the final edit of the book *Hitchcock/Truffaut*, published in 1966. When Truffaut praised Robert Walker's performance and the character as "probably your best villain; he becomes more likable than Farley Granger and even more touching," Hitchcock responded,

> The weaknesses of *Strangers on a Train* are Farley Granger and the girl [Ruth Roman]. I wanted William Holden and Warner Bros. said I had to take the girl because I didn't have any Warner Bros. players in the film. So, the faults

> of *Strangers on a Train* lie in the lack of the two leading people and also in not good enough writing in the final script where we could have had stronger characterizations of [those two characters]. You see, the big problem in these sorts of pictures is that your leading characters tend to become just figures. I was pleased by the general shape of the picture. I like the woman who got murdered—a really bitchy wife who worked in the phonograph record store. And the mother, who was just as screwy as [Bruno].

Despite Hitchcock's reservations, *Strangers on a Train* ignited the beginning of his artistic and commercial renaissance. It certainly marked a financial windfall for him and for Warner Bros. On a budget of somewhere between $1.2 and $1.6 million, it made $7 million—almost $86 million today. Hitchcock's first *Strangers on a Train* check from Warner Bros. was $20,886, or today's equivalent of $253,000. By contrast the same studio cut Hitchcock's first check for *Dial M for Murder* at $12,079.86 (roughly $140,000 today) three years later.

More significantly, *Strangers on a Train* helped restore Hitchcock's confidence and prove his artistic viability. Although his next film for Warner Bros., the somber *I Confess*—much compromised by the studio—would make nowhere near the impact of *Strangers*, a confluence of smart creative decisions and good luck laid the groundwork for what we today consider his most inventive, artistically exciting, and influential moviemaking decade.

With Warner Bros. suffering continuing financial decline, in 1953 Jack Warner clamped a ninety-day hold on the studio's entire production slate; Hitchcock was among those asked to accept a 90 percent salary cut. Agent Lew Wasserman immediately went hunting for a richer deal for Hitchcock and found it at Paramount Pictures. All Hitchcock had to do was agree to make as his first film an adaptation of Cornell

Woolrich's short story "It Had to Be Murder," a project the director had at first rejected when agent Leland Hayward offered it to him on the heels of the success of *Strangers*. Paramount offered Hitchcock greater freedom and technical resources, not only allowing him to hire James Stewart and Grace Kelly to star in that first film—a masterwork based on Woolrich's work, retitled *Rear Window*—but also the opportunity to surround himself with a formidable production team composed of such top-of-the-line professionals as cameraman Robert Burks, editor George Tomasini, costumer Edith Head, production designer Hal Perreira, assistant director Herbert Coleman, and, eventually, composer Bernard Herrmann. Finally, Hitchcock had a team capable of meeting his demand for the level of taste, invention, and expertise he required to help create an astonishing run of films, several of which are most synonymous with his cinematic legacy, including *Rear Window*, *To Catch a Thief*, *The Trouble with Harry*, *The Man Who Knew Too Much*, and *Vertigo*. Paramount also released to massive success the modestly budgeted *Psycho*, which Hitchcock filmed at Universal using members of his TV series crew strictly out of financial necessity when Paramount executives expressed such distate for the project that they even denied him use of the studio's soundstages.

Meanwhile, though, *Strangers on a Train* became a gift that kept on giving.

CHAPTER THIRTEEN

FAMILIAR STRANGERS

As was a frequent event in the 1940s and 1950s, CBS broadcast an abbreviated radio version of *Strangers on a Train* on the popular Lux Radio Theater on December 3, 1951. It starred Ray Milland (as Guy), Ruth Roman, Pat Hitchcock, and Frank Lovejoy as Bruno Antony. Warner Bros. collected $1,000 for granting Lux permission to adapt the screenplay for radio. On April 8, 1954, WCBS aired another radio version starring Virginia Mayo, Dana Andrews (as Guy), and Robert Cummings (as Bruno) on WCBS.

In Paris in 1955, *Strangers on a Train*, *Dial M for Murder*, and *Rebecca* got reissued and consistently sold out in first-run theaters. In the United States, Warner Bros. rereleased *Strangers on a Train* nationally to theaters on May 15, 1956, and again in 1961 to capitalize on the smash worldwide success of *Psycho*. In 1961, Seven Arts Associated Corp. licensed the broadcast rights to "Films of the Fifties," a package of forty Warner Bros. films, including *Rebel Without a Cause* (1955), *The High and the Mighty* (1954), *The Searchers* (1956), *A Star Is Born* (1954), and *Strangers on a Train*. Self-proclaimed "the nation's #1 movie station," the New York–centric WOR–as well as others, including WJAR in Providence, Rhode Island–kept these movies in heavy rotation, bringing them back for nostalgia fans and helping to create new generations of film addicts and filmmakers.

May of 1961 saw the movie receiving a unique theatrical reissue release throughout the United Kingdom. Rather than simply selling off *Strangers on a Train* to TV or opening the ten-year-old movie at the usual second- and third-run theaters, Arthur Abeles, Warner Bros.' head of film distribution throughout Europe, hatched a smarter, more ambitious idea than his American counterparts had. He gambled by booking the movie into the prestigious 1,175-seat flagship Warner Theater in Leicester Square. Sparkling new film prints were struck, and Abeles created a new advertising campaign centered around Hitchcock, not the cast. He promoted the rerelease as an event. Theater owners were coached on how to create buzz through smart showmanship. In advance of the opening, stills from the movie decorated windows of tennis and sporting goods shops. Theater lobbies displayed life-size cardboard images of Hitchcock equipped with speakers that broadcast prerecorded messages warning, "Alfred Hitchcock says never speak to *Strangers on a Train*!" Several theaters, including the Warner, featured lobby display cases containing such objects as cigarette lighters, men's gloves, shattered eyeglasses, revolvers, train tickets, and crossed tennis rackets, with posters reading, "Ordinary enough items individually—but collectively they spell terror and death to *Strangers on a Train*!" Warner Bros.' London offices also took the unusual step of inviting critics to an advance screening to generate new reviews for the ten-year-old film. And review the critics did, responding far more enthusiastically than they had originally. The *Daily Mail* called the movie "breathtaking," *News of the World* said, "It makes your hair stand on end," and the *Daily Mirror* opined, "Even on a second viewing, it comes up fresh and gripping. The excitement never lets up. Honestly, the best bet of the week is *Strangers on a Train*."

Asked by his European and US counterpoints why he would go to such lengths for an "old" movie, Abeles replied,

> Since his tv shows and *Psycho*, Hitchcock's name has become—next to Elizabeth Taylor and Cary Grant—a major box-office attraction. All the stars of *Strangers on a Train* have disappeared . . . faded from public view so that we are not cursed with the usual drawback of a reissue, which is seeing Gary Cooper or Burt Lancaster or Susan Hayward, say, looking ten or fifteen years younger than we saw them looking in their latest release just a week ago.

The risk paid off handsomely. Internal studio memos acknowledged the European theatrical reissue as "an unprecedented moneymaker." At the Warner Theater alone, the box-office results—the theater's third-highest opening in a decade and three times what the film made in 1951—were declared so "truly phenomenal" that the film ran for almost one month and would have played another week if the Warner Theater hadn't been contractually obligated to open *Girls of the Night*, starring Anne Francis.

In 1969 and advertised, ironically, as "Suggested by a Novel by Patricia Highsmith," Warner Bros. released a Malibu Beach–set remake, *Once You Kiss a Stranger*, in which pretty, pouty Carol Lynley seduces golf pro Paul Burke, kills the rival golfer Burke despises, and then tries blackmailing the golfer into killing her psychiatrist, apparently the only person in sunny Southern California who has figured out that she's certifiable. Patricia Highsmith said of the movie, "God knows it was certainly done behind my back. *Strangers on a Golf Course*." In 1971, the floridly baroque Italian oddball *The Designated Victim*, with hippy count Pierre Clémenti playing cat to adulterous businessman Tomas Milian's mouse, put a mostly bloodless, *giallo* (and unofficial) spin on Highsmith. In the 1987 parody *Throw Momma from the Train*, mother-dominated dim bulb Danny DeVito (who also directed) overhears failed writer Billy Crystal's death threats against his ex-wife and literally advises him to take inspiration from *Strangers on the Train*. The film has ardent fans, but what does it say when the best and most memorable character in the whole thing is the victim, played by Oscar-nominated Anne Ramsey? The year 1996 brought *Once You Meet a Stranger*, a disappointing made-for-TV remake starring Jacqueline Bissett as a former child star whose husband refuses to divorce her and Teresa Russell playing mother-hating psychopath Margo Anthony.

During the 2013–2014 season in London's West End, playwright-screenwriter's Craig Warner's well-received staged production at the Gielgud Theater, directed by Robert Alan Ackerman and produced by 007 film series producer Barbara Broccoli, leaned a bit less on Hitchcock's movie version than on Highsmith's novel. Singled out for praise were Jack Huston as Bruno, Imogen Stubbs as his fading Southern belle mother, Miranda Raison as Anne, Christian McKay as the detective, as well as the black-and-white sets and what one critic called "Bernard Herrmann–like music." In fact, the music was Herrmann, from his score for the Nicholas Ray–directed crime thriller starring Robert Ryan and Ida Lupino, *On Dangerous Ground* (1951).

In 2002, Warner Bros. announced a remake to be set in England, with David Seltzer (*The Omen* [1976]) penning the screenplay and Noam Murro (*300: Rise of an Empire* [2014]) to direct, but nothing came of it. In 2015, it was widely reported that *Gone Girl* director David Fincher and screenwriter Gillian Flynn would reteam for an updated version, retitled *Strangers*, with Ben Affleck producing and apparently starring as a burned-out actor whose private plane breaks down during awards season, forcing him to hitch a ride on the private plane of a wealthy psychotic. With little word on the progress since, the prospects look increasingly hazy.

As tantalizing as the prospect of such singular talents as Fincher and Flynn putting their spin on *Strangers on a Train* sounds, what chance does a contemporary version stand in a world of smartphones, advanced forensic technology, and our high-surveillance city streets dense with CCTV security cameras? Or, more simply, do we need another version minus Alfred Hitchcock himself, who seems to have taken with him so many of the secrets of great suspense moviemaking when he died in 1980?

ACKNOWLEDGMENTS

I'm grateful to my editor, Randall Lotowycz—as exacting as he is enthusiastic—and to Running Press for recognizing the saga of *Strangers on a Train* as one long overdue for telling and for trusting me to be the writer who had to tell it. Hats off to my representatives, Lee Sobel and Marc von Arx, for their know-how, faith, persistence, and for being such *mensches*. Big thanks to Bree Russell, keeper of the keys of the Warner Bros. archive at the Cinematic Arts Library of the University of Southern California, the world's largest single studio collection, and to those capable and helpful associates who work alongside her. I appreciated her guidance, patience, and unflagging excitement for this project every step of the way. My thanks to Gary Rubenstein and to Eileen West for their hilarity and the first-rate research help. Thanks, too, to so many knowledgeable professionals at the Margaret Herrick Library of the Academy of Motion Arts and Sciences, including Matt Severson, the library's director, for their years of assistance and support on this and other book and film projects.

Much love to my circle of loved ones, friends, colleagues, internet pals, and family who listened, shared, opined, and—best of all—made me laugh when I most needed it. Gary Rubenstein, Deborah Corday, Howard and Steinnun Green, Douglas Soesbe, Steve De Jarnatt, James Grissom, Christopher Heard, Brian Dupont, Elizabeth Karlin, Nat Segaloff, Paul Farrar, Robert Hofler, Sam Irvin, Mark Westlund, Barbara Hall, Rocky Lang, Louis Heaton, Alan Barnette, Bob Gutowski, Pat McFadden, Marie Merrill, Barbara Bosco, Kevin O'Brien, Bob Gutowski, Edward Williams, Kathy Silva, Todd Tams, Paul Ramuz, Sue Cameron, Kevin Howell, Steven C. Smith, and Tracey Goessell. Deep thanks to Hitchcock associates Henry Bumstead, Robert Clatworthy, Bill Gold, Jere Henshaw, Hilton A. Green, Pat Hitchcock, Joseph Hurley, Paul Jasmin, Arthur Laurents,

Howard Fast, H. N. Swanson, Janet Leigh, Kim Novak, Anthony Perkins, Rita Riggs, Marshall Schlom, Joseph and Marilyn Stefano, Lurene Tuttle, Albert Whitlock, and many others for sharing years of personal and professional memories that shed light on the paradox that was Hitchcock. Undying affection and gratitude to my parents, Evelyn and Arthur, who watched me fall in love with the movies right alongside them. And of course, deep love and gratitude to my soulmates and magical familiars, Rudy, Jack, Magnus, and Callie.

APPENDIX I
Pages on the Cutting-Room Floor

Six screenwriters brought unique perspectives and talents to their work on *Strangers on a Train*. Not all their ideas survived. The following are some of their abandoned screenplay ideas. A few of these ideas found their way into such later Hitchcock films as *Psycho* and *Frenzy*.

Deleted from Whitfield Cook's version:

- The movie was to open with a close-up of a fly landing on a table in Bruno's private train compartment. Bruno—described as "obviously slightly intoxicated, in his early 20s, with a sensitive, almost adolescent type of face, expensively but carelessly dressed"—spots and then "grabs the fly, crushes it, examines it with a faint smile, drops it to the floor, and wipes his hands." In fairness, did Hitchcock himself invent this nasty bit of business? After all, only the technical limitations of the era thwarted Hitchcock's intention to open *Psycho* from the point of view of a fly zooming over the Phoenix, Arizona, skyline straight into the open window of the hotel room shared by clandestine lovers Marion and Sam—the "fly shot" was meant to be a bookend. Near the end of *Psycho*, a fly lands on the hand of Norman Bates in the holding cell. In a revised Cook treatment, Bruno sadistically pulls the legs off the fly as if he were plucking petals off a daisy.

- The train conversation between Guy and Bruno focuses almost exclusively on murder, Bruno's fantasies of killing his despised father (should it be the busted light socket? Carbon monoxide in the garage?), and his warning to Guy about how he envisions his own death ("I want to commit suicide and fix it so it looks like my worst enemy murdered me."). Bruno laments the unhappy life he lives with his parents in "the doghouse" in Great Neck, Long Island, where, according to his father, everyone has done something wrong and must be punished for it.

- On the train, Guy more aggressively tries to get away from Bruno. There are also several descriptions of the boozy Bruno's physical proximity to Guy. For example, "Bruno sways very close to Guy's face. Guy pushes him away, hard."

- When Guy joins Bruno in his private cabin, Cook describes it as littered with fancy luggage, empty liquor bottles, detective novels, and tennis rackets.

- Guy meets his estranged wife, Miriam ("a slight girl in a flowered skirt, bobbysocks and . . . [with] harlequin glasses and myopic lenses, small eyes"), at a crowded student hangout, a "milkshake bar."

- Back from meeting with Miriam, Guy is picked up in a limo by Senator [Morton], his daughters, and the senator's unmarried, older sister. During the limo ride, Guy informs the others that Miriam refuses to divorce him. Guy tells Anne and her sister, Barbara, that Miriam is threatening to come to Washington to live with him and have her baby there. "I could kill her!" Barbara blurts out, calling Miriam one of those people "who'd be better off dead," a phrase that echoes Bruno's philosophy. Barbara persists, "I wonder how much Murder Inc. would charge to do the job?" The senator reproaches her silently, but Barbara always voices what–she says–others are too "intelligent and normal" to admit aloud.

- When Bruno loses Guy's lighter, he overpays a municipal street cleaner to retrieve it from the storm drain.

- Guy rides his train and shudders when he sees a passenger accidentally tap the foot of the traveler sitting opposite him. They begin to converse; Guy stops himself from warning, "Don't!"

- Lurking outside the amusement park, Bruno pours bourbon into his Coke while waiting for nightfall. The boatman calls out to a long line of thrill seekers, "This way to the scene where the murder was committed!"

- Detectives arrive at the amusement park just before Guy does. The cops tell the boatman that Miriam's murderer will return to the scene of the crime at any moment. Boatman pleads with them not to do anything that could ruin his booming business. Boatman agrees to signal the police once he spots the killer. The detectives row out to the island and await Guy, the "murderer." Bruno watches from a distance, concernedly. Guy threads through the crowd, knowing he's being watched. Guy spots Bruno heading toward him. When the boatman yells, "That's him!", Bruno leaps onto the moving merry-go-round.

- In the Antonys' "expensively but tastelessly furnished and decorated" Great Neck, New York, home, Bruno (in pajamas and a silk dressing robe) broods angrily and plays with Guy's lighter as his aunt Clara tends to Bruno's mother, Elsie's, latest black eye and bruises, inflicted by Bruno's father. Clara reminds Elsie, who is "a faded blonde" former actress and Ziegfeld Follies showgirl, that despite her husband's despicable behavior and womanizing, Elsie's own recent marital indiscretions would make divorce a challenge. Says Clara, echoing Barbara Morton's sentiments about Miriam, people like Mr. Antony are such "horrors" that they ought to be dead.

- When Mrs. Antony wails that maybe she herself would be better off dead, Bruno's expression turns from sadness to a steely sense of purpose. Hearing the front door slam, Bruno heads for the door and, to Elsie's horror, threateningly confronts his father—a "vigorous, well-built man in his 50s." Mr. Antony taunts his son, "Oh, are you going to try and kill me again? Which way is it this time, mother's boy? Undetectable poison?" Mrs. Antony hears her husband tell Bruno, "I think it's about time you were put away again." Says Mr. Antony, seeing Bruno twisting Guy's cigarette lighter in his hands, "Oh, a new way? Murder by cigarette lighter?" Bruno's mother drags Bruno out of harm's way. (Note: In the mid-1960s, Universal blocked Hitchcock from making *Kaleidoscope*, in which a charming, perhaps latent homosexual psychopath seduces and murders several women while his estranged, domineering, military-man father wants him institutionalized and his narcissistic, aging Broadway-actress mother aggressively denies her son's psychopathology. The dramatic possibilities for this family dynamic apparently intrigued Hitchcock, and it was Cook who originally laid down the template for Hitchcock over a decade prior.)

- Bruno arrives in Metcalf and looks up the address of a dress shop, Joyce's (Joyce is Miriam's family surname). On the way, he escorts a blind man to safety on the other side of the busy street. Staring into the window of the dress shop, Bruno studies his reflection among the fancy mannequins posed in small-town fashions. In shadow, he watches as Miriam tells her mother that she and the two "college boys" are off to the amusement park; Mrs. Joyce tells Miriam to be careful because of "the way she is" (i.e., pregnant).

- Montage: After Miriam's murder, various Metcalf residents in different parts of town gossip about what a "dreadful girl" Miriam was and how volatile a married couple she and Guy were.

- Two detectives show various people photos of Guy. Later, the detectives remark how nobody saw Guy leave New York. Called in for questioning by the police, Guy realizes his alibi is thin. Reporters take notes at the courthouse–one repeats Guy's statement, "The murder must have been committed by a maniac–with no motive whatsoever!"

- Senator Morton upsets Anne by telling her that Guy's only alibi–a roadside gas station attendant who fixed his car–claims not to remember Guy. Barbara bristles that her father and sister are suspicious of Guy and says, "It would be sort of wonderful to find a man who loved you enough to go out and kill for you!"

- One of the books being read by Anne's sister, Barbara, is *Sexual Behavior in the Human Male*, Dr. Alfred Kinsey's empirically documented 1948 assault on American myths about sexual behaviors, including homosexuality.

- Guy turns up unexpectedly at the senator's office, making his boss and his fellow staff members acutely uncomfortable. Senator Morton advises Guy to throw himself into tennis and take a break from his senate work. Guy arouses further suspicion by answering a phone call from Bruno and pretending the call wasn't for him.

- At the Smithsonian, where Anne works as a volunteer, she tries to console Guy when he says, "Your father thinks I killed Miriam." They walk through the museum's Hall of Fossils, where the giant remains of prehistoric creatures loom over them. Through the bones of the skeleton of the giant brontosaurus, Guy glimpses the shadowy, eerie figure of Bruno staring at him. As Guy and Anne make their way, Bruno zigzags closer and closer, always glimpsed through the light and shadows of the dinosaur bones. (Note: This reads like a purely Hitchcockian montage sequence, prefiguring the impressionistic cutting of the *Psycho* shower sequence. It also suggests a sequence proposed for the aforementioned but never-made late-1960s three-women-and-a-psycho thriller *Kaleidoscope*, in which a young woman's pursuit and murder would have been glimpsed entirely in chiaroscuro "zebra-like shadows and lights" cast by moonlight shining through the rotted wooden deck of an abandoned Navy ship.)

- Cook creates many more instances of Bruno watching Guy from afar.

- Bruno approaches Guy, complaining that he isn't "cooperating" and his "attitude is forcing me to come out into the open." Bruno follows, but Guy shoves him back. Guy rejoins Anne, who has been watching from afar, and asks who Bruno is; Guy says he is "probably a tennis fan." After the match, Guy is troubled seeing Bruno sitting with Anne and her aunt Sarah. He joins them and hears Bruno and Sarah reminisce about his mother's career in musical theater. When Bruno reminds Sarah of his first name, Anne glances at his "Bruno" tie chain, then at Guy, angry about his lying.

- Bruno crashes the party and disarms Senator Morton with his brash irreverence. Guy swears to Anne he did not invite Bruno, who drunkenly confronts a judge whom he once saw sentence a man to the electric chair: "Can you really go home and eat dinner after having to perform such an unpleasant job?" (Hitchcock not only evoked this question in his own interviews but also in the character of the sadistic judge played by Charles Laughton in *The Paradine Case*.)

- Anne monitors her aunt Sarah and Bruno dueting on a song Bruno's mother made famous in her stage career. When Aunt Sarah exclaims what a fan she is of Bruno's mother, Bruno says, "So am I! Of course, I'm like my father, too, in a way. But you know the old bromide—*a boy's best friend is his mother.*" (The moviegoing world would finally hear that old Victorian-era bromide delivered for the ages in *Psycho* nine years later by Norman Bates.)

- Anne confronts Guy while he is trying to rush Bruno out of the Morton house: "What is there between you and this man? What hold has he got over you? Please, both of you, go! I don't know what it all means but I won't have my father embarrassed while he's among friends!"

- After the party, in Guy's apartment, Anne says, "How did you get him to do it? How did you get him to kill Miriam?" He confesses and tells her, "You sound almost disappointed that I didn't do it!" She confronts him on his passivity, and he says, "Maybe I haven't fought for you hard enough. Maybe I was weak where Miriam was concerned." She challenges him to fight for his life.

- Anne goes to Bruno's mother (clad in a negligee in the middle of the day) to warn her of her son's alarming mental state and his diabolical plan to swap murders. Mrs. Antony warns/pleads with Anne not to tell her husband about Bruno, with a chillingly ambiguous line, "You don't understand what this family is like." Finally, she says, "You can't expect a mother to turn against her only son–no matter what he's done." (Cook's last line of dialogue for Mrs. Antony makes an interesting companion piece with *Psycho* screenwriter Joseph Stefano's climactic speech for Mrs. Bates that begins, "It's sad when a mother has to speak the words that condemn her own son . . .")

- At the Forest Hills tennis meet, Bruno warns Guy that his inaction has forced a crisis: "I'm going to give myself up. I'll get the chair. Or I'll kill myself first but you're going with me. I'm going to say we planned it together." Guy punches Bruno.

- During a tennis match at Forest Hills, Bruno slips into the men's locker room and asks the trainer which locker is Guy's, saying, "Guy wants a handkerchief." At the locker, Bruno pockets a handkerchief and the cigarette lighter, then slips out. Later, the trainer asks Guy if he sent anyone for a handkerchief, and Guy says he did not. Guy searches his locker and realizes his lighter is gone. He tells Barbara she must drive him to the train station right after the tennis match. He warns her to avoid the detectives who are watching him. Guy plays tennis and tells the umpire he plans to finish things off in three matches. Barbara heads for the stands and sits with clueless Aunt Sarah, who keeps asking why Anne isn't there.

- Bruno rushes from Guy's tennis match to the train station, where he sees a newspaper sports page with Guy's picture. From Bruno's POV, the newspaper columns disappear and are replaced in his imagination by a headline announcing the arrest of Guy Haines—the subheading reveals that Guy's lighter was found at the scene of the crime.

- From the first, Hitchcock wanted the amusement park carousel to be decorated with ornate mechanical cherubs crashing cymbals together; they would be filmed in close-up and cut to, as if applauding the fistfight between Guy and Bruno. After fighting on the carousel, Guy and Bruno are led off in handcuffs, and the police announce, "No occupants are seriously hurt!" (*Seriously?*) The boatman points out Bruno as the killer.

- Gathered at the police station are Anne, Bruno's mother, and her lawyer. Bruno, believing Guy is the one under suspicion, starts ranting insanely to the police before realizing he has sealed his fate: "You see, the trouble with most everybody is they just don't have the guts to put people out of the way who deserve to be put out of the way. Isn't that right, Chief? Isn't that right, Mom? Don't tell me you've never wanted to murder someone, Chief. But you police are lucky. You get all that killing off your chest by shooting fellas on the run and you get paid for it. Most people don't get that chance and they wouldn't have the guts. That was the trouble with Guy. I sure picked the wrong guy when I picked him. Here I figure out a swell scheme—best game I ever had to get rid of a couple of people ought to be got rid of—but he let me down." Bruno looks at the stenographer taking down his [highly unlikely] accidental confession, then at the chief and says, "You wouldn't care to cross out those last few lines, would you?" He says, "I just made it OK for you, Guy."

- Bruno's mother, no longer in denial, offers Guy and Anne a lift, saying, "Would you like a ride to Forest Lawn?" [*sic*, Cook surely meant Forest Hills . . . not one of Southern California's six well-known cemeteries, one of which is famously known as a final resting place for film industry notables.]

Deleted from Raymond Chandler's version:

- As the men meet and talk on the train, when Guy offers to light Bruno's cigarette, the latter "takes Guy's hand to bring the lighter up close to his face." When Bruno comments on how swank the lighter is, says Guy, "I just carry it for other people. I don't smoke." Chandler comments on Bruno's overly familiar, almost intimate gestures and tone by noting how, "This is moving a little fast for Guy's taste."

- Bruno tells Guy he lives with his family in Alexandria, Virginia, but he is on the way to join his mother (no longer a former stage star) at a Lake Oconomowoc, Wisconsin, resort. "I love my mother. She's wonderful. She's everything–everything my father isn't. I hate my father." Guy talks too much and with too much exposition about his career prospects ("Forest Hills is my last chance. I'm twenty-five years old. That's the beginning of middle age for a tennis player"). He also complains about his marital troubles with Miriam, prompting Bruno to observe, "Women. They're all selfish. All they think of is themselves. Of course, my mother's an exception." Chandler turns Guy's cigarette lighter into a fetish object, as he describes Bruno taking the lighter and rubbing it between his palms, caressing the embossing, watching Guy "all the while."

- Describing Guy exiting the train in Metcalf, Chandler offers some of the most sharp, atmospheric writing he gave Hitchcock. Describing

Metcalf, "If you want to be sentimental, it is the face of America. If you want to be cynical, it is the mirror of a half-baked civilization."

- In the "milkshake bar" scene where Guy and Miriam rendezvous, Chandler describes Miriam as "rather cute in an immature way. She's been to the beauty parlor . . . she wears a summery dress, fancy glasses with rhinestones. She orders something disgusting." The other customers eavesdrop on this famously argumentative, well-known couple.

- At the Wisconsin lake resort hotel, Bruno watches one of Guy's tennis matches on television. Mrs. Antony, in her late forties, early fifties and "elegant," let alone "cool and fascinating," draws her son's attention to a handsome young man in a linen suit crossing the hotel lobby. She says she wishes Bruno would take similar pride in his appearance, and he sneers, "That's the desk clerk." Bruno calls Guy at the Westside Tennis Club in South Bend, Indiana, then he lies to his mother, saying that he's going to Chicago to see a girl. Says Mrs. Antony, "I'm so glad. You so seldom take any interest in girls."

- When Bruno is about to strangle Miriam on the island at the amusement park, Chandler has the psychopath sadistically dragging out the preliminaries.

  BRUNO
  Is your name Miriam?
  MIRIAM
  Yes, my name is Miriam, but I don't think I've had the pleasure–

  He comes to her, smiling politely. [Referring to the boorish, "husky" male friend who brought Miriam to the park and is vomiting in the bushes after drinking too much] . . .

BRUNO

Your friend can't hold his liquor.

MIRIAM *(bitterly)*

Don't I know it! Haven't we met somewhere?

BRUNO

Yes and no. Cigarette? You shouldn't go out with people like that. You shouldn't go out at all.

Bruno takes out Guy's cigarette lighter.

MIRIAM

Why, that's Guy's . . .

He grips her throat.

BRUNO

And I don't think you will go out at all anymore.

Yet Chandler goes Whitfield Cook one better with this:

Her hair falls over her glasses. Bruno casually moves her hair aside and retrieves the glasses.

Chandler's depiction of this brutal, icy-cold moment prefigures a similarly disturbing one in Hitchcock's *Frenzy*, when the psychopath strangles to death and sexually assaults the hero's ex-wife at the business she owns, then, on his way out, chomps on the apple his victim brought for lunch.

- Guy stops at a service station on a remote road when the senator's Cadillac he's transporting develops a broken fan belt. The money-grubbing attendant (Chandler calls him "a bucolic character") gets off some sardonic dialogue that reveals his disdain and distrust for city-slicker Guy as he fleeces him. One senses Chandler indulging himself in overwriting a scene that only exists to establish Guy's whereabouts and, later, the bucolic character trying to throw him under the bus.

- In a Metcalf montage sequence after newspapers report Guy's alibi, Miriam's mother, "haggard with weeping," says to a neighbor, "Who says he was driving from New York to Washington? He hated her. I'm her mother and I know it had to be somebody that knew that amusement park mighty well." Meanwhile, Miriam's reputation as "fast" prompts a callous carhop to say, "I guess she was a pretty awful type at that. But it's a nasty break for Guy Haines. You know what the [Mortons] are."

- Guy faces a mob of reporters and photographers, whose flash bulbs dissolve into the image of the flames of Guy's lighter as Bruno flicks it on and off in his bed.

- Chandler attempts to make Anne a more active, essential presence while also having her utter inane things. While on a date with Guy as she tries to build up his optimism and strengthen his resolve, she says, "It's a peach of a day. I feel sort of light and airy and free." As she and Guy leave a fancy restaurant after dinner, Bruno watches them, and in a "sort of carrying, breathed voice and caressing tone says, 'Guy?'. . ." Anne asks, "Didn't someone call you?" Bruno watches Anne and Guy leave a bar and calls out to him again, making Anne ask, "Is that someone I should know?"

- In the Smithsonian Museum scene, Chandler, perhaps taking visual direction from Hitchcock, details the choreography of Bruno as a "tall figure moving [with Anne and Guy] as they stroll past the mounted skeletons of prehistoric monsters." Bruno is "always seen behind the skeletons. . . [moving with] a drifting sort of movement which has the effect of bringing him ever closer to Guy and Anne as they reach the point near the entrance where there is a gigantic brontosaurus skeleton. Suddenly, Anne stops and turns and there–framed in the bones of the brontosaurus–is the face and figure of Bruno staring at her. And whispering, Anne says to Guy, 'There's that man again. I think he's following us. I think you know that man. I think he's following you. I think you know why he's following you.'" They leave the museum and argue over Guy's refusal to fess up to Anne.

- Bruno calls Guy's apartment: "Guy, I like you. Why can't we get together? I suppose that girl you're with all the time is Anne [Morton]. . . . You know I don't like girls an awful lot as a rule, but I think I'd like her." Guy slams down the phone.

- During a moment of tense silence when Guy is about to serve the ball during his crucial tennis match at Chevy Chase Country Club, Bruno riotously laughs out loud, deliberately rattling Guy's composure.

- In contrast to Cook, who keeps Bruno an almost ghostly presence who suddenly appears and vanishes, Chandler describes Bruno arriving and departing such locales as hotels, tennis clubs, ticket booths, and so on, always interacting with extraneous characters, like a little girl whom he pats on the head but who recoils from him, sending him into a fury. When he calls Guy asking if his divorce went through, Bruno and his mother are shown vacationing at the Wisconsin lake resort; we see him send Guy a telegram: "Guy, when we talk, you're always with someone. Call me at the Statler. Bruno." When Bruno urges Guy to "keep his end of their bargain," he specifies the dates Mr. Antony will be alone in the house while he and his mother are bound for Bermuda by clipper.

- Chandler makes Guy an even weaker, more ambivalent character. As he buckles under the pressure of being stalked by Bruno, Guy tells Senator Morton that he plans to back out of a tennis tournament because he isn't a strong enough player.

- Guy goes to Bruno's home armed with Bruno's gun. Bruno realizes Guy is bluffing, so he knocks him out, grabs the gun and cigarette lighter, and heads to his father's room to commit the murder himself. In his father's room, Bruno knocks back some liquor and, imagining Miriam's and Guy's faces in a mirror, shoots the mirror but not his father. Guy escapes.

- Anne repeatedly says things the audience already knows, telling Guy "There is some clandestine link between you two men." Lunching with Guy, she confronts him with "Why don't you tell me what's the matter? . . . I think it's one thing in particular. And I think it has something to do with that man. . . . Guy, let's not fence. You know what I mean. Don't pretend with me, that's all I ask."

- Bruno deliberately jostles a messenger boy who has just delivered him a package. The boy drops his cigarette, but Bruno replaces and lights it with Guy's lighter, but "there is something about Bruno's appearance and clothes and manner which [the boy] doesn't like." As the messenger boy mounts his bike and rides off, he feels Bruno watching him. The boy "jerks the cigarette out of his mouth, throws it away, and spits contemptuously. Bruno's face convulses with fury." Writes Chandler, "The messenger makes a contemptuous gesture as he rides away. And it is obvious to any sophisticated person what the messenger thinks Guy is."

- Bruno phones Guy and, pestering him that they must talk about his "agreeing" to kill his father, suggests coming up to Guy's apartment. Guy puts him off, proposing they instead rendezvous on the Arlington Memorial Bridge. There, Guy bristles when Bruno keeps pressing him about killing his father. "You love to act. Your type always does!" says Guy. "What type?" Bruno hisses. He angers Guy by babbling nervously about Miriam's glasses: "I stepped on them. I don't know why I brought them along. The whole thing was silly. It's almost comical, Guy. Miriam . . . one minute we were bouncing up and down on the merry-go-round. I think she might have liked me, Guy. But I hated her. She wasn't good for you, Guy. She wasn't good for you at all." Bruno giggles, and Guy floors him with a roundhouse punch. Bruno whimpers, "You hit me, Guy. You hit me. And I like you so much . . . better than anybody I've ever met, except my mother. What did you hit me for? I didn't mean to offend you." Guy storms away, leaving Bruno bruised and brooding.

- A society party hosted by Senator Morton and Anne. (Note: Chandler queries Hitchcock, "Perhaps we need another scene at Chevy Chase Country–Guy plays and loses the semi-finals? Perhaps we need a scene with Bruno and mother again or an attempt at a scene with his father or something of that sort? I don't know.") Anne pretends to know Bruno, hoping to avoid upsetting her father. Writes Chandler, "Bruno is delighted. He beams and pays her a deft compliment if Chandler can think of a deft compliment." Bruno grows increasingly drunk, performing impromptu card tricks that charm the older Washington society women.

After Bruno nearly strangles a fellow party guest, Leo G. Carroll, as Senator Morton, orders Guy to eject Bruno as quickly and discreetly as possible. Despite what daughter Barbara says, apparently Daddy *does* mind a little scandal.

- Bruno produces a full house from the coattails of Guy's jacket. When one socialite asks if Bruno is about to materialize a white rabbit, he says, "I had a white rabbit once. A very dear little white rabbit. In a moment of absent-mindedness, I strangled it." Eyeing Bruno across the room, Barbara says to Anne, "There's a flashy little number. Think I ought to make a pitch?" After demonstrating the art of strangulation on a French woman (whom Chandler names, wittily but pointlessly, "Madame Récamier," after the early nineteenth-century French socialite beauty who mesmerized European society), Bruno passes out, and Guy carries him to a private study to let him recuperate. Barbara says, "That fellow's a psycho if I ever saw one."

- Anne and Guy bicker (again) over his continued refusal to go to the police for help. Guy finally explains, "[Bruno] would get off because his father is rich. They'd say he was crazy and irresponsible and didn't know what he was doing. But I wouldn't get off and you and your father and Barbara wouldn't get off."

- Chandler's unnecessarily complex geography for the narrative sends Guy on an uneventful plane trip and a taxi ride to the Antony mansion. When Guy goes to the Antony home and finds Bruno waiting in his father's bed, Bruno angrily says, "You're not a killer, Mr. Haines. The double cross is more in your line, isn't it?"

- Guy drives back to the backwoods service station hoping to reestablish the alibi for his whereabouts at the time of Miriam's death. "The bucolic man" who overcharged him to fix the Cadillac's fan belt is gone. The place is vacated.

- Anne shows up at the Antony house to tell Bruno's mother everything her son has done. Initially, Mrs. Antony denies reality; when cornered, she becomes calculating and threatening. She backhands Anne's face. Anne leaves in angry disbelief.

- Another meeting between Bruno and Guy on the Arlington Memorial Bridge, and Bruno pleads with Guy to kill his father, "He's like a great weight on my chest. Sometimes, when he's around, I feel as if I couldn't breathe." (Compare this to Thornton Wilder writing to his sibling about their father, "There are times when I feel his perpetual and repetitive monologue is trying to swamp my personality and I get an awful rage." Did Hitchcock share Wilder's privileged personal information about his father with Chandler?) When Guy offers to meet with Bruno's father to untangle their "big misunderstanding," Bruno warns he will kill Guy and Anne. Guy says, "No, I'll kill you–slowly."

- During the Morton house party scene, Chandler proposed a lot of new material, including Anne confronting Bruno about how he almost strangled Madame Récamier (whom Chandler renames Madame Père Lachaise–after the largest, most "star-studded" Parisian cemetery, named for the French Jesuit priest and father confessor of King Louis XIV.) When Bruno insists he doesn't know any "French lady," Anne says, "Do you only strangle people you know?" Guy confesses everything to Anne and, kissing her, observes, "You're as cold as ice. I think you're almost as crazy as [Bruno] is." (Wait, *what?*)

- Guy and Bruno–on the Jefferson Memorial Bridge again–discuss Bruno's father. Bruno says, "When all this is over–we can see each other–without skulking around corners. We can really be friends." Bold stuff for the early 1950s during the dark shadow of the Lavender Scare and Red Scare. All this material was deleted.

- On the tennis court, Guy is winning his biggest game yet. Anne attempts to detain Bruno by inviting him to sit in their family's private viewing box. When Bruno overreacts to a minor verbal slip he makes, Barbara taunts him, "What's the matter? You kill somebody?" Bruno realizes what Anne and Barbara are up to. He rushes off, telling them, "I've got an appointment with the moon." During a break in the tennis match, Anne urges Guy to default so he can get to the amusement park before Bruno. Guy refuses to throw the game. He resolves to reclaim his power and restore his battered pride.

- En route to the amusement park, Chandler repeatedly describes Bruno "fondling" Guy's lighter. At the train station, a newsboy jostles Bruno, accidentally sending the lighter tumbling down into the sewer grating. Bruno remains passive as a work crew rescues the lighter for him.

- On the midway, a keyed-up Bruno barely holds himself back from randomly killing a pigeon with a stone. Meanwhile, Guy and Anne arrive at the park but, from here on, Chandler barely accounts for Anne's whereabouts.

- Bruno, at the murder scene on the island at the amusement park, tells a stranger he is revolted by the crowds of ghoulish rubber-neckers ogling the scene of the crime. The boatman has turned the area into a thriving tourist attraction, roped off and with a stone placed where Miriam's head had lain. A young wise guy shines a flashlight over the crime scene–it shines on Guy's lighter, right where Bruno placed it. As the excitement over the discovery builds, Bruno boards a boat and smugly rows back to the main part of the park.

- On the merry-go-round, when a policeman aims his gun at Guy, Anne's scream startles the shooter, who accidentally clips the ride attendant instead. (Note: This is a variation on the famous Albert Hall sequence in *The Man Who Knew Too Much* [made by Hitchcock in England in 1934 and remade in America in 1956], in which a scream from the mother of a kidnapped child foils an attempted political assassination.)

- Guy and Bruno fight on the merry-go-round, where Bruno nearly strangles Guy before whimpering, "I don't like the merry-go-round. Tell them to stop it. I'm dizzy. It makes me sick to my stomach." (One might expect Chandler to link Bruno's dizziness—his vertigo, if you will—to some childhood psychological trauma, as in such earlier Hitchcock works as, say, *Shadow of a Doubt* or *Spellbound*. . . . But he doesn't.) The police nab Bruno.

- A brawl at the Metcalf police station leaves an unhinged Bruno in a straitjacket. He confesses to Miriam's murder and espouses his theories on human nature in a similar (but far less persuasive) way as does Norman Bates in the holding cell at the end of *Psycho*.

Deleted from Czenzi Ormonde's version (with contributions by Alfred Hitchcock, Barbara Keon, and Alma Reville):

- A moment on the Metcalf bus when Bruno nearly attacks a little Pekingese dog sitting on the lap of a woman sitting next to him—the friendly dog licks Bruno's cheek.

- Guy offers to resign from his job with Senator Morton.

- The following dialogue exchange between Barbara and Senator Morton, after Miriam's murder:

  BARBARA
  This will certainly give our dinner party next week a shot in the arm.
  SENATOR MORTON
  I've never been aware that our little gatherings needed stimulating.
  BARBARA
  I can just hear the old gossips licking their chops.
  SENATOR MORTON
  Can't you ever be serious?

- An angry confrontation in the police station between Guy and Miriam's mother. (Hitchcock apparently filmed the scene but cut it early in postproduction because it made Guy much less sympathetic to the audience.)

- A lengthy police interrogation scene in which Guy gets asked whether he felt angry enough to inflict bodily harm on Miriam once she denied him the divorce.

- Bruno's process of worming his way into the Mortons' circle of friends—especially the French woman Madame Darville—by lying about having mutual acquaintances and shared foreign travel experiences.

- Several brief comic scenes between the two detectives who are shadowing Guy. There is one in which one detective reports to the other that Guy put the drunken Bruno into a car, then Anne ran out of the Morton house during the party:

  DETECTIVE HENNESSEY
  People like Haines and the Mortons don't have arguments on the sidewalk. I hope it was just a lover's quarrel.
  DETECTIVE HAMMOND
  You're soft, Hennessey. You got illusions. A detective can't afford illusions. They always bust right in your face.
  DETECTIVE HENNESSEY
  Just do your job, Hammond, and shut up.

APPENDIX II
Preview Screening Differences

The version of *Strangers of a Train* shown to audiences at the California sneak previews underwent numerous refinements and changes before the final theatrical release version. The variations are as follows:

Additional footage and alternate takes in the train conversation between Guy and Bruno amp up the latter's flamboyant and seductive personality, as well as his flirtation with and unspoken attraction to Guy. The undertones that dare not speak their name become more like overtones–for 1951, anyway.

- 03:05–03:07: After Bruno promises to let Guy go back to reading his book, the shots before and after are held longer.

- 04:08–04:16: The dialogue "Yes, I am. Ask me anything," is heard in both versions, but in the preview, it continued, "from today's sports news or stock report to Li'l Abner, I got the answer. Even news about people that I don't know."

- 04:35–04:40: The preview version stays throughout on Bruno. The released version cuts back (pointlessly) to Guy for a single shot.

- 05:57–06:19: Bruno presses Guy to stay with him and to order food from the server. The preview version of this train scene features more dialogue, more frequent and longer shots of Bruno looking at Guy, and more fey playing from Walker, slightly elevating the tone of homoerotic attraction and seduction. Contemporary viewers, accustomed to blunt, direct dialogue and imagery, might find all this too subtle or miss it entirely.

BRUNO

Waiter! Bring me some lamb chops, French fries, and chocolate ice cream.

WAITER

Yes, sir.

BRUNO

Compartment B, car 121.

The waiter wants to leave, Bruno holds him back.

BRUNO *(continued)*

And, waiter . . .

The waiter turns around again.

WAITER

Yes, sir?

BRUNO

Guy, what'll you have?

GUY

Thanks, just the same . . .

BRUNO

Go on, go on, order.

GUY

Well, I'll just have a hamburger and a cup of coffee.

This was the gourmand Hitchcock's code for a strictly working-class character. Similarly, in a roadside restaurant scene in *Marnie* (1964), the heroine orders a frankfurter and a cup of coffee.

- 08:24–08:28: Guy finally tries to interrupt Bruno; Bruno takes a verbal swipe at Anne, Guy's fiancée:

  GUY
  Let's not talk about it anymore.
  BRUNO
  A woman like that can sure make a lot of trouble for you . . .

- 8:52–09:06: Bruno is quicker on the uptake when Guy reminds him that murder is illegal. Bruno pivots by mentioning Guy's estranged wife's gentleman friends.

  BRUNO
  My theory is that everybody is a potential murderer. Didn't you ever feel like you wanted to kill somebody? Let's say, one of those useless fellas that Miriam was playing around with?

  Guy ponders it a moment.

  GUY
  You can't go around killing people just because you think they're useless.

- 10:28 / 11:16–11:18: Longer shots of the train's arrival.

- 64:40–64:45: Guy paces slightly longer before answering the phone.

- 65:46–66:33: Guy's walk to Bruno's family home is different. In the theatrical release version, the detective appears on screen before we see Guy on the fire escape. The preview version offers another shot of the detective before Guy retrieves Bruno's schematic of the layout of the Antony house and then climbs out to the fire escape.

- 66:38–67:05: In the preview version, Guy climbs over the fence of the Antony house and hides from the detective. Then we see him as a tiny figure crossing the vast lawn as he moves toward the house.

- 67:12–67:13: The preview version lingers longer on Guy moving toward the door of the mansion. Once inside the Antony house, there is an insert from Guy's POV of Bruno's drawing of the layout of the house with emphasis on the location of "My Father's Room," raising suspense as to whether Guy entertains notions of actually killing Bruno's father as he does in Highsmith's novel.

- 75:15: The version shown in previews features a shot of Bruno holding the cigarette lighter while talking to Anne.

- 90:51–90:58: The preview version features an additional shot of Guy on the train, then cuts to a shot of Bruno at the amusement park.

- 91:32–91:33, 89:55–92;04, 92:05–92:06: All shots of Bruno on the midway are held marginally longer.

- 93:06–93:09: Wider perspective on the midway shows more of the carousel and Ferris wheel and remains longer on Bruno at the ticket booth.

- 100:13–100:49 / 102:41–102:57: Immediately after Guy's relieved phone call, the original version directly fades to the last scene in the train with Anne and Guy. When another passenger, a cleric, recognizes Guy and asks whether he is Guy Haines, Guy and Anne share a look, then move to another compartment, leaving the cleric momentarily confused before he simply returns to his newspaper.

For those keeping score, the preview version offers thirty-two moments of additional footage and six moments of alternative footage.

The second sneak preview in April ended with Guy and Anne on the train and the clergyman bemused when they rebuff him. But Hitchcock made other small but telling changes and refinements.

- Hitchcock shot a close-up of Bruno's hand training a gun on Guy as the latter descended the Antony house staircase. Hitchcock shot the staircase, from Guy's POV, two ways. One, with the camera normally locked down and, two, at the tilted, or Dutch, angle. The latter was used in the final film, suggesting not only menace but also dramatizing (and commenting upon) Guy's psychological state.

- Hitchcock reshot the scene of Bruno on the phone with his parents (in rear projection, in the background), putting Walker in a more impactful close-up.

- Hitchcock filmed two different versions of Guy opening the senior Mr. Antony's bedroom door—one without movement and the other with a push-in to a close-up of Guy. He used the shot without movement for the film released to theaters. Guy takes the gun from his pocket, looks at it, then replaces it in his pocket and opens a door. The hesitation and Granger's reaction suggests Guy has a moment in which he considers committing the murder and then decides against it. Another version makes it clear that the gun is not loaded, alerting Bruno that Guy has another motive entirely.

APPENDIX III
Filming Locations

National Gallery of Art, Washington, District of Columbia

Union Station, 50 Massachusetts Avenue NE, Washington, District of Columbia

Jefferson Memorial, 900 Ohio Drive SW, Washington, District of Columbia

Penn Station, New York City, New York

Danbury Railway Station, 120 White Street, Danbury, Connecticut

West Side Tennis Club, 1 Tennis Place, Forest Hills, Queens, New York

Warner Bros. Studios, Burbank, California, Soundstages 1, 14, 15

Rowland V. Lee Ranch, Fallbrook Avenue, Canoga Park, Los Angeles, California

SELECTED BIBLIOGRAPHY

Cline, Sally. *Dashiell Hammett: Man of Mystery.* New York: Arcade Publishing, 2014.

Gottlieb, Sidney, and Alfred Hitchcock. *Alfred Hitchcock: Interviews.* Jackson: University Press of Mississippi, 2003.

Granger, Farley, and Robert Calhoun. *Include Me Out: My Life from Goldwyn to Broadway.* New York: St. Martin's Press, 2007.

Greven, David. *Intimate Violence: Hitchcock, Sex, and Queer Theory.* Oxford: Oxford University Press, 2017.

Highsmith, Patricia. *Strangers on a Train.* New York: Harper & Brothers, 1950.

Hiney, Tom. *Raymond Chandler: A Biography.* New York: Grove Press, 1997.

Hiney, Tom, Frank MacShane, and Raymond Chandler. *The Raymond Chandler Papers: Selected Letters and Non-Fiction, 1909–1959.* New York: Atlantic Monthly Press, 2001.

Johnson, David K. *The Lavender Scare: The Cold War Persecution of Gays and Lesbians in the Federal Government.* Chicago: University of Chicago Press, 2023.

Johnson, Diane. *Dashiell Hammett: A Life.* New York: Random House, 1983.

Krohn, Bill. *Hitchcock at Work.* London: Phaidon Press, 2003.

Layman, Richard. *Shadow Man: The Life of Dashiell Hammett.* New York: Harcourt Brace Jovanovich, 1981.

LoBrutto, Vincent. *By Design: Interviews with Film Production Designers.* Westport, CT: Prager, 1992.

McGilligan, Patrick. *Alfred Hitchcock: A Life in Darkness and Light.* Chichester, UK: Wiley, 2003.

Niven, Penelope. *Thornton Wilder: A Life.* New York: Harper, 2012.

Schenkar, Joan. *The Talented Miss Highsmith: The Secret Life and Serious Art of Patricia Highsmith.* New York: St. Martin's Press, 2009.

Spoto, Donald. *The Dark Side of Genius: The Life of Alfred Hitchcock.* Boston: Little, Brown and Company, 1983.

Sullivan, Jack. *Hitchcock's Music.* New Haven, CT: Yale University Press, 2006.

Thomas, Bob. *Clown Prince of Hollywood: The Antic Life and Times of Jack L. Warner.* New York: McGraw-Hill, 1990.

Truffaut, François *Hitchcock/Truffaut.* New York: Simon and Schuster, 1967.

Wilder, Thornton. *The Selected Letters of Thornton Wilder.* New York: HarperCollins, 2008.

Williams, Tom. *A Mysterious Something in the Light: The Life of Raymond Chandler.* Chicago: Chicago Review Press, 2013.

Index

Page numbers in italics indicate photographs and illustrations.

INDEX

INDEX

INDEX